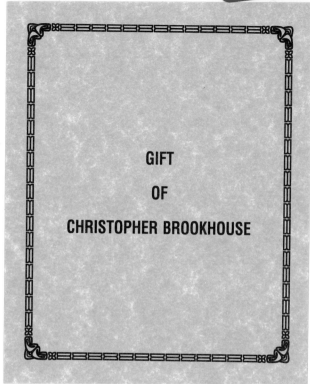

North by Northwest

Rutgers Films in Print

Charles Affron, Mirella Jona Affron, and Robert Lyons, editors

My Darling Clementine, John Ford, director
edited by Robert Lyons
The Last Metro, François Truffaut, director
edited by Mirella Jona Affron and E. Rubinstein
Touch of Evil, Orson Welles, director
edited by Terry Comito
The Marriage of Maria Braun, Rainer Werner Fassbinder, director
edited by Joyce Rheuban
Letter from an Unknown Woman, Max Ophuls, director
edited by Virginia Wright Wexman with Karen Hollinger
Rashomon, Akira Kurosawa, director
edited by Donald Richie
8½, Federico Fellini, director
edited by Charles Affron
La Strada, Federico Fellini, director
edited by edited by Peter Bondanella and Manuela Gieri
Breathless, Jean-Luc Godard, director
edited by Dudley Andrew
Bringing Up Baby, Howard Hawks, director
edited by Gerald Mast
Chimes at Midnight, Orson Welles, director
edited by Bridget Gellert Lyons
L'avventura, Michelangelo Antonioni, director
edited by Seymour Chatman and Guido Fink
Meet John Doe, Frank Capra, director
edited by Charles Wolfe
Invasion of the Body Snatchers, Don Siegel, director
edited by Al LaValley
Memories of Underdevelopment, Tomás Gutiérrez Alea, director
introduction by Michael Chanan
Imitation of Life, Douglas Sirk, director
edited by Lucy Fischer
Ugetsu, Kenji Mizoguchi, director
edited by Keiko I. McDonald
Shoot the Piano Player, François Truffaut, director
edited by Peter Brunette
My Night at Maud's, Eric Rohmer, director
edited by English Showalter
North by Northwest, Alfred Hitchcock, director
edited by James Naremore

North by Northwest

Alfred Hitchcock, director

James Naremore, editor

Rutgers University Press

New Brunswick, New Jersey

#27431510

North by Northwest is volume 20 in the Rutgers
Films in Print Series

Library of Congress Cataloging-in-Publication Data

North by northwest: Alfred Hitchcock, director /
James Naremore, editor.
    p.   cm.—(Rutgers films in print; v. 20)
    Includes continuity script.
    Filmography: p.
    Includes bibliographical references.
    ISBN 0-8135-2006-1 (cloth)
    ISBN 0-8135-2007-X (pbk.)
    1. Hitchcock, Alfred 1899–   —Criticism and
interpretation. 2. North by northwest (Motion
picture). I. Naremore, James. II. Series.
PN1997.N5373N67   1993
791.43′72—dc20   93-18283
                              CIP

British Cataloging-in-Publication information available

The continuity script is published by permission of
Turner Entertainment, Inc.

FOR DARLENE

Acknowledgments

My thanks to Charles and Mirella Affron for giving me an opportunity to write about Hitchcock, and to Leslie Mitchner for waiting so patiently for the manuscript. Robert Lyons was a remarkably helpful, witty, and intelligent reader of my work, and Peter Strupp was sharply attentive to the many complexities and details involved in a project of this kind. As usual, Darlene Sadlier helped in more ways than I can count.

Contents

Introduction

Spies and Lovers / 3
James Naremore

Alfred Hitchcock: A Biographical
Sketch / 21

North by Northwest

Credits and Cast / 31

The Continuity Script / 35

**Interviews, Reviews,
and Commentaries**

Interviews

An Interview with Alfred
Hitchcock / 177
Jean Domarchi and
Jean Douchet

An Interview with
Ernest Lehman / 186
John Brady

Reviews

Time / 193

The New Republic / 194
Stanley Kauffmann

Cahiers du Cinéma / 195
Luc Moullet

Commentaries

North by Northwest / 201
Robin Wood

The Designs of Authorship:
An Essay on *North by
Northwest* / 210
Marian Keane

The Hitchcockian Blot / 221
Slavoj Žižek

Filmography and Bibliography

Hitchcock Filmography,
1925–1976 / 231

Selected Bibliography / 237

Introduction

Spies and Lovers

James Naremore

Although Alfred Hitchcock is identified with a certain type of thriller or murder story, he actually made a wide variety of films—including two costume pictures, a prize fight melodrama, an adaptation of a Sean O'Casey play, a screwball comedy, and (believe it or not) an operetta. His reputation as the "master of suspense" evolved slowly and was determined in large part by a series of critically and commercially successful spy movies he directed at Gaumont British and Gainsborough Pictures between 1934 and 1938. In Hollywood during the early 1940s, he filmed two patriotic adventures about espionage, and over the next twenty years he periodically returned to the theme, treating it in a somewhat more ambiguous style appropriate to the cold war. Of his dozen features in this vein, however, none was more popular, influential, or commonly associated with his authorial signature than the comic-romantic epic, *North by Northwest* (1959).

Produced by Hitchcock under a special one-picture arrangement with Metro-Goldwyn-Mayer, the film drew on the talents of the director's most brilliant collaborators, including actor Cary Grant, cinematographer Robert Burks, composer Bernard Herrmann, production designer Robert Boyle, and graphic artist Saul Bass; it was released at the peak of Hitchcock's celebrity on American television, and in many ways it functioned as a capstone to or summary of his career. Thus, in the course of their book-length interview, François Truffaut told Hitchcock that "just as *The Thirty-nine Steps* may be regarded as the compendium of your work in Britain, *North by Northwest* is the picture that epitomizes the whole of your work in America."[1]

Hitchcock neither supported nor denied Truffaut's claim, perhaps because many of his most characteristic films were less about political intrigue than about sexual guilts and anxieties in private settings. But screenwriter Ernest Lehman has confirmed that *North by Northwest* was intended as a kind of homage or retrospective. In 1957,

---

1. *Hitchcock* (New York: Simon & Schuster, 1967), p. 190.

Lehman was hired by Hitchcock to develop a script from Hammond Innes's novel, *The Wreck of the Mary Deare;* he soon abandoned the job, feeling that neither he nor Hitchcock had any real interest in it. According to Lehman, the two men continued to hold conversations until a better idea emerged:

> One day I said, "I want to do a Hitchcock picture to end all Hitchcock pictures. . . ." And by that I meant a movie-movie—with glamour, wit, excitement, movement, big scenes, a large canvas, innocent bystander caught up in great derring-do, in the *Hitchcock* manner.
>
> And then one day he said, a little wistfully, "I've always wanted to do a chase sequence across the faces of Mount Rushmore."[2]

Hitchcock had been fond of staging melodramatic chases against the backdrop of imperial monuments ever since *Blackmail* (1929), which climaxes with the police scurrying across the roof of the British Museum. The mere idea of a cliff-hanging scene on Mount Rushmore was enough to start Lehman working on a new project, entitled *In a Northwesterly Direction.* (At later stages, the film was called *Breathless* and *The Man on Lincoln's Nose;* MGM's story editor, Kenneth MacKenna, suggested the title that was eventually adopted.) Lehman's screenplay, developed after a series of story conferences in which Hitchcock described various surrealistic episodes that might be used, was an obvious attempt to draw together themes and situations from at least three of the director's previous films about international espionage, blending them into a spectacular and definitively "Hitchcockian" entertainment. As in *The Thirty-nine Steps* (1935), an ordinary man falls by accident into a bizarre adventure; falsely accused of a murder, he leads the police on a treacherous and amusing cross-country chase, in the course of which he meets a beautiful woman, exposes a group of foreign agents, and proves his innocence. As in *Saboteur* (1942), the protagonist finds himself locked in a climactic life-and-death struggle with a sadistic spy atop a national monument. And as in *Notorious* (1946), a coolly pragmatic American bureaucracy persuades an insecure woman to sleep with the enemy for "patriotic" reasons; when the woman complies, the hero and the villain become jealous rivals for her love, and neither side in the ideological struggle can lay claim to moral or ethical purity.

Most criticism of the film has concentrated on such issues, although it should be noted that Lehman's screenplay was equally predicated on Hitchcock's ability to "get a Cary Grant with the greatest of ease."[3] Indeed there is a sense in which

---

2. Quoted in Donald Spoto, *The Dark Side of Genius: The Life of Alfred Hitchcock* (New York: Random House, 1983), p. 423. Spoto's biography contains much useful information about the production of the film.

3. Ernest Lehman, interviewed by John Brady in *The Craft of the Screenwriter* (New York: Touchstone Books, 1982), p. 205, reprinted in this volume.

Grant "coauthored" *North by Northwest:* he was as big a star as Hitchcock, he received a larger share of the film's profits, and he significantly influenced both the tone and the content of the narrative. Hence Grant and Lehman sometimes argued passionately about the script:

> Cary Grant and I had a few fierce battles in the back seat of a limousine on location at Bakersfield during the crop-duster sequence. . . . He would sit there and go over some of his scenes with me. "This is ridiculous," he'd say. "You think you are writing a Cary Grant picture? This is a David Niven picture."[4]

Despite Grant's occasional reservations, the completed film is obviously designed to exploit his acting skills and his star image. The famous crop-dusting sequence, for example, derives most of its wit from the mere sight of Grant running across a prairie, garbed in the same costume he had worn in countless movie drawing rooms. Throughout, Hitchcock and Lehman joke about the actor's unrumpled charm, and they sometimes allow him to peep through his role. ("I know," Grant says at one point, adjusting a pair of Hollywoodish sunglasses, "I look vaguely familiar.") Our constant awareness of his stardom is enhanced by Hitchcock's lifelong interest in the paradoxes of theatricality and identity, and by Lehman's story of a person who is created out of nothing. "George Kaplan," the fake spy manufactured by government agents, is similar in many ways to "Roger O. Thornhill," a sterotypical Madison Avenue executive whose middle initial stands for zero; by extension, both characters have something in common with "Cary Grant," who was created by Archie Leach and the entertainment industry out of a made-up proper name, a set of performing skills, and a series of narrative functions.

I have elsewhere commented at length on Grant's performance, showing how he mixes the light-comic sophistication of an Alfred Lunt and the music hall clowning of a Charlie Chaplin with the glamour of a fashion model and the atheleticism of a Hollywood action hero.[5] He sharpens the timing of the film's dialogue and gives literal pace to the sequences in which he strides across hotel lobbies or runs away from his pursuers; equally important, the decision to cast him affected the very writing of the screenplay, which is not only a "wrong man" thriller, but also a "comedy of remarriage," similar to the pictures that secured his reputation in the 1930s. Stanley Cavell has noted that *North by Northwest* shifts the emphasis of the remarriage plot from the "creation of a new woman" to the "revival" of a much-divorced man;[6] nevertheless, elements of the old formula are preserved, and Grant's uniquely attractive romantic style remains intact. As

---

4. Lehman interview, p. 226.
5. James Naremore, *Acting in the Cinema* (Berkeley and Los Angeles: University of California Press, 1988), pp. 213–235.
6. Stanley Cavell, "North by Northwest," in *A Hitchcock Reader,* ed. Marshall Deutelbaum and Leland Poague (Ames: Iowa State University Press, 1986), pp. 249–261.

Andrew Britton has remarked, one of the actor's important achievements was to embody an unorthodox male heterosexuality, arrived at through a relationship "in which the woman appears so often as the educator of the male, and of his pleasure."[7] Notice, for instance, Grant's behavior in his love scenes with Eva Marie Saint, which are erotic without suggesting a masculine dominance. Partly because of these scenes, and partly because of the film's affinities with Grant's work in the 1930s, *North by Northwest* offers a greater sense of utopian playfulness than one usually expects from Hitchcock. As in *Suspicion* (1941) and *Notorious,* Hitchcock suggests that dark impulses lie beneath Grant's charm, but here the actor's cheerful and courteous attributes seem more evident; his beautifully judged comic reactions recall the antic grace of his screwball comedies, and he lends a polite, ironic reserve to his intimate moments. In fact, a close comparison of the continuity script with the published screenplay (issued by Viking Press in 1972, and now out of print) reveals that Grant rarely speaks his lines exactly as they were written. He invests his smallest phrases and gestures with an air of modest discretion, and in most ways the personality he creates is very different from the boozing playboy Lehman had envisioned.

Certainly others of Hitchcock's collaborators had a significant effect on the film. Bernard Herrmann's score provides a feeling of expansive adventure and Gothic tension, and Saul Bass's graphic designs may have influenced the gridlike, geometric minimalism of certain of the photograpic images. Suffice it to say that *North by Northwest* is both a collaborative effort and a "Hitchcock picture to end all Hitchcock pictures." Before examining Hitchcock's style in detail, however, it is important to emphasize that the film also partakes in a large-scale economic and cultural history. At the level of generic conventions, for example, *North by Northwest* is symptomatic of a transitional moment in the evolution of spy fiction: it draws many of its best effects from an extensive (and mostly British) tradition of narratives about international intrigue to which Hitchcock himself had been a major contributor; at the same time, it predicts certain features of the sleekly commodified James Bond movies that followed in its wake.

The full extent of the film's generic background is suggested by Michael Denning's useful study of British spy fiction, *Cover Stories,* which points out that all the major changes in narratives about espionage have been marked by shifts in the economics and cultural politics of book publication. Not surprisingly, the form emerged at the beginning of the twentieth century, when "the existence of rival imperialist states made it increasingly difficult to envision the totality of social relations."[8] Several of the most distinguished authors of the period—including

---

7. Andrew Britton, *Cary Grant: Comedy and Male Desire* (Newcastle upon Tyne, England: Tyneside Cinema, 1983), p. 17.
8. Michael Denning, *Cover Stories: Narrative and Ideology in the British Spy Thriller* (London: Routledge & Kegan Paul, 1987), p. 13.

Rudyard Kipling, Henry James, and Joseph Conrad—were interested in the activities of secret agents; generally speaking, however, the original masters of the spy story were popular craftsmen who aimed their fiction at a downmarket readership, borrowing effects from the American dime novel to praise the civilizing effects of the British empire. The genre did not achieve full-fledged respectability until the 1930s, when it was embraced by the cultural arm of the Popular Front—notably by writers like Graham Greene and Eric Ambler, who brought a new artistic "realism" to the old melodramatic plots, winning approval from literary reviewers and the growing middle-class membership of subscription book clubs. Finally, during the cold war, with the rise of the paperback industry and *Playboy* magazine, the James Bond craze began; although the realist tradition remained alive, a great deal of spy fiction reverted to the square-jawed heroics of the original stories, all the while providing luxurious and sexually explicit fantasies that were symptomatic of a burgeoning consumer economy.

Hitchcock's work needs to be understood in the context of these events. Even though his medium was the movies rather than literature, many of his characteristic themes and stylistic effects were developed in close relation to the British novel of espionage—a type of entertainment that sometimes lives a double life, supporting patriotic agendas even while it explores a Kafkaesque borderland between the individual subject and the authoritarian state. *North by Northwest* is a highly self-conscious example of such narrative duplicity, poised neatly between a heroic adventure story and a nightmarish scenario in which personal identity and the sense of "knowable community" are threatened with dissolution. And because it appeared at a relatively late stage of Hitchcock's career, it had an unusually pivotal effect: looked at today, it seems to encapsulate the entire history of a genre, gathering up familiar motifs from all of Hitchcock's sources and transforming them into a new style, perfectly keyed to a changing marketplace.

Among the major British novelists of the early twentieth century, Joseph Conrad and Somerset Maugham were especially adept at describing the social and psychological ironies of the borderland where spies operate. Hitchcock adapted their novels for two of his best pictures of the 1930s, but he had even more in common with John Buchan, the "father" of mass-market spy fiction, who published *The Thirty-nine Steps* in 1915.[9] A Scottish businessman and later the Governor General of Canada, Buchan was essentially a writer of boy's adventure stories designed to promote British national interests. The key to his success lay in the fact that his protagonists were amateurs rather than members of a high diplomatic service; as Graham Greene later observed, Buchan realized "the enormous dramatic value of adventure in familiar surroundings happening to unadventurous men, members of Parliament and members of the Athenaeum,

9. Hitchcock's film adaptation of Buchan's novel was entitled *The 39 Steps*. I have maintained this distinction in format throughout.

lawyers and barristers, businessmen and minor peers: murder in 'the atmosphere of breeding and simplicity and stability.'"[10] Thus Richard Hannay, the protagonist of *The Thirty-nine Steps,* is a well-bred citizen, thoroughly at home in the modern city, who accidentally plunges through the orderly surface of British society into a primal underworld of national warfare. His discovery of a hidden network of power is dangerous but thrilling, allowing him to behave rather like a swash-buckling hero. Along with the therapeutic derring-do comes a knowledge of a fundamental truth. In the words of one of Buchan's other protagonists,

> Now I saw how thin is the protection of civilization. An accident . . . a false charge and a bogus arrest—there were a dozen ways of spiriting one out of this gay and bustling world.[11]

Hitchcock acknowledged the importance of this theme during his interview with Truffaut, in which he noted that "Buchan was a strong influence on my work long before I undertook *The Thirty-nine Steps,*" chiefly because of his "under-statement of highly dramatic ideas."[12] A film like *North by Northwest* may seem anything but understated, but notice how much it depends on a vivid contrast between a breathtaking adventure and a cast of polished, reserved actors. Nearly all the comedy, suspense, and sexual unease derive from the threat of violence in an atmosphere of "breeding and simplicity and stability." Meanwhile, Roger O. Thornhill, the complacent Madison Avenue executive who finds himself inter-pellated under the name of George Kaplan, is a lineal descendant of Buchan's heroes, inhabiting a more thoroughly modernized and politically treacherous society.[13] Like Hannay, he is accused of murder (in this case, the victim is a kindly diplomat who is knifed in broad daylight in the crowded reception lounge of the

10. Graham Greene, "The Last Buchan," in *Graham Greene: Collected Essays* (Harmondsworth, England: Penguin, 1970), p. 167.

11. Quoted by Greene, ibid., p. 168.

12. *Hitchcock,* p. 65.

13. In using the verb *interpellate,* I am referring to Louis Althusser's highly influential and widely reprinted essay, "Ideology and Ideological State Apparatuses," which first appeared in English in 1971. (See also the commentary by Slavoj Žižek reprinted in this volume.) Althusser argues that ideology reproduces itself across successive generations through a process of *naming,* or calling out to individuals; as he puts it, ideology "recruits" its subjects "by that very precise operation which I have called *interpellation* or hailing, and which can be imagined along the lines of the most commonplace everyday police (or other) hailing: 'Hey, you there!'" The process occurs not only in the public world of the police and law courts, but also in the more primal or intimate world of the family: "it is certain in advance that [a child] will bear its Father's Name, and will therefore have an identity and be irreplaceable. Before its birth, the child is therefore always-already a subject, appointed as a subject in and by the specific ideological configuration in which it is 'expected.'" Seen in Althusserian terms, *North by Northwest* could be understood as a comic allegory about interpellation, in which the name "George Kaplan" is revealed as nothing more than an empty signifier. (See Althusser, *Lenin and Philosophy,* trans. Ben Brewster [New York: Monthly Review Press, 1971], pp. 174, 176.)

United Nations); and like Hannay, he flees the menacing structures of urban life, heading north and west, where he tracks an archvillain to his lair (Hannay ran to Scotland, whereas Thornhill heads for South Dakota).

It seems only natural that Buchan's novels should have provided an inspiration for Hitchcock, since mainstream cinema has always relied on the conventions of melodrama and romance.[14] But the widespread critical recognition and artistic legitimacy Hitchcock achieved in the interwar years came at least in part from his ability to temper Buchan's rather dated plots, which were based in a polite ethos of gentlemanly games, with an opposite quality, sometimes called irony or realism. Hitchcock always regarded himself as a serious artist working in a popular medium; he was keenly aware of vanguard artistic movements such as expressionism and surrealism, and he seems to have recognized quite early on that the key to success (especially in the class-conscious world of British cinema) lay in capturing the attention of reviewers and intellectuals. Hence his work in the 1930s shared certain traits with figures like Greene and Ambler, who were his approximate contemporaries.[15] Together with several other writers and directors of the period, he took popular formulas and "crossed over" into a realm admired by critics, transforming melodramatic values and establishing what Michael Denning calls a full-fledged aesthetic ideology.[16] To understand properly what a later Hitchcock picture like *North by Northwest* inherits from this ideology, we need to view the film in light of four essential features of what I shall term the modernist or "artful" suspense story:

1. *Skepticism toward established legal and political institutions.* Hitchcock's British spy films were antifascist, and during the early 1940s he made occasional gestures on behalf of wartime propaganda; on the whole, however, he was a disengaged artist, and in this respect he was quite different from Greene and Ambler. His frequently discussed plot device, the "MacGuffin," is actually the

14. The best discussion of Hitchcock's indebtedness to the romance mode is Lesley Brill, *The Hitchcock Romance: Love and Irony in Hitchcock's Films* (Princeton, N.J.: Princeton University Press, 1988). See especially the remarks on *North by Northwest,* pp. 4–21.

15. Greene and Hitchcock have several things in common, including the fact that they were both British Catholics who were fond of Buchan. But the relationship between Hitchcock and Ambler was more specific. David O. Selznick attempted to bring the two men together when Hitchcock first came to America, and in 1943 Hitchcock wrote the introduction to an omnibus of Ambler's fiction, entitled *Intrigue.* Hitchcock never adapted Greene or Ambler to the screen, but Ambler married Hitchcock's associate, Joan Harrison, in 1958, and then took over the script for *The Wreck of the Mary Deare* (1959, directed by Michael Anderson), the project Hitchcock and Ernest Lehman had abandoned before starting *North by Northwest.*

16. See Denning, *Cover Stories,* especially pp. 59–90. My listing of the formal and thematic attributes of the "art" thriller is indebted to this more detaied and nuanced discussion. Denning remarks that the major thrillers of the 1930s "are marked by the 'literary' as it was defined in the early twentieth century . . . perhaps crucially, by the concern for the issue of point of view" (pp. 63–64).

expression of an easy cynicism about politics, since it reduces the causes of espionage to an absurdity.[17] (In *North by Northwest,* the MacGuffin becomes a self-reflexive joke: a statuette containing government secrets breaks open to reveal what looks like a roll of 35mm motion picture film.) Even so, Hitchcock was in some ways a critic of government orthodoxy: the agents or officers of the law in his pictures are nearly always depicted ironically, and the narratives focus relentlessly on the psychic anxieties of middle-class characters who are in danger of being arrested, punished, or manipulated by an ideological apparatus.

Hitchcock's relatively anxious or cynical attitude toward the state is apparent in *North by Northwest,* where he and Lehman satirize the cold war. The film was released in the final year of the Eisenhower presidency, at a time when the daily news was filled with conflicting stories about diplomacy and international conspiracy. In the same issue of *Time* magazine in which *North by Northwest* was originally reviewed, readers were informed of a "cold thaw," precipitated by a forthcoming visit to the United States by Nikita Khrushchev; the magazine also noted that Richard Nixon had just returned from the Soviet Union, bringing a report on the poor condition of the Russian consumer economy, and that the United States was launching its ninth satellite into space, hoping to overcome the military advantage achieved by Sputnik in 1957. At almost the same moment, Allen Dulles, the director of the CIA, had emerged from a meeting with forty-five U.S. governors in San Juan, Puerto Rico, at which he announced that "the Soviets intend to use nuclear blackmail as a major weapon to promote their objectives— namely, to spread Communism throughout the world." In response to Dulles, New York's Nelson Rockefeller was proposing a nationwide system of private bomb shelters and a federally sponsored army of civil defense experts for every community in the country.[18]

---

17. According to Donald Spoto, the term "MacGuffin" was coined not by Hitchcock, but by one of his British collaborators, Angus MacPhail (see *Dark Side,* pp. 159–160). Hitchcock loved to explain the term to interviewers—for example in his conversations with Truffaut, where he describes the MacGuffin as "the device, the gimmick, if you will, or the papers the spies are after. . . . in the picture the plans, documents, or secrets must seem to be of vital importance to the characters. To me, the narrator, they're of no importance whatever" (*Hitchcock,* p. 98). The name for this unimportant but necessary element of the plot was derived from a shaggy dog joke involving two men traveling aboard a train. Hitchcock told the joke as follows:
>One man says, "What's that package up there in the baggage rack?"
>And the other answers, "Oh, that's a MacGuffin."
>The first one asks, "What's a MacGuffin?"
>"Well," the other man says, "it's an apparatus for trapping lions in the Scottish Highlands."
>The first man says, "But there are no lions in the Scottish Highlands," and the other one answers, "Well then, that's no MacGuffin!" So you see that a MacGuffin is actually nothing at all. (ibid., p. 99).

18. These various news items appear in the "National Affairs" section of *Time,* August 17, 1959, pp. 17–22.

Given such an atmosphere, Hitchcock and Lehman poked fun at the CIA, subtly linking its activities to the "expedient exaggerations" and image-making techniques of Madison Avenue (a favorite target of Hitchcock's television programs during the same years). They gave the chief of their fictional U.S. spy agency (Leo G. Carroll) a vague resemblance to Dulles; they salted the film with joking allusions to real-life conspiracies (as when a pre-Columbian statuette containing microfilm is described as "the pumpkin," in reference to the Alger Hiss–Whittaker Chambers case); and they even allowed Cary Grant to suggest that the United States "ought to start learning how to lose a few cold wars." Hitchcock's almost Wildean aestheticism added to the feeling of irreverence. "For me, art comes before democracy," he told *Cahiers du Cinéma* when the film was released,[19] and he reinforced the point in the chase atop Mount Rushmore, where he ironically juxtaposed two movie stars and a small, dark, native American sculpture against the massive, chalky carvings of the presidents. When the U.S. Park Service refused him permission to depict characters suspended from the presidential faces, he reluctantly moved all the action to the rocks between them; and to demonstrate his contempt, he withdrew all acknowledgment of the Park Service from the credits.[20]

2. *A morally ambiguous, quasi-psychoanalytic treatment of character.* Unlike Buchan's novels, which preserved the firm moral categories of popular melodrama, the major spy stories of the 1930s were psychologically and ethically complex. The characters often suffered from an ontological insecurity, and the familiar doppelgänger theme of Gothic ficton was given a clinical twist, as if to suggest that the nominal hero was motivated by the same dark impulses as the villain. All of Hitchcock's films were marked by these qualities, although *North by Northwest* treats its psychoanalytic subtext lightly. Vandamm (James Mason), the master spy, is in many ways an anachronistic figure, reminiscent of the evil Germans in Buchan's work or in countless Hollywood melodramas about World War II; nevertheless, he physically resembles Roger Thornhill, and he has a similar urbanity and self-confidence. The film suggests that he is bisexual, emphasizing his closeness to Leonard (Martin Landau), but it also suggests that Roger has a sublimated, romantic attachment to his delightfully cynical mother (Jessie Royce Landis). Above all, the two men are alike in their desire for Eve Kendall

19. Jean Domarchi and Jean Douchet, "Entretien avec Alfred Hitchcock," *Cahiers du Cinéma* 102 (December 1959): 18, reprinted in this volume.

20. The action in the Mount Rushmore sequence was of course staged entirely in a studio, but the National Park Service was concerned by the fact that actors *appeared* to be suspended from the monument. According to Donald Spoto, Hitchcock refused to give any credit to the Department of the Interior (*Dark Side*, p. 443). However, in the interview with *Cahiers du Cinéma* reprinted in this volume, Hitchcock claims that it was the Department of the Interior that refused credit, because the film showed a park ranger punching Cary Grant in the jaw.

(Eva Marie Saint)—an affinity Hitchcock underlines in his clever staging of the auction house sequence, in which Roger and Vandamm stand face to face, with Eve sitting between them, looking impassively forward, like an objet d'art they are in competition to possess.

3. *Systematic control of focalization or point of view.* In its move toward psychological realism, modern literature as a whole became increasingly subjective, exploring the tension between individual consciousness and a problematic, unknowable totality. Henry James and Joseph Conrad were early exponents of the technique, and their work had an important influence on the 1930s generation of British spy novelists. Thus Graham Greene's *Ministry of Fear* (1943) is centered in the mind of a protagonist who doubts his own sanity, and Eric Ambler's *A Coffin for Dimitrios* (1939) borrows its plot from Conrad's *Heart of Darkness,* allowing the central character to take shape impressionistically, through the scattered accounts of various narrators.

Hitchcock's own interest in modernized narrative was stimulated not only by espionage fiction, but also by a number of vanguard developments in the style of late silent movies. He shares many qualities with Lev Kuleshov and the Soviet montage school of the 1920s—a group of directors who were intensely concerned with "pure cinema," and who tried to exert a Pavlovian mastery over the audience by means of graphic design and the skillful juxtaposition of images. (Ivor Montague, one of Hitchcock's associates at the London Film Society and a scriptwriter for both *The Lodger* and *The Man Who Knew Too Much,* was an early translator of Eisenstein.[21]) Above all, however, Hitchcock's style was affected by his apprenticeship during the 1920s at UFA, the German studio where F. W. Murnau and other expressionist filmmakers experimented with subjective narration for the camera. Perhaps because of his formative experiences in Germany, he became the cinema's most famous exponent of a kind of psychological editing, in which the meaning of a sequence derives from careful alternations between "inner" and "outer" points of view. James Agee was aware of this fact in 1946, when he reviewed *Notorious.* "One would think," he wrote, "that the use of the camera subjectively—that is, as one of the characters—would for many years have been as basic a movie device as the closeup, but few people try it and

---

21. As I've suggested elsewhere in this essay, Hitchcock also had many things in common with the surrealists—especially an interest in the Freudian subconscious, a romantic attitude toward male heterosexual passion, and a tendency to value what he called "imagination" over "logic." (See the interview reprinted in this volume, in which he declares, "Logic, we should pitch out the window!") He often remarked that his favorite movie director was Luis Buñuel; indeed the sound of a toilet flushing in Buñuel's *L'Age d'or* (1930) seems to be echoed three decades later in a famous scene in *Psycho.* The relation between these two filmmakers is further explored by Robert Stam in "Hitchcock and Buñuel: Authority, Desire, and the Absurd," in Walter Raubicheck and Walter Srebnick, ed., *Hitchcock's Rereleased Films: From* Rope *to* Vertigo (Detroit: Wayne State University Press, 1991), pp. 116–146.

Hitchcock is nearly the only living man I can think of who knows just when and how to."[22]

Hitchcock's technique, which reminded Agee of that of "a good French novelist," actually depends upon a careful manipulation of two formal extremes: the purely subjective shot/reverse shot, focalized through a character; and the purely objective shot, often positioned from a "bird's-eye" vantage, looking down on a scene. Again and again, his films veer back and forth between an uncanny private perspective and a schematic, godlike omniscience (or between what the psychoanalyst Jacques Lacan would call the Imaginary and Symbolic registers). These interdependent formal effects can be seen everywhere in *North by Northwest,* and they make us especially aware of the director's control over the story. The bird's-eye view occurs at several important junctures, usually at the beginning or end of a sequence, as in the conclusion of the murder scene at the United Nations building. In the sequence in which Roger Thornhill speeds down a dark highway in a stolen Mercedes, Hitchcock keeps the camera inside the car, viewing all the near accidents from Roger's drunken point of view; then at the end, in the comic collision with the police, he cuts to an almost proscenium-style shot that declares his coolly detached presence. The best example of his method, however, is the crop-dusting episode, which opens with a lofty view of a straight highway running through a barren prairie, and then fragments the landscape into a series of ground-level shots. Lehman's original script had proposed cross-cutting between the pilot of the biplane and Roger; but Hitchcock designed the episode in a rigorously subjective manner, showing virtually everything from Roger's perspective, until the moment when he sneaks offscreen and rides away in a stolen pickup truck.

Elsewhere, the film cleverly manipulates narrative information, controlling how much the audience knows in relation to the characters. During the first part of the story, we are placed almost completely in Roger's position, so that we are certain of his innocence even if we are baffled by the sinister goings-on; then the perspective shifts to an intelligence agency, where Hitchcock looks down on the action from a lofty angle, allowing us to learn important information that Roger does not possess. From this point onward, we alternate between two positions, sometimes sharing in Roger's surprise or anxiety, sometimes watching helplessly while he tries to cope with a dangerous situation that we fully comprehend. The technique is raised to the level of tour de force in the penultimate episode, when Roger attempts to rescue Eve from Vandamm's mountain retreat: at strategic moments, the camera substitutes for the eyes of Roger, Vandamm, Leonard, and Anna the housekeeper; all the while, the film plays a series of Hitchcockian tricks, sometimes revealing information to create suspense (as when Leonard conceals a gun from Vandamm), and sometimes withholding information to create surprise (as when Vandamm discovers that the gun contains blanks).

22. *Agee on Film,* vol. 1 (New York: McDowell, Obolensky, 1958), p. 214.

4. *The use of melodramatic violence to depict an eruption of the real into imaginary social relations.* Of all the "artful" characteristics I have been describing, this is the most important, not only for Hitchcock's films but for all sorts of noirish adventure or mystery in the modern period.[23] Popular melodrama at the turn of the century—in the hands of such different artists as David Belasco, D. W. Griffith, and John Buchan—had used violence cathartically, in the service of an ostensibly moral attitude: virtuous characters were crushed by brutes, but evil was usually punished by righteous force. In sharp contrast, Hitchcock and his contemporaries imagined a world where justice triumphed ironically, and where violence had deep-seated psychological motives. Hitchcock in particular was fond of giving a Freudian emphasis to Buchan's idea about the "thin" protection afforded by civilization, showing chaotic desires and acts of cruelty breaking through an orderly, middle-class propriety, as if the "real" forces of the id were attacking the imaginary or rationalized defenses of the superego.

Much of the violence experienced by Roger Thornhill in *North by Northwest* has this feeling, rather like a comic nightmare in which the political and sexual unconscious return, exploding the surface of a smug, Madison Avenue life-style. Repeatedly, the film subjects Roger to threats, embarrassment, and exposure in public places; at the same time, however, it resembles a wish-fulfilling, Mitty-esque dream, allowing him to become an old-fashioned adventurer who triumphs over evil and wins the hand of a fair lady. Hitchcock keeps the two implications in perfect balance, so that romance and irony intermingle. The daring chase across Mount Rushmore, for example, is hallucinatory (all the more so because of the artificial look of back projection and optical printing), and the brilliantly economical conclusion operates by free association, lifting Roger and Eve out of one kind of dream and into another. Especially in the second half of the film, suspense is generated less by the spy plot than by a fantastic network of male jealousies and fears of betrayal, extending from Roger to Vandamm to Leonard, with Eve always in danger of being savagely exterminated. Meanwhile, the love scenes have the same darkly suggestive logic as the action sequences. Eva Marie Saint plays a typical Hitchcock blonde (elegant, buttoned-up, repressed on the surface but exuding a smoldering carnality), and when she and Grant embrace on the Twentieth-Century Limited, Hitchcock introduces a characteristically sado-masochistic note: "Maybe you're planning to murder me right here, tonight," she

---

23. Hitchcock was not the only director to suggest that civilized life was but a protective veneer covering a "reality" of sordid violence. In Fritz Lang's *Ministry of Fear* (1944, adapted from the Graham Greene novel), there is a remarkably Hitchcock-like scene in which a Bond Street tailor, pursued by government agents, enters a plush dressing room and stabs himself to death with a pair of shears in order to avoid capture. Likewise, in Lang's *Cloak and Dagger* (1946), there is a scene rather like the one Hitchcock later staged in *Torn Curtain* (1966), in which a protracted and clumsy fight to the death takes place amid placid surroundings.

murmurs seductively. He raises his hands to her shimmering hair as if he would like to strangle her. "Shall I?" he asks. "Please do," she responds.

But if *North by Northwest* is everywhere shaped by these four defining features of modernist melodrama, it also represents something new. Significantly, the film was released at the very moment when American show business was about to enter a postmodern phase. In 1959 the classic studio system had been replaced by a variety of package-unit arrangements, and Hollywood had become the chief purveyor of material for television. The artifacts left behind by the old industry were being recycled and mythologized, while the new industry worked toward a more thorough consolidation of the different media. Hitchcock was in an excellent position to take advantage of the changing conditions. Partly because of his special relationship with Lew Wasserman of the MCA talent agency, he had become the "editor" of *Alfred Hitchcock's Mystery Magazine* and the impresario of *Alfred Hitchcock Presents,* one of the most popular television shows in America; he was also in charge of his own unit for theatrical films, so that he could oscillate between sardonic, low-budget television programs and colorful, star-filled theatrical shows. (In 1960, he synthesized the two forms in *Psycho,* his single most profitable undertaking.) Meanwhile, in France, the critics of the New Wave were reevaluating classic Hollywood, elevating Hitchcock to canonical status.[24]

Little wonder, then, that *North by Northwest* should manifest so many of the attributes Fredric Jameson has attributed to the "cultural logic of late capitalism."[25] It is not simply a film directed by Alfred Hitchcock and starring Cary Grant, but a film in the Hitchcock and Grant "manner"—an ultraglamorous "movie-movie," employing a pastiche of their previous work. Its tongue-in-cheek style and direct appeals to romantic fantasy seem to predict subsequent developments in the industry, affecting not only the James Bond cycle but also such pictures as Stanley Donen's *Charade* (1963), Arthur Hiller's *Silver Streak* (1976), Brian De Palma's *The Fury* (1978), and Jonathan Demme's *Something Wild* (1986). By the same token, its special effects and exhilarating spirit of high adventure are echoed in the blockbuster films of Steven Spielberg and George Lucas. Consider *Close Encounters of the Third Kind* (1977), in which a man and a woman clasp hands across a mountaintop, and in which François Truffaut makes a speech about ordinary people caught up in extraordinary adventures. Consider, too, *Raiders of the Lost Ark* (1981), in which most of the chase sequences try to achieve a feeling of extreme peril in travelogue settings.

24. For an account of the critical reception accorded Hitchcock's films in these years, see Robert E. Kapsis, *Hitchcock: The Making of a Reputation* (Chicago: University of Chicago Press, 1992).
25. See Jameson's *Postmodernism, or, the Cultural Logic of Late Capitalism* (Durham, N.C.: Duke University Press, 1991).

To be sure, *North by Northwest* is different in many ways from the films I have mentioned. My point is simply that Hitchcock was a shrewd commercial artist, and that *North by Northwest* allowed him to develop new, more spectacular possibilities for a kind of entertainment narrative he had perfected many years earlier. By the late 1950s, he had become such a valuable commodity that his directorial signature could be foregrounded as never before: *North by Northwest* is therefore designed as a special and blatantly intertextual event, recapitulating his earlier triumphs and containing one of his most ostentatious appearances as an extra.

It should be remembered that, even though Hitchcock was a sophisticated ironist who could openly mock the pieties of Hollywood melodrama (as in *Vertigo* and *Psycho,* the films he made before and after *North by Northwest*), he was able to maintain his position in the industry only because he respected certain traditional standards of production. He frequently relied on the star system, and he combined a gift for sexual suspense with a highly developed taste for luxury and charm. Actually, he never strayed far from the values of Selznick, who had brought him to Hollywood in the 1940s. He merely arranged his career so that he could mix glamorous projects involving upper-class characters, such as the Cary Grant vehicles, with somber pictures like *Shadow of a Doubt* (1943), in which the psychotic Uncle Charlie tells his innocent, small-town niece that "the world is a foul sty," and that "if you ripped the fronts off houses you'd find swine."

Hitchcock's fastidious, suspenseful treatment of love and violence has often been related to his private obsessions, and to a more systemic pathology of masculine desire underlying the classic cinema.[26] But these same qualities, reinforced by his polished commercialism, have equally important social implications. Interestingly, his spy movies seldom ventured into "Greeneland"—the term literary critics have given to the spiritually seedy, impoverished mise-en-scène of Graham Greene's novels. In British films like *Sabotage* (1936), Hitchcock tried to achieve what he called a "real lower-middle-class atmosphere,"[27] but in general he took advantage of the genre's tendency to become a species of travel literature. He was fond of describing his method to interviewers, as when he told

---

26. The literature on the second of these topics is extensive, prompted by a feminist interest in psychoanalysis. See, for example, Laura Mulvey's widely reprinted essay, "Visual Pleasure and Narrative Cinema," which appears in her book, *Visual and Other Pleasures* (Bloomington: Indiana University Press, 1989), pp. 14–26. See also Jacqueline Rose, "Paranoia and the Film System," in Constance Penley, ed., *Feminism and Film Theory* (New York: Routledge & Kegan Paul, 1988), pp. 141–158. The most ambitious discussion of *North by Northwest* in psychoanalytic terms is Raymond Bellour, "Le Blocage symbolique," in *Communications,* Volume 23 (Paris: Seuil, 1975), pp. 235–350. The best of many feminist accounts of Hitchcock is Tania Modleski, *The Women Who Knew Too Much: Hitchcock and Feminist Theory* (New York: Methuen, 1988).
27. Alfred Hitchcock, "Direction (1937)," in Albert J. LaValley, ed., *Focus on Hitchcock* (Englewood Cliffs, N.J.: Prentice-Hall, 1972), p. 34.

François Truffaut about the need to invest *The Secret Agent* (1936) with entertainment values so that he could compensate for the lack of a happy ending:

The action takes place in Switzerland. I said to myself, "What do they have in Switzerland?" They have milk chocolate, they have the Alps, they have village dances, and they have lakes. All of these national ingredients were woven into the picture.[28]

The only critic to have commented at length on the social implications of Hitchcock's picture-postcard settings is Virginia Wexman, who has suggested that the director was a cultural imperialist and a cinematic "tour guide."[29] The full implications of Wexman's argument become clear if we note a remark Hitchcock himself makes during the interview on *North by Northwest* reprinted in this volume: "[Cary Grant] succeeds in evading the police disguised as a porter in a red cap. Porters in red caps are one of the characteristic features of Chicago." Perhaps so, but Hitchcock fails to mention that a great many of Chicago's red caps in 1959 were black men. (We see blacks on several other occasions in the film, working as porters, as valets, and even in one early scene as a redcap.) The comic escape scene in La Salle Street Station therefore depends on a temporary suspension of verisimilitude—a deliberate transformation of America into a tourist's fantasyland, suitable for the adventures of a well-to-do, somewhat British set of characters. This tendency may explain why *North by Northwest* seems to anticipate Hollywood in the 1970s and 1980s. There is no scene in the picture like the one in *The 39 Steps* in which Richard Hannay spends an evening with a cruel old farmer and his young wife, and there are no intentionally grotesque Hitchcockian jokes that disturb the beautiful surroundings—no dowager putting out a cigarette in a fried egg and no country gentleman holding up his hand to show an amputated finger. The working class and the peasants have been moved to the margins of the action, and nothing occurs outside the boundaries of commercial travel aboard clearly advertised trains, planes, and buses.

Wexman contends that Hitchcock's glossy American thrillers—especially *Vertigo*—entailed not only a kind of tourism but also a "displacement of racial and class issues into the sphere of sexuality."[30] Although I generally agree with this argument, I would put the case somewhat differently: a film like *Vertigo* clearly

---

28. *Hitchcock*, p. 74.

29. "The Critic as Consumer: Film Study in the University, *Vertigo*, and the Film Canon," *Film Quarterly* 39, no. 2 (Spring 1986): 32–41.

30. Ibid., p. 36. Wexman observes the curious fact that no psychoanalytic critic has ever remarked upon the equation Hitchcock made (during a discussion of *Marnie* with Truffaut) between fetishism and miscegenation (*Hitchcock*, p. 227). Notice also that, in the Truffaut interview, Hitchcock recalled newspaper photos of people being taken to jail: "I remember one time when they showed the head of the New York Stock Exchange being jailed. He was handcuffed to a Negro. Later on I used that in *The Thirty-nine Steps*" (ibid., p. 34).

reveals Hitchcock's interest in the relationship between class and sex, even if his attitudes are perversely conservative, controlled by the demands of Hollywood glamour. In similar fashion, the settings in some of his movies have a contradictory function: they seduce the audience into a romantic fantasy, but they seem ironic or surrealistic, as if a bourgeois spectacle were being defaced by something grotesquely inappropriate. Just as Hitchcock used movie stars to implicate us in certain anxieties about voyeurism, so he used what he called "national elements" to disturb our consumerist gaze. In the final analysis, however, he remained firmly committed to his role as commercial entertainer, and he demonstrated a remarkable ability to have everything both ways. On television in the late 1950s, he made fun of his sponsors, but at the same time he brought them high ratings. In *North by Northwest,* he joked about Madison Avenue and the presidential monuments, but he also produced a Technicolor, VistaVision daydream involving two beautiful, superbly dressed people having brook trout and sex on the Twentieth-Century Limited. Even the title of his film was double-edged: on the one hand it alluded to *Hamlet,* reminding critics of his interest in Freudian materials; but on the other hand, it provided an excellent opportunity to stage a scene in an airport, where a sign for Northwest Orient Airlines was prominently displayed.

Perhaps because Hitchcock was chiefly interested in sexual anxiety, he could retain his commercial instincts without forsaking the more unorthodox aspects of his "vision." He sometimes directed social-realist projects like *The Wrong Man* (1956), but even in dealing with quotidian subjects his imagery always had an eerie, dreamlike effect. The fascination of his work derived in part from a conflict between his sinister irony and his pellucid syntax, which gave each sequence the clean, boldly simplified look of a storyboard or a cartoon. There was a vaguely pornographic impulse lurking at the edges of his films, inviting critics to speculate about the psychosexual mechanisms of popular cinema; but his carefully controlled imagery also hinted at a latent, Orwellian fear of descending into the lower classes. In both respects, he was a director who specialized in repression. The anal-compulsive neatness he brought to the construction of his films was rather like an austere dandyism, reinforcing the psychic and social tensions he was trying to dramatize.

These tensions are never far away in *North by Northwest,* which is one of the most crowd-pleasing entertainments of Hitchcock's career. He seems to have been in a lighthearted mood when he produced the film, and yet he gave melodrama the feeling of a guilty dream and romantic comedy an air of danger. Throughout, he made satiric use of American landscape, turning every colorful tourist stop and national icon into a slightly paranoid vision. He depicted spies as insensitive organization men and jealous lovers, and when he gave us the pleasure of watching Cary Grant and Eva Marie Saint, he tinged each moment with anxiety. Ultimately, he swept away all the troubling ambiguities, concluding the film with a normative, heterosexual marriage between Roger and Eve. The ending, however, is accomplished by a kind of directorial sleight of hand, in the form of a match cut; and if the release of tension works better here than in *Strangers on a Train* (1951), that is only because it is more swiftly and playfully executed.[31] In the delightful concluding scene, Hitchcock shows Roger and Eve aboard a luxury sleeping car, speeding away into a night of sexual bliss. But his last shot—a bird's-eye view of the phallic train entering a tunnel—signals his derisive sense of humor, provoking ironic laughter and a chastened awareness that every fairy tale has hidden meanings.

31. Several commentators on the film, including Robin Wood, Stanley Cavell, and Lesley Brill, have treated the marriage plot in somewhat moralistic terms, as if it signified progress toward a mature and loving relationship. By contrast, Raymond Durgnat has argued that the film ought not to be read as if it were a *Bildungsroman*. Durgnat points out that several problems remain unresolved at the end—notably the fact that Roger Thornhill seems to be returning to his life as a Madison Avenue executive: "As so often, Hitchcock slips neatly past any real moral crux, and those who see him as a challenging moralist only demonstrate how effectively his melodramatic and conformist preassumptions and his absurdist poetry conceal the real moral issues" (Raymond Durgnat, *The Strange Case of Alfred Hitchcock* [Cambridge, Mass.: MIT Press, 1974], p. 309).

Alfred Hitchcock: A Biographical Sketch

lfred Joseph Hitchcock, Great Britain's most important film director, was born in Leytonstone, England, a suburb of London's East End, on August 13, 1899. The third child of greengrocer William Hitchcock and his wife Emma, young Alfred was raised in a lower-middle-class neighborhood, and was one of the first members of his family to receive a secondary education. Because his mother was an Irish Catholic, he was sent to St. Ignatius College, a Jesuit day school for boys, where he was taught the rudiments of literature, mathematics, languages, and religion. Not long after the death of his father in 1914, he took a job at the Henley Telegraph Company, meanwhile enrolling in night classes on navigation, draftsmanship, and technical mechanics at the University of London. An avid film buff throughout his youth, he later claimed that his early artistic influences included not only the movies but also Edgar Allan Poe's mystery fiction and Flaubert's *Madame Bovary*. In 1918, he signaled his ambitions by writing a Poe-like story entitled "Gas," which was published in the Henley company's office magazine.

In 1919, Hitchcock took a portfolio of his designs and drawings to the British offices of the Famous Players–Lasky Film Corporation, and was hired as an illustrator of title cards for silent movies. For several years he worked alongside Mordant Hall (later the film critic of the *New York Times*), acquiring a distinctly Americanized introduction to the film industry. An eager employee, he was valued for his quick intelligence and willingness to assume any task. Among the directors he encountered at Famous Players was George Fitzmaurice, a meticulous designer of storyboards and settings, who probably influenced his later methods of planning films in advance of shooting. He also attracted the attention of producer-playwright Seymour Hicks, with whom he codirected *Always Tell Your Wife* (1923). Eventually, he was assigned to direct a picture entitled *Mrs. Peabody* or *Number Thirteen,* which remained unfinished.

When Famous Players merged with Paramount and dissolved its British offices, Hitchcock moved to an independent company headed by Michael Balcon, where he was involved in scripting, editing, and art direction. He became an assistant to director Graham Cutts, and he sometimes traveled abroad to work on Anglo-German productions. At UFA, the German studio responsible for many ex-pressionst masterpieces, he observed F. W. Murnau directing *The Last Laugh* (1924). Back in England, he attended the newly formed London Film Society, a group of filmmakers and literary intellectuals (including critics Iris Barry and Ivor Montagu) who were attempting to improve the artistic quality of British cinema. During the same formative period, he met the talented film editor Alma Reville; the two were married in 1926, and Reville often received credit as a writer of Hitchcock's later films.

In 1925, Michael Balcon started Hitchcock on his career by sending him to Munich to direct *The Pleasure Garden,* a Griffith-style melodrama about the love life of two London chorus girls. The completed picture is in some ways character-istic, particularly in its high artistic polish and its titillating mixture of sex and suspense; but the assignment that helped to form Hitchcock's subsequent profes-sional identity was his third film for Balcon, *The Lodger* (1926), a Jack the Ripper murder story based on the novel by Marie Belloc Lowndes. Hitchcock filled this state-of-the-art production with stylistic effects he had learned from the Germans, and he subtly advertised his own work by making two "cameo" appearances as an extra in crowd scenes. A dazzling synthesis of Germanic artistry with American entertainment values, *The Lodger* became one of the most celebrated events of the British silent cinema, immediately transforming its director into a major celebrity.

Film production in Britain during the mid-1920s was chiefly devoted to low-budget movies, most of which were designed to profit from a law requiring theater owners to exhibit a certain amount of domestic product for every feature they imported from Hollywood. Partly because of the success of *The Lodger,* Hitch-cock was able to create a special niche for himself, above the crowd of ordinary directors. After two more films with Balcon, he signed a contract with British International Pictures (BIP), a large, well-equipped studio that was trying to counter the national trend toward "quota quickies." His first undertaking was his own original screenplay for *The Ring* (1927), a love triangle set in a prize-fighting milieu, which once again showed his interest in Murnau, together with a distinc-tive flair for surrealist juxtapositions. Two years later, he employed a similar style in *Blackmail,* the first British all-talking picture. Cleverly scripted by Hitchcock, Benn W. Levy, and playwright Charles Bennett from Bennett's play, this thriller about a woman blackmailed for murder was distinguished for its expressive use of sound; but perhaps more importantly, it contained several motifs that would recur in Hitchcock's later work: an emphasis on the subjectivity of a person who fears apprehension by the police; an "exchange of guilt" between the protagonist and a criminal; and a spectacular chase staged against the backdrop of a public monument.

Hitchcock remained at BIP until 1932, taking charge of a variety of films, including an adaptation of a Sean O'Casey play (*Juno and the Paycock,* 1930), a whodunit (*Murder!,* 1930), and a slightly autobiographical comedy (*Rich and*

Strange, 1932). Unfortunately, his relationship with the studio was detached and businesslike, and he soon began to feel professionally adrift. The low point of his career came when he left BIP to direct a costume musical for the independent producer Tom Arnold (*Waltzes from Vienna,* 1933). At about this time, Michael Balcon, head of the newly formed Gaumont-British film company, learned of Hitchcock's dissatisfaction and offered him the chance to make a series of films with Charles Bennett, his collaborator on *Blackmail.* Joining forces with Ivor Montagu and Alma Reville, Hitchcock and Bennett forged an ideal working relationship, and the string of pictures they created together were celebrated throughout the world.

Balcon and Montagu were political activists, and, in keeping with the atmosphere of the times, they encouraged Hitchcock to make films about international intrigue. *The Man Who Knew Too Much* (1934) concerned a British family on vacation in Switzerland; the family accidentally learns about an assassination plot, and a group of spies kidnaps their child in order to ensure their silence. *The 39 Steps* (1935) was a modernization of the John Buchan novel, involving an innocent Canadian visitor to England who is framed for murder by a ring of espionage agents. *The Secret Agent* (1936), loosely based on two of Somerset Maugham's Ashenden stories, dealt with the grimly ironic adventures of a reluctant British spy working in Switzerland. *Sabotage* (1936), derived from Joseph Conrad's *The Secret Agent,* told the story of a middle-aged anarchist who operates a movie theater in a London suburb; when one of the spy's bombs accidentally kills his wife's little brother, the wife takes her revenge with a bread knife. *Young and Innocent* (1938), the only film in the series that did not allude to violent political events in contemporary Europe, was a "wrong man" thriller in a comic mode, centering on a young woman who becomes a detective, helping a male friend to clear his name of a murder charge. All of these films involved a characteristically "Hitchcockian" mixture of sex, narrative tension, and mordant wit; they were filled with visual set pieces or "director's moments," and they forever established his reputation as a master of suspense. Not surprisingly, Hitchcock chose a similar format when he subsequently moved to Gainsborough Pictures: in *The Lady Vanishes* (1938), a charming little old lady disappears from a train traveling through the Balkans, and a young English couple discovers that she is in reality a secret agent, kidnapped by spies.

The great success of Hitchcock's British thrillers soon attracted the attention of Hollywood, and in 1937 he was offered a contract by David O. Selznick, who was planning a film about the sinking of the *Titanic.* Two years later, as war broke out in England, Hitchcock completed his last British film, *Jamaica Inn* (1939), and moved to America, making California his home for the rest of his life. The project concerning the *Titanic* failed to materialize, but he directed *Rebecca* (1940), an elaborately produced adaptation of Daphne du Maurier's best-selling Gothic romance. Like so much of Selznick's work, *Rebecca* was told from a woman's point of view; Hitchcock's intensely subjective camera heightened the audience's identification with the insecure heroine, and everywhere intensified the atmosphere of masochistic delirium. The completed film, which won an Academy Award for best picture of the year, gave Hitchcock a secure position from which to manage his American career.

During the 1940s, Hitchcock remained one of Selznick's favorite directors, making two more films in a Gothic style: the pop-Freudian thriller *Spellbound* (1945) and the courtroom melodrama *The Paradine Case* (1947). He also did freelance work on two wartime films that strongly resembled his British espionage pictures: *Foreign Correspondent* (1940) and *Saboteur* (1942). Among his most interesting films of the decade were *Suspicion* (1941), the story of a suspected wife murderer, in which Hitchcock began his long collaboration with Cary Grant; *Shadow of a Doubt* (1943), a Thornton Wilder script about a psychotic bluebeard who hides from the police by visiting his sister's family in Santa Rosa, California; *Lifeboat* (1944), an ironic political allegory set entirely aboard a small lifeboat adrift at sea; and *Notorious* (1946), a perverse love triangle involving Nazi espionage in postwar Brazil. Partly because of the continuing influence of Selznick, most of these films were told from the perspective of women; they were also marked by a brooding, romantic anguish and a seductive fatalism that seemed to pervade Hollywood throughout the heyday of film noir.

From 1948 onward, Hitchcock was essentially his own producer, working mainly for Warner Brothers, Paramount, and Universal. His Warners films included two adaptations of drawing-room thrillers by British playwrights—*Rope* (1948) and *Dial M for Murder* (1954)—the first involving a complex experiment with extended takes, all of them carefully designed to preserve a sense of the invisible "fourth wall" in proscenium theater, and the second making artful use of the 3-D process. Also at Warners, Hitchcock began his collaboration with cinematographer Robert Burks. Their best films at the studio were *Strangers on a Train* (1951), Hitchcock's most humorous and exciting exploration of the theme of doubles or "secret sharers"; and *The Wrong Man* (1956), a harrowing, critically underrated docudrama, in which the terrors besetting the protagonist are more economic than sexual.

Hitchcock's most influential work was done at Paramount, where he began to employ composer Bernard Herrmann, and where he specialized in handsomely mounted, VistaVision pictures starring Cary Grant, James Stewart, and Grace Kelly. He had long been fond of introducing self-reflexive elements into his films (as in the movies-within-the-movie in *Sabotage* and *Rebecca*), but in this period he seemed to turn further inward, closely examining the formal basis of his art. Occasionally he revisited his past triumphs, as in the remake of *The Man Who Knew Too Much* (1956), and in *North by Northwest* (1959) (released by MGM, but involving all the key Paramount personnel). More significantly, he became increasingly preoccupied with the psychology of voyeurism and the ethics of cinematic spectatorship. The theme of sadistic voyeurism is treated playfully in *Rear Window* (1954), where the protagonist witnesses a murder through the window of a neighbor's apartment; it becomes much more troubling in *Vertigo* (1958), where Hitchcock's treatment of an obsessed, somewhat necrophiliac private eye reveals a deep indebtedness to Poe and the ur-surrealist romantics; and it reaches a violent climax in *Psycho* (1960), where the male audience is made complicit in the savage knifing of a beautiful woman.

Throughout most of these years, Hitchcock was also involved in television production. In 1955, the Columbia Broadcasting System and Bristol-Myers offered him one of the most lucrative contracts in entertainment history to supervise *Alfred Hitchcock Presents,* a series of half-hour and one-hour television dramas about murder. Hitchcock was only peripherally involved with the show, leaving most of the details to his associates Joan Harrison and Norman Lloyd; nevertheless, his presence as narrator and occasional director helped to give *Alfred Hitchcock Presents* some of the highest ratings of the late 1950s. Each week, to the strains of Gounod's "Funeral March of a Marionette" (a theme Hitchcock had first heard while watching Murnau's *Sunrise* [1927]), the director's portly shadow moved across the screen, filling the outline of a caricature he had sketched of himself. His satiric remarks on the sponsors, combined with his cherubic looks and deadpan, ultradignified treatment of graveyard humor, made him the most famous movie director in the world.

Hitchcock directed nineteen short films for *Alfred Hitchcock Presents,* plus one episode that was broadcast on an NBC series called *Ford Startime.* Meanwhile, in vanguard European film journals, his work was receiving unprecedented critical attention. As the auteur theory spread from France to America, his critical success transcended even his box office appeal, until he was recognized everywhere as a major artist. The films he made in the late 1950s and early 1960s exerted a massive influence on Hollywood directors down to the present day, and the best-known scenes from those films became touchstones of cinema history. The brutal shower murder in *Psycho,* for example, has been analyzed as thoroughly as Eisenstein's Odessa Steps sequence in *The Battleship Potemkin* (1925).

After 1960, as a result of *Psycho* and the darkly humorous television show, Hitchcock's audience had come to think of him as a man who played sadistic practical jokes, especially in pictures involving gruesome attacks on women. When he moved to Universal, he exploited this new image to the fullest. *The Birds* (1963) was an apocalyptic horror movie in which birds inexplicably turn against humans, unleashing most of their fury on a mink-coated heroine. *Marnie* (1964) was a variation on the psychoanalytic themes of *Spellbound,* but it was also a more violent, Buñuellian film, suited to the newly relaxed standards of the Production Code. *Frenzy* (1972), the most disturbingly explicit of these experiments in sexual violence, marked Hitchcock's return to London and the serial killer motif of *The Lodger,* thereby neatly rounding off his almost fifty years in show business.

In his declining years Hitchcock made two more espionage thrillers—*Torn Curtain* (1966) and *Topaz* (1969)—but he seemed out of his element when he treated the cold war realistically. His last picture was *Family Plot* (1976), based on an ingenious script by Ernest Lehman, in which he discreetly employed one of Lev Kuleshov's famous principles of film editing: he photographed a heterogeneous mixture of images from northern and southern California, and, by combining these images in continuity, he created an entirely cinematic space.

At the time of his death on April 29, 1980, Hitchcock was a legendary personality. He never received an Oscar (although he was nominated for the award five times), but the Academy of Motion Picture Arts and Sciences presented him with the Irving G. Thalberg Memorial Award in 1968. ("Thank you," he said, in the shortest acceptance speech on record.) In 1971, the French made him a Chevalier of the Legion of Honor, and over the next two decades he was repeatedly honored by imitation, parody, and analysis. Generations of filmmakers have tried to emulate his greatest achievements, and discussions of his work have been at the center of every new development in film theory since the early 1950s. In effect, his very name has become one of the definitions of cinema.

North by Northwest

North by Northwest

This transcription is based on the 136-minute release print of *North by Northwest,* which is widely available in videotape and 16mm formats. I have tried to be as factual as possible in describing what appears on the screen, although a project of this kind cannot avoid becoming somewhat interpretive. Except for a few instances, I have not attributed emotions to the actors' speeches ("sadly," "anxiously," "ironically," and so forth), and I have made my formal descriptions of shots as brief as possible. Unless otherwise noted, all references to the left or right side of the screen refer to the perpective of the audience. I have sometimes used the theatrical term "upstage" to indicate a playing area in the background, but otherwise my language is drawn entirely from the world of cinema. The following standard abbreviations for camera distance are employed througout the text:

C U   close-up
E C U   extreme close-up
M S   medium shot

L S   long shot
E L S   extreme long shot
P O V point of view

"Nondiegetic music" is any form of musical accompaniment that does not have an apparent source within the fictional space of the film.

Hitchcock and film editor George Tomasini made a habit of joining the shot/reverse shots of verbal exchanges between characters at just the point where character A is ending a speech or where character B has begun to reply. There are many occasions in the film when the last word of a speech carries over into the next shot, or where the first shot ends with a syllable like "go-" and the second shot begins with a syllable like "-ing." In the interest of clarity and readability, I have not tried to reproduce the exact timing of these cuts.

A note on special effects: Hitchcock was particularly fond of the "glass shot," in which a painting on a sheet of glass is positioned so as to blend with live action. He was also one of the last major directors to employ the Schüfftan process, a more complex type of glass shot that involves mirrors, allowing live action, models, and paintings to be photographed simultaneously. In one version of this technique, the paintings or models are photographed through a transparent sheet of glass positioned at a 45° angle to the lens of the camera; a single area of the glass contains a mirrored surface that reflects live action from the opposite side of the set, making it appear to blend with the model. (In an alternate version of the process, live action is viewed through the glass and artwork is reflected in the mirror.) The Schüfftan process was widely used in Germany and Britain during the 1920s and 1930s—for example in scenes involving the city of the future in Fritz Lang's *Metropolis* and in the chase sequence at the end of Hitchcock's *Blackmail*. To appreciate how the technique was used

in *North by Northwest,* see the illustration for shot 301 of the continuity script—an apparent high-angle view from atop the United Nations Secretariat, showing the tiny figure of Roger Thornhill running across a walkway on the grounds below. The Mount Rushmore episode also uses the Schüfftan process frequently, although a few shots in this part of the film were accomplished with back projection or optical printing. In order to simplify descriptions in the continuity script, I have used the term "matte" to indicate any shot that combines a model or painting with live action—no matter whether the technique in use is the glass shot, the Schüfftan process, or optical printing. I use the term "process" to indicate those shots in which live action was staged in front of process screens or back projection.

Credits

Producer-Director
Alfred Hitchcock

Production Company
Metro-Goldwyn-Mayer

Screenplay
Ernest Lehman

Music
Bernard Herrmann

Director of Photography
Robert Burks, A.S.C.

Production Designer
Robert Boyle

Art Direction
William A. Horning and Merrill Pye

Set Decoration
Henry Grace and Frank McKelvey

Special Effects
A. Arnold Gillespie and Lee LeBlanc

Titles
Saul Bass

Film Editor
George Tomasini, A.C.E.

Color Consultant
Charles K. Hagedon

Recording Supervisor
Franklin Milton

Hair Styles
Sydney Guilaroff

Makeup
William Tuttle

Assistant Director
Robert Saunders

Associate Producer
Herbert Coleman

Process
Technicolor

Length
Time
136 minutes

Shooting Schedule
Shot between August 27 and
    December 24, 1958, on locations in
    Hollywood; also New York City,
    Long Island, and Chicago, and at
    Mount Rushmore National
    Memorial, South Dakota.

Release Date
August 6, 1959 (Radio City Music
    Hall, New York)

Cast

Roger Thornhill
Cary Grant

Eve Kendall
Eva Marie Saint

Phillip Vandamm
James Mason

Clara Thornhill, Roger's Mother
Jessie Royce Landis

The Professor
Leo G. Carroll

"Mrs. Townsend"
(Vandamm's Sister)
Josephine Hutchinson

Lester Townsend
Philip Ober

Leonard
Martin Landau

Valerian
Adam Williams

Victor Larrabee
Edward Platt

Licht
Robert Ellenstein

Auctioneer
Les Tremayne

Dr. Cross
Philip Coolidge

Captain Junket
Edward Binns

Chicago Policemen
(Sergeant Flamm, Charlie)
Patrick McVey, Ken Lynch

Sergeant Emil Klinger
John Beradino

Housekeeper (Anna)
Nora Marlowe

Maggie
Doreen Lang

Judge Anson B. Flynn
Alexander J. Lockwood

Lieutenant Harding
Stanley Adams

Intelligence Agents
Larry Dobkin, Harvey Stephens,
Walter Coy, Madge Kennedy

Elevator Starter (Eddie)
Tommy Farrell

Captain of Waiters (Victor)
Harry Seymour

Herman Weltner
Frank Wilcox

Larry Wade
Robert Shayne

Fanning Nelson
Carleton Young

Lieutenant Hagerman
Paul Genge

Patrolman in Glen Cove Station
Robert B. Williams

Maid (Elsie)
Maudie Prickett

Valet
James McCallion

First New York Taxi Driver
Baynes Barron

United Nations Receptionist
Doris Singh

Attendants at United Nations
Sally Fraser, Susan Whitney,
Maura McGiveney

Ticket Agent
Ned Glass

Conductor
Howard Negley

Steward
Jack Daly

Man on Road
Malcom Atterbury

Assistant Auctioneer
Olan Soule

Woman Bidder
Helen Spring

Woman in Hospital
Patricia Cuts

Ranger
Dale Van Sickel

Rapid City Taxi Driver
Frank Marlowe

Assistant Conductor
Harry Strang

Telephone Operator
Sara Berner

Man Who Misses Bus
Alfred Hitchcock

The Continuity Script

1. *A flat, pale green surface. To the sounds of Bernard Herrmann's "fandango," parallel lines enter the screen from the right, moving at a slightly irregular rate, as if drawn by an invisible stylus. From above and below, another set of lines moves vertically across the screen, forming a geometric grid. When the grid is completed, titles scroll onto the screen from the top and bottom, situating themselves along the diagonal lines and creating a sense of perspective. The following titles appear:* METRO-GOLDWYN-MAYER PRESENTS. CARY GRANT. EVA MARIE SAINT. JAMES MASON. IN ALFRED HITCHCOCK'S. NORTH BY NORTHWEST.
   Dissolve.

2. L S : *the green surface transforms into the glass façade of an office building, seen from a slight angle. The geometric lines become windows, reflecting traffic on the street below. Titles:.* CO-STARRING JESSIE ROYCE LANDIS, WITH LEO G. CARROLL, JOSEPHINE HUTCHINSON, PHILIP OBER, MARTIN LANDAU. ADAM WILLIAMS, EDWARD PLATT, ROBERT ELLENSTEIN, LES TREMAYNE, PHILIP COOLIDGE, PATRICK McVEY, EDWARD BINNS, KEN LYNCH. WRITTEN BY ERNEST LEHMAN. MUSIC BY BERNARD HERRMANN. DIRECTOR OF PHOTOGRAPHY ROBERT BURKS, A.S.C.; TECHNICOLOR. PRODUCTION DESIGNED BY ROBERT BOYLE; ART DIRECTORS WILLIAM A. HORNING & MERRILL PYE; SET DECORATIONS HENRY GRACE & FRANK McKELVEY; SPECIAL EFFECTS A. ARNOLD GILLESPIE & LEE LeBLANC; TITLES DESIGNED BY SAUL BASS. IN VISTAVISION. FILM EDITOR GEORGE TOMASINI, A.C.E.; COLOR CONSULTANT CHARLES K. HAGEDON; RECORDING SUPERVISOR FRANKLIN MILTON; HAIR STYLES BY SYDNEY GUILAROFF; MAKE UP BY WILLIAM TUTTLE; ASSISTANT DIRECTOR ROBERT SAUNDERS.
   Dissolve (credits continue over the following sequence of shots).

3. L S : *the entrance to a Manhattan office building at the end of the day. A crowd of pedestrians moves back and forth along the sidewalk, and office workers emerge from the doors.*

4. L S : *from a high angle, the camera views a crowd of people moving down a subway entrance.*

5. L S : *at a stoplight, a city bus rushes past and a crowd of pedestrians crosses the street.*

6. L S : *a crowd of well-dressed commuters bustles down the steps of Grand Central Station. Title:* ASSOCIATE PRODUCER HERBERT COLEMAN.

7. L S : *a taxi pulls up to a curb and two women shoppers break into a fight over who will take it. Title, appearing over this and the next two shots:* DIRECTED BY ALFRED HITCHCOCK.

8. L S : *a dense crowd moves shoulder to shoulder across a street.*

9. L S : *the director runs up to a corner, trying to catch a bus. He arrives too late; the door slides shut in his face and the bus drives off.*

10. L S, *as in 3: Workers continue to exit an office building.*
    The nondiegetic music draws to a close.
    A Madison Avenue Office Building, interior, day
11. L S: *an elevator door opens and a crowd exits. From the rear of the*
    crowd, we can hear a voice.
    R O G E R T H O R N H I L L: "Even if you accept the belief that the high
       Trendex automatically means a rise in the sales curve, . . ."
    Roger Thornhill emerges from the elevator, dictating a letter to Maggie,
    his secretary, who moves alongside, writing everything onto a pad. He is
    a tall, handsome advertising executive, dressed in an elegant gray suit
    and tie. The camera tracks backward, following him out into the corridor.
    R O G E R: ". . . which, incidentally, I don't, . . ."
    E L E V A T O R S T A R T E R: Mr. Thornhill?
    R O G E R (*glances briefly over his shoulder and continues to walk for-*
       ward): Goodnight, Eddie. Say hello to the missus.
    E L E V A T O R S T A R T E R (*shouting*): We're not talking!
    Roger glances back over his shoulder and smiles, then returns to his dic-
    tation. The camera continues to track backward as he and his secretary
    walk rapidly down the hallway.
    R O G E R: ". . . my recommendation is still the same. Dash. Spread the
       good word in as many small time segments as we can grab, and let the
       opposition have their high ratings while we cry about it all the way to

the bank." (*He pauses at a newsstand to buy a paper.*) "Why don't we colonize at the Colony one day next week for lunch? Let me hear from you, Sam. Happy thoughts." Etcetera, etcetera. (*He has now reached the exit to the building. The camera pans as he turns left and moves toward the doors.*) Come on, better walk me to the Plaza.

MAGGIE: I didn't put a coat on!

ROGER: Use your blood sugar, child. Come on. (*They exit.*)

Madison Avenue, exterior, day

12. MS: *the camera tracks backward as Roger and Maggie step out onto the street and walk briskly along, weaving through crowds.*

ROGER: Next?

MAGGIE: Gretchen Sabinson.

ROGER: Oh, yes. Send her a box of candy from Blum's. Ten dollars. You know the kind. Each piece wrapped in gold paper. She'll like that. She'll think she's eating money. Just say to her, "Darling, I count the days, the hours, the minutes. . . ."

MAGGIE: You said that one last time.

ROGER: I did? Oh, well, put, "Something for your sweet tooth, baby, and all your other sweet parts." (*Maggie glances up at him.*) Oh, I know, I know!

MAGGIE: (*glancing and pointing off to the right*): Oh, could we take a cab, Mr. Thornhill?

ROGER: What, for two blocks?

MAGGIE: You're late and I'm tired.

ROGER: You know, that's your trouble Maggie, you don't eat properly. All right. Taxi!

13. MS, *reverse angle: a red and yellow taxi enters the screen from the right and comes to a stop. The man who has hailed it reaches for the door. From behind the camera and to the right, Roger enters, rapidly pulling Maggie along, reaching out to grasp the man's shoulder just as he is about to step inside the cab.*

ROGER: I beg your pardon, I have a *very* sick woman here. You don't mind, do you? (*He pushes Maggie into the cab and and gets in after her.*)

MAN: Well, no.

ROGER (*closing the door*): Thank you.

MAN: Perfectly all right.

Inside the Taxi, interior, day

14. MS (*process*): *Roger climbs into the back seat and sits beside Maggie, who turns to glance out the rear window as they drive off.*

ROGER (*to the driver*): First stop, the Plaza. Don't throw the flag.

MAGGIE: Poor man.

ROGER: Oh, come, come, come! I made him a happy man. I made him feel like a Good Samaritan.

MAGGIE: He knew you were lying.

ROGER (*opening his newspaper*): Ah, Maggie, in the world of advertising there is no such thing as a lie. There is only The Expedient Exaggeration, you ought to know that. (*Glances down at his waist.*) Say, do I look heavyish to you?

MAGGIE: What?

ROGER: I feel heavyish. Put a note on my desk in the morning: "Think thin."

MAGGIE (*writing in her pad*): "Think thin."

ROGER (*to driver*): Better make it the Fifty-Ninth Street entrance, driver.

15. CU (*process*): *in the front seat, the driver turns slightly and speaks over his shoulder.*

DRIVER: Okay.

16. MS (*process*), *as in 14.*

ROGER (*to Maggie, as he continues to read the paper*): Oh, soon as you get back to the office, call my mother. Remind her we've got theater tickets for tonight. Dinner at 21, seven o'clock. I'll have had two martinis at the Oak Bar, so she needn't bother to sniff my breath.

MAGGIE: She doesn't do that!

ROGER (*smiling*): Sure she does, like a bloodhound.

MAGGIE (*reading from her notes*): Bigelow at ten-thirty is your first for tomorrow. You're due at the Skin Glow rehearsal at noon, then lunch with Falcon and his wife.

ROGER: Oh, yes, where was that?

MAGGIE: Larry and Arnold's. One o'clock. (*Roger lowers the paper and reaches for his wallet as the cab slows.*) Will you check in later?

ROGER: Absolutely not.

17. MS (*process*): *a view from the front seat, looking past the driver at Roger and Maggie.*

ROGER (*as the cab stops*): Driver, take this lady back where she belongs.

DRIVER: Right.

ROGER: That ought to cover it. (*To Maggie*): And don't forget, call my mother right away.

MAGGIE: I won't. Goodnight, Mr. Thornhill.

ROGER: Goodnight, Maggie. (*He exits the cab.*)

Entrance to the Plaza Hotel, exterior, day:

18. LS: *Roger steps out onto the curb and closes the door of the cab. He glances at his wristwatch. Suddenly a thought occurs to him. He turns to shout after the departing cab.*

ROGER: Oh, wait, Maggie! You can't call her, she's at Mrs. . . .

But Maggie is already gone. Frowning, Roger consults his watch again and turns back toward the hotel. The camera pans to follow him as he crosses to the entrance.

Lobby of the Plaza Hotel, interior, day

19. LS: *the lobby. In the distance, Roger enters through a revolving door and walks along the marble floor toward the desk. In the background, the hotel Muzak is playing "It's a Most Unusual Day." Roger consults his watch again. The camera pans to follow him as he rounds the corner beyond the desk and walks toward the Oak Room bar.*

20. LS: *turning the corner beside the elevators, Roger walks through the entrance of the bar.*

The Oak Room Bar, interior, day

21. MS: *Roger enters from the left rear of the camera, and the captain steps up to greet him.*

CAPTAIN: Good evening, Mr. Thornhill.

ROGER: Good evening, Victor. I'm looking for Mr. Weltner and two other gentlemen.

CAPTAIN: Yes, sir. Right this way.

He leads Roger over to a nearby table.

22. MS: *Roger steps up to the table, and a distinguished-looking man rises to shake his hand. Two other men rise as they are introduced.*

ROGER: Herman? Sorry I was a little late.

WELTNER (*making introductions*): Roger Thornhill, Fanning Nelson.

NELSON (*cups his hand over his ear, trying to hear the name*): How do you do.

ROGER (*shakes Nelson's hand*): How do you do.

WELTNER: Larry Wade.

WADE: How do you do.

ROGER (*shaking hands*): How do you do.

WADE (*indicating his martini as everyone sits down*): We've got a little head start here, Mr. Thornhill.

ROGER: That won't last long.

Roger consults his wristwatch again, frowns, and looks around the room somewhat anxiously.

WELTNER: I was just telling Larry and Fanning, you may be slow in starting, but there's nobody faster coming down the homestretch. (*Pause.*) What's the matter, Roger? You've got the fidgets.

23. MCU: *Roger, over Weltner's shoulder.*

ROGER: Oh, I just did something pretty stupid. I told my secretary to call Mother, and I realized she won't be able to reach her where she is.

WELTNER: Why not?

ROGER: Well, she's playing bridge at the apartment of one of her cronies.

24. MS: *the three martini drinkers from over Roger's shoulder. Nelson leans across the table and cups a hand over his ear. At the extreme right, beyond Weltner's shoulder, two men can be seen standing just outside the bar, near the window of one of the hotel shops. One of them, Licht, wears a hat. They appear to be holding a serious conversation.*

WELTNER: Your secretary?

ROGER: No, my mother. One of those brand new apartments—all wet paint and no telephone yet.

From offscreen, a bellboy's voice can be heard.

BELLBOY: Paging Mr. George Kaplan!

25. MCU, *as in 23, with the bellboy slightly visible in the distance behind Roger.*

BELLBOY: Mr. Kaplan!

ROGER (*turning to look over his shoulder*): Perhaps if I sent a telegram.

BELLBOY: Mr. George Kaplan!

ROGER (*reaching out and snapping his fingers as he calls*): Boy!

26. MCU: *Wade and Weltner. The camera tracks quickly to the right, looking past them and across the room at the men in the distance. It zooms from LS to MCU, viewing the two figures from a slightly low angle. The men stare grimly and intently in Roger's direction.*

27. LS *from the POV of the two men. The bellboy crosses to Roger.*

28. MCU: *the two men, seen from a lower angle. Licht speaks quietly to his companion, Valerian, from out of the side of his mouth, never taking his eyes from Roger.*

LICHT: Kaplan.

29. M S : *the bellboy steps up to Roger, who remains seated at the table.*

    R O G E R : I've got to get off a wire immediately. Can you send it off for
    me if I write it out for you here?

    B E L L B O Y : I'm not permitted to do that, sir, but if you'll follow me. . . .

    R O G E R : Oh. (*Looks disappointed, and then turns to his companions.*) If
    you'll excuse me, gentlemen. (*Starts to rise.*)

30. M S : *the three martini drinkers, with Nelson still cupping his hand over
    his ear.*

    W A D E : Go right ahead.

31. M S , *as in 29: Roger stands.*

    R O G E R : Thank you.

    *The camera tracks backward as he and the bellboy walk toward the exit.
    They stop for a moment, and the camera pauses with them. The bellboy
    points ahead.*

    B E L L B O Y : Right through there, sir.

    R O G E R : Thank you.

    *The bellboy steps out of the frame to the left, and Roger continues for-
    ward. The camera tracks ahead of him, but it reframes the action, viewing
    him in* C U *. Suddenly a hand enters from offscreen right, grasping him
    hard on the shoulder. He and the camera stop. He looks down at the
    hand.*

    R O G E R : Hey, wait a minute. What's that supposed to be?

    The camera moves back slightly to M C U *and pans to the right, revealing
    the two sinister men who have been standing outside the bar. Licht is
    holding Roger by the shoulder. Roger tries unsuccessfully to remove the
    hand.*

    V A L E R I A N (*speaking in low voice, with an accent*): A car is waiting out-
    side. You will walk between us, saying nothing.

    R O G E R : What are you talking about?

    L I C H T (*moving in close, pulling roughly at Roger's shoulder, and shov-
    ing a small gun in his side*): Let's go!

    *A dark chord of nondiegetic music. The music will continue throughout
    this and the next sequence, until Roger is taken to his destination.*

    R O G E R : Let's go? Where? Who. . . . Who. . . . (*He looks down at the
    gun.*) Who are you?

    V A L E R I A N : Mere errand boys carrying concealed weapons. His is
    pointed at your heart, so please, no errors of judgment, I beg of you.

    R O G E R (*trying to pull free*): Oh, come on, fellas, what is this, a joke or
    something?

    L I C H T (*also, it is now apparent, with an accent*): Yes, a joke. We will
    laugh in the car.

    V A L E R I A N : Come. . . .

The two men each seize Roger by the arm and turn him around, walking him toward the hotel exit. The camera tracks forward, following them.

ROGER: This is ridicu—

32. MCU: *a tightly framed view of the small of Roger's back. A gun is pressed into his side and the two men are holding his arms. They walk forward into* LS, *out the open door of the hotel, and force him into the back seat of a Cadillac limousine waiting at the entrance.*

Limousine, interior, day

33. MCU (*process*): *the back seat of the limousine. Roger sits between the two men, leaning forward with his elbows on his knees, clasping his hands and adopting a conversational tone.*

ROGER: Well. (*The two abductors ignore him, staring straight ahead.*) Don't tell me where we're going. Surprise me. (*Pause.*) You know, I left some friends back there in the Oak Bar. They're going to think I'm awfully rude. I mean, oh, couldn't we stop off at a drugstore for a moment so that I could explain I'm being, uh, kidnapped? Well, That is what's happening, isn't it?

No response. Roger looks grimly forward, and then at the car door on the left. Suddenly he lunges for the door handle.

34. MCU (*process*): *looking over Roger's shoulder out the side of the limousine. Roger tries unsuccessfully to open the door.*

35. CU (*process*): *Roger returns to his seat. The two men are continuing to ignore him. He smiles slightly and turns to Valerian, on his right.*

ROGER: Locked.

He looks ahead, and his smile fades.

Dissolve.

Road to the Townsend Estate, exterior, day

36. LS: *late afternoon on a country road leading to a Glen Cove estate. The limousine approaches and turns into an elaborate wrought iron gateway. A wrought iron sign on the lawn outside reads* "TOWNSEND."

37. MCU, *as in 33: Roger looks over his shoulder out the back window and then turns to Valerian.*

ROGER: Who's Townsend?

The man looks forward, ignoring him.

ROGER: Really? Interesting.

38. LS: *Roger's* POV, *looking across the back of the front seat and out the window of the front passenger door. The roof of a mansion can be seen just beyond some trees in the distance.*

39. CU: *Roger frowns slightly, reacting to what he sees.*

40. LS, *as in 38: the mansion comes into full view.*

41. CU, *as in 39: Roger looks intently out the window.*

42. LS: *the limousine moves away from the camera, down the driveway toward the mansion.*

43. LS : *a parking area near the entrance to the mansion; the camera pans as the limousine turns and comes to a stop before the front steps. Viewed from a low angle, the two men and Roger exit the car and walk up the steps to a doorway. Roger looks around, amazed by the surroundings.*

44. MS : *low angle. The front door of the mansion is opened by a grim-faced woman, Anna, dressed as a housekeeper. Roger and Valerian enter. The nondiegetic music ends.*

45. LS , *as in 43: Licht remains outside and walks away toward the side of the mansion. We hear the sound of his footsteps.*

Townsend Estate, interior, day

46. LS : *a slightly low-angle shot of Roger and Valerian entering the front room of the tastefully decorated mansion, followed by Anna. The camera pans with Roger as he crosses into the center of the room.*

VALERIAN : Where is he?

ANNA : Upstairs, dressing.

VALERIAN : Tell him I'm here.

ANNA (*closing the door*): The dinner guests are expected.

VALERIAN : Never mind that. Say to him, "Kaplan."

ROGER : By the way, what are we having for dessert?

VALERIAN : Is there anyone in the library?

ANNA : No.

VALERIAN (*to Roger*): This way.

The camera pans as he crosses with Roger to the library door. In the background, Anna goes upstairs. At the door, Valerian pauses. Roger looks at him, then at the closed door. Valerian waits until Roger opens the door.

Library, interior, day

47. LS : *Roger and Valerian enter the spacious, warmly colored library, which contains a white fireplace, plushly upholstered furniture, oriental rugs, and floor-to-ceiling bookcases. Valerian reaches down to press the lock on the door.*

VALERIAN : You will wait here.

ROGER : Don't hurry. I'll catch up on my reading.

Nondiegetic music begins.

Valerian steps out, closing the door behind him. Roger tests the door handle and finds it locked. The camera pans as Roger crosses the room to a desk, looking around at the bookshelves. When he approaches the desk, the camera tracks forward a bit, viewing him from a relatively low angle. He picks up a magazine wrapped in a mailing tube lying on top of the desk and studies it.

48. CU (*insert, from Roger's* POV): *An address label:* "MR. LESTER TOWNSEND, 109 BAYWOOD, GLEN COVE, N.Y."

49. LS, *as in 47: Roger considers what he has read, puts down the tube, and glances out the windows behind the desk.*

50. LS: *Roger's* POV, *looking out the window. On the lawn outside, a man in a dark suit is playing croquet. Licht walks up and tells him something. They seem to be conversing intently. The man in the dark suit tosses his croquet mallet on the ground, and both figures walk rapidly off to the right, toward the front of the house.*

51. LS: *reverse angle, looking across the desk toward the door of the library. We hear the sound of the door being unlocked.*
   The nondiegetic music ends.

52. MCU: *Roger is crouched beside the window. He turns quckly and looks toward the door.*

53. LS, *as in 51: the door opens and a handsome, distinguished-looking stranger enters the room, dressed in a three-piece suit. He closes the door and stands for a moment, gazing toward Roger.*

54. MCU, *as in 52: Roger straightens up, looking toward the stranger.*

55. LS: *a slightly closer view of the stranger, seen from Roger's approximate* POV.
   STRANGER: Good evening.

56. MCU, *as in 54: Roger does not reply.*

57. LS, *as in 55: keeping his eyes fixed on Roger, the stranger crosses forward toward the left side of the desk. The camera pans to follow him.*

58. MCU, *as in 56: Roger moves to the left, looking offscreen right toward the stranger. The camera tracks left to follow him.*

59. LS, *as at end of 57: looking offscreen left toward Roger, the stranger crosses to the left. The camera pans left, viewing him from a slightly low angle as he moves into a* MS.

60. MCU, *as at end of 58: Roger moves farther left, around his side of the desk, looking offscreen right toward the stranger. The camera pans left. The panning movements in this and the previous shots are matched, creating a vertiginous, 360° effect.*

61. MS, *as at the end of 59: the stranger pulls the drapes closed over the window, darkening the room.*

62. MCU, *as in 60: Roger's face in darkness, looking off to the right at the stranger.*

63. MS, *as in 61: the camera pans as the stranger steps to the end of the desk and turns on a lamp. He is viewed from a slightly low angle, with his face partly shadowed.*
   STRANGER (*speaking in a cultivated British accent, while intently scrutinizing Roger*): Not what I expected. A little taller, a little more polished than the others.

64. MCU, *as in 62, with the lamplight striking Roger full in the face.*
   ROGER: Oh, I'm so glad you're pleased, Mr. Townsend.

65. MS, *as in 63.*
    STRANGER: But I'm afraid just as obvious.
    He crosses in front of the lamp and moves to the right, the camera panning with him.

66. MCU: *reverse shot, with Roger viewed from a slightly low angle.*
    ROGER: Now what the devil is this all about? Why was I brought here?

67. MS, *as as end of 65: the stranger turns on a lamp beside the couch and sits down beneath it, continuing to scrutinize Roger.*
    STRANGER: Games? Must we?

68. MCU, *as in 66: Roger advances a few steps toward the stranger and the camera tracks backward.*
    ROGER: Not that I mind a slight case of abduction now and then, but I have tickets for the theater this evening. . .

69. MCU *(reverse angle): the stranger sits at the edge of the couch in a meditative pose, his elbow on the armrest and his forefinger lightly touching his temple.*
    ROGER *(offscreen)*: . . .to a show I was looking forward to.

70. MCU, *as in 68.*
    ROGER: And I get, well, kind of unreasonable about things like that.

71. MCU, *as in 69.*
    STRANGER: With such expert playacting, you make this very room a theater.
    The stranger looks off to the right as we hear the sound of a door opening.

72. LS: *the stranger's* POV—*a low angle, across the back of the couch, from beneath the lighted lamp, looking toward the library door. The door opens and the dark-suited man whom we have seen playing croquet enters the room. He stares toward Roger with reptilian interest.*
    STRANGER *(offscreen)*: Ah, Leonard. Have you met our distinguished guest?

73. LS: *Leonard's* POV, *looking across the room at Roger. Roger stands to the left of the screen, frowning back at the camera.*

74. LS, *as in 72.*
    LEONARD: He's a well-tailored one, isn't he?

75. MCU, *as in 71: during this shot, Leonard can be seen crossing the room behind the couch, to stand near the stranger.*
    STRANGER: My secretary is a great admirer of your methods, Mr. Kaplan. Elusiveness, however misguided. . . .

76. MS: *Roger, looking offscreen right, crosses toward the stranger. The camera pans, bringing all three characters into view.*
    ROGER: Wait a minute. Wait a minute. Did you call me "Kaplan"?
    STRANGER: Oh, I know you're a man of many names, but I'm perfectly willing to accept your current choice.

The stranger begins patting his coat pockets, looking for cigarettes. Finding none, he holds out a hand toward Leonard, who immediately produces a cigarette case and opens it for him. Both he and Leonard continue to stare at Roger throughout this business.

ROGER: Current choice? My name is Thornhill. Roger Thornhill. It's never been anything else!

STRANGER: Of course.

ROGER: So obviously your friends picked up the wrong package when they bundled me out here in the car.

STRANGER: Do sit down, Mr. Kaplan.

77. MCU: *Roger, looking down toward the stranger.*

ROGER: I told you! I'm *not* Kaplan, whoever he is. I. . . .

The sound of the door opening. Roger turns and looks up.

78. LS: *nearly the same as in 72, looking across the back of the couch toward the door. An attractive, rather matronly woman enters, dressed as if for a dinner party.*

WOMAN (*looking toward Roger*): Excuse me.

STRANGER (*offscreen*): Yes?

WOMAN (*looking toward the stranger*): The guests are here, dear.

STRANGER (*offscreen*): Look after them. I'll be with you in a few minutes.

The woman nods and exits, closing the door.

79. LS: *a bird's-eye view looking down on the three men, with Roger on the left and Leonard standing at the apex of the triangle.*

STRANGER: Now, shall we get down to business?

ROGER: I'm all for that.

Leonard takes a step closer to Roger, who eyes him cautiously.

STRANGER: Quite simply, I'd like you to tell me how much you know of our arrangements, and of course how you've *come* by this information.

Roger sighs with exasperation.

STRANGER: Naturally, I don't expect to get this for nothing.

ROGER: Of *course* not.

STRANGER: Don't misunderstand me. I don't really expect you to fall in with this suggestion.

Roger puts his hands in his pockets and turns away, crossing slowly back toward the desk as the stranger speaks. The camera pans with him, leaving the other two figures behind.

STRANGER (*offscreen*): But the least I can do is afford you the opportunity of surviving the evening.

80. MCU: *astonished, Roger stops in his tracks and turns, removing his hands from his pockets and looking offscreen right toward the stranger.*

ROGER: What the devil is *that* supposed to mean?

81. MS: *the stranger and Leonard seen from a low angle, with the camera positioned at the end of the couch.*

STRANGER: Why don't you surprise me, Mr. Kaplan, and say yes?

ROGER (*offscreen*): I've already told you. . . .

LEONARD: We know where you're headed for.

82. MCU, *as in 80, Roger looking offscreen right at Leonard.*

ROGER: And *I* know where I'm headed. I'm headed for the Winter Garden Theater in New York and I think I'd better get going.

The camera makes a 180° pan as he moves briskly to the right and crosses the room. He opens the library door, and the camera tracks forward slightly, closing in for a tight CU of Valerian, who takes a step inside the room.

83. MS: *looking over Roger's shoulder at Valerian. Roger turns around, looking down to the left, toward the stranger.*

ROGER: Townsend, you're making a serious mistake.

84. MS: *from the end of the couch, looking toward the stranger and slightly up toward Leonard, who is standing in the background. Leonard has lit the stranger's cigarette. He stares at Roger and begins to cross slowly toward the right, into LS.*

STRANGER: This is not going to lead to a very happy conclusion, Mr. Kaplan.

The stranger rises and crosses toward the desk, the camera panning and viewing him in long shot, from a low angle.

ROGER (*offscreen*): I'm *not* Kaplan!

STRANGER: I do wish you'd reconsider.

85. MS, *as in 83: Roger looks offscreen to the left of the camera, toward the stranger. The library door is now closed, and Leonard crosses to stand behind Roger.*

LEONARD: We also know your contact in Pittsburgh since Jason . . . committed suicide.

ROGER (*turning to look at Leonard and then back toward the stranger*): What contact? I've never even *been* in Pittsburgh!

86. LS, *as at end of 84: the stranger is standing behind the desk. He puts on glasses and picks up a piece of paper, reading aloud.*

STRANGER: On June the sixteenth, you checked into the Sherwyn Hotel in Pittsburgh . . .

87. MS: *Roger and Leonard, standing near the door. As the stranger reads, Roger crosses the room to the stranger and the camera pans, framing the two figures at a low angle from the end of the desk.*

STRANGER: . . . as Mr. George Kaplan of Berkeley, California. A week later you registered at the Benjamin Franklin Hotel in Philadelphia as Mr. George Kaplan of Pittsburgh. On August the eleventh you stayed at the Statler in Boston. On August the twenty-ninth George Kaplan of Boston registered at the Whittier in Detroit. At present, you are registered in room seven ninety-six at the Plaza Hotel in New York as Mr. George Kaplan of Detroit.

ROGER (*standing with his hands in his pockets*): Really.

STRANGER (*putting down the paper and removing his glasses*): In two days you're due at the Ambassador East in Chicago, . . .

ROGER: Oh.

STRANGER: . . . and then at the Sheraton-Johnson Hotel in Rapid City, South Dakota.

ROGER (*shakes his head*): Not me.

STRANGER: So you see, there's very little sense in maintaining this fiction that you're deceiving us, any more than *we*'re deceiving *you*, Mr. Kaplan.

ROGER (*reaching for his inner coat pocket*): I don't suppose it would do any good to show you a wallet . . .

88. MS, *as in 85: Leonard takes a few steps forward, the camera tilting up to view him at a low angle.*

ROGER (*offscreen*): . . . full of identification cards, a driver's license, things like that?

LEONARD: They provide you with such good ones.

89. MS: *the stranger and Roger at the desk. The stranger consults his watch.*

STRANGER: It's getting late. I have guests. Do you intend to cooperate with us? I'd like a simple yes or no.

ROGER: A simple no. For the simple reason I simply don't know what you're talking about!

The stranger pauses, then crosses behind Roger toward the other side of the library. The camera remains behind, tracking in to a CU of Roger as he turns to look toward the stranger.

90. MS, *reverse angle: the stranger enters the shot from behind the camera and crosses toward the library door, passing Leonard on the way. The camera tracks forward, past Leonard, moving toward the door.*

STRANGER (*speaking with his back to us*): Give Mr. Kaplan a drink, Leonard. A pleasant journey, sir.

Opening the door, the stranger pauses in the hallway, looks off to the right, and then exits to the left. Suddenly Valerian and Licht appear in the doorway. The first to enter is Licht. He has removed the hat, and we can see that he is balding. He stares offscreen left toward Roger with sadistic pleasure; in his right hand, he holds a cigarette between thumb and forefinger, Gestapo style. The camera tracks back slightly as he and Valerian enter the room, closing the door behind them.

91. MS, *as at end of 89: Roger looks apprehensively toward his captors, putting his wallet back in his coat pocket.*

92. MS: *the three assailants, with Leonard standing in the middle distance and the other two beside the door. As he speaks, Leonard crosses the room to the right, toward a liquor cabinet installed in one of the bookcases. The camera pans.*

LEONARD: Scotch? Rye? Bourbon? . . .

93. MS: *Leonard is seen from a slightly low angle as he opens the cabinet and looks at the display of bottles.*

LEONARD: . . . Vodka?

94. MS, *as in 91.*

ROGER: Nothing, thank you. I'll just take a quick ride back to town.

He starts to cross the room to the right, the camera panning.

LEONARD (*offscreen*): Oh, that has been arranged.

Roger pauses.

95. MS, *as in 93: Leonard selects a bottle of bourbon and a large tumbler.*

LEONARD: But first, a libation. Bourbon.

He steps toward Roger, the camera tilting up slightly as he moves forward.

96. MS: *Roger is at the left and Leonard enters the shot from the right, bearing the bottle and the glass.*

ROGER: You drink it. I've had enough stimulation for one day.

LEONARD: It'll be easier if you take this yourself. Otherwise, it will be necessary for us to insist.

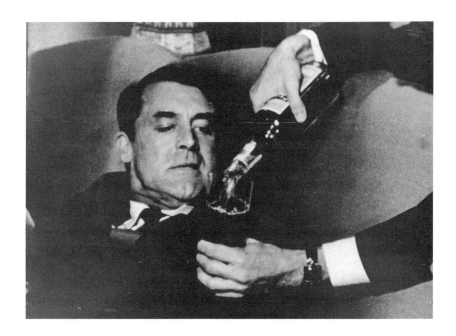

*Glancing past Leonard, Roger decides to make a desperate run for the
door. He lunges to the right, shoving Leonard aside.*

97.   CU: *At the doorway, Roger is stopped by Valerian and Licht, who each
grab him by the arm and drag him back into the room. The camera pans,
watching his face as he is pulled along. He struggles mightily, but to no
avail. The camera pans and tilts, keeping his face in* CU *as he is shoved
down on the couch and held tight. At the right of the frame, Leonard's
hands enter, pouring bourbon into an exceedingly tall glass while Roger
watches.*

LEONARD (*offscreen*): Cheers.

*Holding the glass under Roger's nose, Leonard continues to pour. Roger
watches with growing anxiety as the glass fills to the brim.*

*Nondiegetic music begins with a series of slow base chords; this music
will modulate into the "fandango" theme, and will continue throughout
the next sequence.*

Dissolve.

A Road beside the Ocean, exterior, night

98.   LS (*matte*): *a moonlit road winding along sharp cliffs beside the sea. A
white Mercedes convertible is parked on the road; behind it, the Cadillac
limousine from the earlier scene is parked with its headlights turned on.
Valerian and Licht remove Roger from the back seat of the limousine and,
supporting his body by the arms, drag him to the Mercedes.*

99. CU: *the two men shove Roger into the driver's seat of the convertible. Roger mumbles and sings a drunken, undecipherable song.*
100. LS (*matte*): *a view down the road from the front of the car, showing a hairpin curve and a sheer cliff falling off to the sea.*
101. MCU, *as in 99: Valerian and Licht prop Roger against the steering wheel and close the door.*
102. MCU: *Roger at the steering wheel. Licht reaches into the car to prop Roger up, and in the background we see Valerian getting into the passenger seat. He does not close the door.*
    ROGER (*singing drunkenly*): I've grown accushtomed to your fashe. . . . *Valerian reaches across and starts the car.*
    ROGER (*weaving and propping his head sleepily against Valerian's shoulder*): Don't worry 'bout me, fellas—I'll take the bus.
103. LS: *Licht walks toward the limousine, turning to look back over his shoulder.*
104. MCU, *as in 101: the Mercedes starts to roll forward, with Valerian guiding the steering wheel. Roger slumps drunkenly against the door. The camera tracks alongside the car. Roger looks up and squints toward the road ahead.*
105. LS (*matte*): *Roger's* POV, *looking out the front of the car and past the Mercedes hood ornament. The car is veering to the left, toward the cliff.*
106. MCU, *as in 104: Roger reacts, sitting up.*
107. LS, *as in 105: the car moves closer to the cliff, swerving sharply toward the edge.*
108. MCU: *tracking shot. Roger and Valerian are viewed through the front window of the Mercedes. Roger turns toward Valerian and tries to focus. Mustering his strength, he pushes against his assailant.*
109. MS: *tracking shot. A high-angle view of Roger shoving Valerian completely out the open passenger door as the car continues to roll forward and off the screen to the lower left.*
110. CU: *tracking shot. Viewed from the side of the car, Roger tries to steady himself behind the wheel. His head bobs back and his eyes close.*
111. LS, *as in 107: Roger's* POV. *He manages to point the car slightly more toward the road.*
112. LS: *Valerian recovers and runs toward the limousine, jumping into the passenger side as it starts off toward the Mercedes.*
113. CU, *as in 110: Roger's head bobs sleepily. The car moves forward at a slightly faster rate than the camera, almost getting out of frame to the left.*
114. LS, *as in 111: The nose of the car swerves straight out toward the sea.*
115. MS: *a view through the front window of the limousine, looking toward the two assailants. They come to a stop, as if they expect the Mercedes to go over the cliff.*

116.   LS (*matte*): *from the assailants' POV, we see the Mercedes swerve onto a dirt shoulder beside the cliff.*

117.   CU: *tracking shot, slightly larger than 113. Roger's head bobs. His eyes close and his mouth falls open.*

118.   MCU (*matte*): *the rear wheel of the Mercedes slides over the cliff edge and spins in the air. The car lurches to a stop.*

119.   CU, *slightly larger and from a lower angle than 108: Roger leans out from the side of the car, bending to look straight down.*

120.   CU: *deep focus. Roger's POV, looking down at the wheel, which is suspended in midair over the rocky seashore. The car engine races and the wheel spins, throwing out exhaust.*

121.   CU, *as in 119: Roger does a double take: first he raises his head and looks slightly off to the right, then down, and then up again.*
       ROGER: Ooooh.
       He turns to the steering wheel.

122.   MCU, *as in 118: the rear wheel of the Mercedes moves forward, back onto the road.*

123.   MCU, *as in 115: the two assailants react, starting the limousine and setting off in pursuit.*

124.   LS, *as in 116: the Mercedes drives off, around the hairpin curve and out of sight.*

125.   CU (*process*): *Roger, viewed from straight on as he tries to steer the car along the winding road. His collar is turned up and he is focusing intently ahead.*

126.   MCU (*process*): *the two assailants, viewed from straight on as they pursue Roger.*

127.   CU, *as in 125: Roger squints slightly and yawns. Suddenly his eyes bulge open.*

128.   LS (*process*): *Roger's POV out the front window, looking past the hood ornament. The headlights reveal a sharp turn in the road, bounded by trees. Roger swerves to the left, encountering another sharp curve and an oncoming station wagon, which honks its horn and narrowly avoids a collision by using the wrong lane.*

129.   CU, *as in 127: Roger turns the steering wheel sharply and struggles to keep his eyes open.*

130.   LS, *as in 128: the curving road.*

131.   CU, *as in 129: Roger tightens his lips, frowns, blinks, and tilts his head back, trying to focus.*

132.   LS, *as in 130: more sharp curves in the road.*

133.   CU, *as in 131: Roger opens his eyes wide and then squints.*

134.   LS, *as in 132: turning a corner, the Mercedes approaches another car from the rear and passes it, forcing it off onto the shoulder.*

135. CU, *as in 133: Roger sits up straight and tries to behave with aplomb. In the distance, we hear the angry driver of the other car honking his horn. Suddenly Roger's eyes bulge wide open in alarm. He spins the steering wheel wildly to negotiate a curve, and his tires squeal.*

136. MCU *(process), as in 126: Valerian and Licht, still following Roger.*

137. CU, *as in 135: Roger tries to see something ahead. His eyes narrow to slits and he leans forward over the steering wheel, struggling to focus. Then he frowns, sits up straight, and looks out the corners of his eyes.*

138. LS: *double exposure. From Roger's* POV, *looking past the hood ornament, we see two images of the road—one curving to the right and the other going straight.*
Dissolve.

139. LS, *as in 138: a single image of the road. The car has moved off onto the shoulder and is heading straight for a telephone pole.*

140. CU, *as in 137: Roger's eyes grow wide in fear and he spins the steering wheel. The tires squeal and the car throws up dust behind.*

141. LS, *as in 139: the car has moved back onto the road, but is now in the wrong lane.*

142. CU, *as in 140: Roger heaves a sigh, tightening his lips and closing his eyes. He looks forward sleepily.*

143. LS: *the road ahead from Roger's* POV, *but without the hood ornament that was visible in the earlier shots. A car ahead is moving slowly away from a stop sign, and Roger is approaching fast.*

144. CU *(process): larger than the previous shots in the sequence. Roger turns the steering wheel rapidly.*

145. LS, *as in 143: the Mercedes swerves to the left to avoid a rear-end collision. In order to escape another car coming toward it in the left lane, it keeps turning toward a side road, where it almost crashes into a third car. The third driver honks angrily.*

146. CU, *as in 144: Roger squints.*

147. LS, *as in 141: the road ahead from Roger's* POV, *with the hood ornament visible again. Turning back onto the main road, the Mercedes narrowly misses the oncoming car.*

148. CU, *as in 142: Roger frowns and looks comically frightened as he tries to steer between the three cars. His eyes open in astonishment and he leans back; then he squints and leans forward.*

149. LS: *from the side of the road, the camera looks diagonally across at a parked car marked* "GLEN COVE POLICE," *with a policeman standing outside. The Mercedes goes speeding past on the wrong side of the road. The policeman jumps into his car, turns on his flasher and siren, and starts off after the Mercedes.*

150. LS: *a view down the road as the police car drives off in hot pursuit.*

151. CU, *as in 148: relaxing a bit, Roger leans back and squints. Behind him, we can see the police car and hear the siren. Roger frowns, turning a bit to listen over his shoulder; then he shakes his head in disbelief and continues driving. Again he listens. Suddenly he grows sleepy and begins to nod.*

152. LS, *as in 147: from a side street, a man pedaling a bicycle moves out of the intersection and onto the main road. The Mercedes is heading straight for him.*

153. CU, *as in 151: Roger squints and looks concerned. Suddenly he slams on the brakes, his eyes growing wide in astonishment.*

154. LS, *as in 152: the Mercedes lurches to a stop as the cyclist crosses in front of it.*

155. LS: *from the side of the road, the camera looks across at the Mercedes. The police car enters from the right, its siren still blaring.*

156. LS: *same angle as 155, but a slightly closer view. The police car crashes into the rear of the Mercedes.*

157. LS, *as in 155: a third car enters from the right, behind the police car.*

158. LS: *same angle as 157, but a closer view of the police car. The third car crashes into the rear of the police car.*

159. LS, *as in 157: the three cars, smashed bumper to bumper.*

160. LS: *the Cadillac limousine bearing the two assailants comes to a stop in the distance, farther back down the road.*
161. MCU (*process*): *the two assailants, viewed from straight on, looking frustrated.*
162. LS, *as in 159: two policemen slowly get out of the patrol car and walk forward to the Mercedes. The patrol car's siren is still wailing, and its light is still flashing.*
163. LS, *as in 160: the limousine backs up, turns around, and drives off.*
164. LS, *as in 162: the policemen walk up to the doors of the Mercedes. The nondiegetic music ends.*
  Dissolve.

Glen Cove Police Station, interior, night

165. MS: *the two policemen, one of whom is Sergeant Klinger, enter, holding Roger by the arms. The camera pans as they cross to the lieutenant in charge of the booking desk.*
  ROGER: Thanks for the lift, fellas.
  KLINGER: Lieutenant, I want this man examined for driving while intoxicated.
  LIEUTENANT (*looking at Roger, who can barely stand*): Really.
  ROGER: You see, they tried to kill me. . . . Now he won't listen to me. . . . In a big house. . . . They tried to kill me!
  KLINGER: All right. Let's just go inside.
  ROGER: I don't wanna go inside. (*He turns and looks squarely into the face of the second policeman.*) Somebody call the police!
  KLINGER: Come on, come on now.
  Klinger takes Roger's arm and leads him toward a courtroom in the distance. The lieutenant gives the second policeman a form to fill out.

Courtroom, interior, night

166. LS: *Klinger and Roger, seen with their backs to the camera, walking into the courtroom. Roger leans at a 45° angle against Klinger, who struggles to lead him over to a bench at the front of the room.*
  KLINGER: Sit down.
  ROGER: I don't wanna sit (*weaving, he slumps toward the bench*).
167. MS: *high angle. Roger plops down on the bench and manages to sit fairly straight. Klinger puts his hands on his hips.*
  ROGER: Perfectly all right. See? (*He cocks one leg over the arm of the bench and leans back on his elbow, trying to lie down.*) We'll get 'em. We'll throw the book at 'em. Assault and kidnapping. Assault with a gun and a bourbon and a sports car.
168. MS: *reverse angle, looking over Roger and up toward Klinger.*
  ROGER: We'll get 'em.
  KLINGER: You'll be all right after a good night's sleep. We've got a nice cell all made up and waiting.

169. MS, *as in 167.*
     ROGER: I don't wanna cell. I wanna policeman.

170. MS: *the second policeman enters. The camera pans as he crosses right toward Roger and Klinger.*
     SECOND POLICEMAN: The car was just reported stolen.
     KLINGER: Uh huh.
     SECOND POLICEMAN: A Mrs. Babson up on Twining Road.
     ROGER (*trying to stand up*): I . . . I gotta call someone. Where's the phone?
     KLINGER: (*helping Roger to stand and guiding him toward the left*): You're allowed one call. Over here. (*The camera tracks left as they move to the door, with Roger still unable to walk.*) Better make it your lawyer.
     ROGER (*to Klinger*): Butterfield eight-one-oh-nine-eight.
     KLINGER (*holding Roger up and opening a door to an inner office with his free hand*): What am I, a telephone operator?
     They enter the office and the camera tracks forward to frame them through the open doorway.
     ROGER: Butterfield eight-one-oh-nine-eight.
     Klinger dials. Roger smiles sleepily, tries to straighten his tie, and bends over to watch the dialing procedure. While Klinger waits for an answer, Roger sits on the edge of the desk, leaving one foot on the floor, and tilts his head forward until it almost touches Klinger's chest.
     KLINGER: Just a minute, please. (*He hands the receiver to Roger.*) Here.
     ROGER: Thank you. Thank you (*He sits up straight and clears his throat.*) Hello, Mother? Mother, this is your son, Roger Thornhill. Yeah. (*Listens.*) Wait a minute and I'll find out. (*To policeman.*) Where am I?
     KLINGER: Glen Cove police station.
     ROGER (*to his mother, trying not to slur the words*): Glen Cove police station. (*He listens, looks serious, and tries to straighten up even more.*) No, no, Mother, I have *not* been drinking. No, no, . . . these two men, they poured a whole bottle of bourbon into me. (*Pause.*) No, they didn't give me a chaser. No, you. . . .
     A man crosses in the near foreground, moving to the right and looking into the office. He and Klinger exchange glances.
     KLINGER (*trying to take the receiver*): Come on, let's go.
     ROGER: Wait, I . . . I . . . I'm not finished yet.
     KLINGER: Yes you are. Come on.
     ROGER (*into telephone*): Mother, I . . . I . . . I gotta go now. You get my lawyer right away and come out and bail me out.
     KLINGER: Tomorrow morning, tell her.
     ROGER: Tomorrow morning, he says. (*Pause.*) Oh. I dunno, I'll ask him. (*To policeman.*) She wants to know who says.

KLINGER: Sergeant Emil Klinger.

ROGER (*into telephone*): Sergeant Emil . . . (*pauses, looks at police-man*). Emil? (*Into telephone.*) Sergeant Emil Klinger. (*Pauses, smiles.*) I didn't believe it either. (*Pause.*) No, I'm all right, Mother. Good night. Good night, dear. (*He hands the receiver to Klinger, who hangs it up.*) That was Mother.

The camera tracks backward as Klinger takes Roger by the arm and leads him out into the courtroom.

KLINGER: Let's go.

The camera pans with Klinger and Roger as they move back to the front of the courtroom, where they are viewed in long shot. The man we saw walking past a few moments earlier is seated at a table near the front of the room. He is Dr. Cross. The second policeman is drawing a chalk line on the floor.

KLINGER (*to the man at the table*): Here's your man, doctor.

Roger looks warily at the chalk line and sits unsteadily in a chair next to the doctor.

171. MS: *Roger and the doctor, facing one another at the table.*

CROSS: What's your name?

ROGER: Roger Thornhill.

CROSS: Stick out your tongue and say "ah."

ROGER: Better move back. Ahhh.

CROSS: Have you been drinking?

ROGER: Doctor, I am gassed.

CROSS: What were you drinking?

ROGER: Bourbon. See, these two fellas, they . . . (*spreads his arms to gesticulate*).

CROSS: How much would you say that you drank?

ROGER: What'd you say?

CROSS: How much would you say that you drank?

ROGER (*sitting up and spreading his arms wider*): Oh, about this much.

CROSS: Mr. Thornhill, it is my opinion that you are definitely intoxi-cated, and I'm now going to have. . . .

ROGER (*overlapping*): No question. I'm stinking. (*He climbs up on the table to lie down.*)

CROSS: And I'm now going to ask your permission to draw blood.

ROGER: How disgusting. (*He stretches out on the table.*)

CROSS (*reading a prepared statement*): "You may refuse to permit a blood test to be made, but if you do refuse, your license will be re-voked. You have the right to notify a physician of your own choosing if you. . . ."

Dissolve.

Courtroom, interior, day

172. LS: *Roger, who is obviously suffering from a hangover, has been brought before a judge. The doctor and the two arresting officers from the previous scene are present, together with Roger's lawyer, Victor Larrabee. To the left, seated in the first row of spectators, is Roger's mother, a handsomely dressed woman wearing a jacket with a high fur collar.*

     LARRABEE (*unconvincingly*): . . . it was at this point that Mr. Thornhill succeeded in escaping from his . . .

173. MS: *looking across the Judge's bench at Roger and Larrabee, with Roger's mother in the background to the far left.*

     LARRABEE: . . . would-be assassins, and when they gave chase he . . .

174. MS: *deep focus, reverse angle, looking toward the highly skeptical judge. In the foreground, Dr. Cross can be seen in profile.*

     LARRABEE: . . . naturally had to drive as best he could under the, uh . . .

175. MS: *Roger's mother. She heaves a sigh and almost rolls her eyes.*

     LARRABEE (*offscreen*): . . . circumstances.

     JUDGE (*offscreen*): Counselor, . . .

176. MCU: *the judge, seated behind the bench.*

     JUDGE: . . . how long have you known your client?

177. MS: *Roger, Larrabee, and Sergeant Klinger.*

     LARRABEE: Seven years, Your Honor.

     JUDGE (*offscreen*): Do you know him to be a reasonable man?

178. CU: *Roger's mother, looking amused.*

     LARRABEE (*offscreen*): Absolutely.

     ROGER'S MOTHER (*loud enough for everyone to hear*): Hah!

179. MCU: *Roger and Larrabee. Roger turns around to the left and looks offscreen, frowning.*

     ROGER: Mother!

180. CU, *as in 178: Roger's mother shrugs.*

     JUDGE (*offscreen*): And you believe there is . . .

181. MCU, *as in 179.*

     JUDGE (*offscreen*): . . . some credence to this story?

     ROGER: Credence!

     LARRABEE: Well, yes, Your Honor. I mean if my client says that this is what happened, I'm . . . I'm certain it must have happened.

     ROGER (*under his breath, as he holds his aching forehead*): You're damn right.

182. MCU, *as in 176.*

     JUDGE: Sergeant, . . .

183. MS, *as in 177.*

     JUDGE (*offscreen*): . . . I want this turned over to the county detectives for investigation.

184. MCU, *as in 182.*
> JUDGE: I suggest you call them up and have them come over here immediately.

185. MS, *as in 177.*
> KLINGER: Right, Your Honor.
> JUDGE (*offscreen*): Counselor, I'm going to set this over for final disposition tomorrow night at seven-thiry, at which time I expect you and the defendant to be here and ready to go to trial.

186. MCU, *as in 184.*
> JUDGE: In the meantime, the county detectives will determine if his story has any basis in fact.

187. MCU, *as in 181.*
> ROGER: Basis in fact! I suppose if I were brought in here *dead* you still wouldn't believe . . .
> LARRABEE: Roger, wait a minute.
> ROGER: Well, I mean . . . after all, Your Honor, would I make up such a story?

188. MCU, *as in 186.*
> JUDGE: That is precisely what we're . . .

189. MCU, *as in 187.*
> JUDGE (*offscreen*): . . . intending to find out, Mr. Thornhill.
> *Roger holds his forehead and shakes his head wearily.*
> *Dissolve.*

Townsend Estate, exterior, day
A foreboding strain of nondiegetic music underlines the transition to this sequence.

190. LS: *an unmarked police car pulls up to the front door of the Townsend estate. Roger gets out, accompanied by his mother, his lawyer, and two plainclothes detectives, Captain Junket and Lieutenant Harding.*

191. MS: *the five of them step up to the door, and Roger rings the bell. Anna, the housekeeper from the previous night, answers. Music ends.*
> ANNA: Yes?
> ROGER: Remember me?
> ANNA: Yes, sir.
> ROGER: Good.
> JUNKET: Is Mr. Townsend at home?
> ANNA: No, I'm sorry, he's left for the day, sir.
> JUNKET: Mrs. Townsend?
> ANNA (*pauses*): Who shall I say is calling?
> JUNKET: County detectives.
> ANNA: Come in, please.

Reception Room of the Townsend Estate, interior, day

192. L S : *The five visitors and Anna enter the reception room of the mansion, which looks exactly as before. The camera pans as Anna leads the group over to the library.*

A N N A : This way, please.

Library, interior, day

193. L S : *Anna opens the library door, allowing the five visitors, led by Roger's mother, to step inside. The camera pans as they cross to the middle of the room.*

R O G E R (*to detectives*): This is the room.

A N N A : I'll call Madame.

J U N K E T (*as she goes out*): You do that.

R O G E R (*camera tracks forward slightly as he moves to the sofa and picks up one of the cushions*): And here's the sofa where they held me down. They spilled bourbon all over it. I'll show you the stains. (*But the cushion is spotless.*) Well, they must've cleaned them off. (*Camera pans as he crosses over to a nearby bookshelf.*) This is the cabinet where they keep the liquor. Scotch, gin, vodka . . . (*He opens the cabinet, only to find that it is now filled with books.*)

194. M S : *across Roger's back toward his mother and the three increasingly skeptical men.*

R O G E R ' S M O T H E R (*smiling*): . . . and bourbon. I remember when it used to come in bottles.

Roger steps back to stand near his mother. He gestures toward the cabinet and frowns, momentarily speechless. Offscreen, we hear the library door open. All five characters look off to the right.

W O M A N (*offscreen*): Roger!

195. M C U : *at the doorway, we see the woman who played "Mrs. Townsend" in the earlier scene. She crosses quickly toward Roger, ignoring everyone else, and the camera pans to follow her.*

W O M A N : Dear! We were so worried about you! (*She embraces him.*)

196. M C U : *looking over the woman's shoulder at Roger's astonished face.*

W O M A N : Did you get home all right? (*Breaking off the embrace, she holds him at arm's length.*) Of course . . .

197. M C U : *the two detectives, looking on.*

W O M A N (*offscreen*): . . . you did!

198. M C U , *as in 196:* Let me look at you. Oh, a little pink eyed, but then aren't we all? It was a dull party. You didn't miss a *thing*!

199. C U : *Roger's mother, keeping her face polite, but apparently believing every word.*

R O G E R (*offscreen*): I want you all to know, I . . .

200. L S :   *the entire group, with Roger and the woman on the left, the four
other visitors on the right. Roger steps away from the woman and crosses
upstage toward the fireplace.*

R O G E R :   . . . never saw this woman before last night!

*The woman looks toward Roger's mother and laughs as if Roger were
making a joke.*

201. M S :   *the two detectives and Roger's mother.*

J U N K E T :   Mrs. Townsend, I'm Captain Junket of the Nassau County detectives. This is Lieutenant Harding.

202. M S :   *as in 200, only closer. Roger has moved back to the group. He and
the woman are on the left, with the lawyer and Roger's mother on the
right.*

W O M A N :   How do you do. (*Turning to Roger.*) You haven't gotten into
trouble, Roger?

R O G E R ' S   M O T H E R (*rolling her eyes*): Huh! Has he gotten into trouble!

R O G E R (*to the woman, overlapping his mother*): Now stop calling me
Roger!

J U N K E T (*offscreen*): Mrs. Townsend, Mr. Thornhill was picked up last
night . . .

203. M S , *as in 201.*

J U N K E T :   . . . driving while under the influence of alcohol, . . .

204. M S , *as in 202.*

JUNKET (*offscreen*): . . . and incidentally in a stolen car.

WOMAN: Stolen car!

JUNKET: Belonging to Mrs. Babson of Twining Road.

WOMAN (*turning to Roger*): Roger, you said you were going to call a cab! You *didn't* borrow Laura's Mercedes?

ROGER (*furious*): No, I *didn't* . . . *borrow* . . . *Laura's* . . . *Mercedes!* (*He winces in pain and puts his hand to his forehead.*)

JUNKET (*offscreen*): Mr. Thornhill has told us that he was brought . . .

205. MCU: *the two policemen.*

JUNKET: . . . to this house against his will last night, . . .

206. MS, *as in 204.*

JUNKET (*offscreen*): . . . and, uh, forcibly intoxicated . . .

207. MCU, *as in 205.*

JUNKET: . . . by some friends of your husband's and then set out on the road.

208. MCU: *the woman and Roger's lawyer.*

JUNKET (*offscreen*): Now, do you know anything about this?

WOMAN: Well, now, Captain, Roger *was* a bit tipsy . . .

209. MCU: *Roger, growing increasingly frustrated.*

WOMAN (*offscreen*): . . . when he arrived here by cab for dinner.

ROGER: She's lying! (*He crosses to stand farther off. The camera pans, framing him in* MS *as he turns and stands alone.*)

WOMAN (*offscreen*): And I'm afraid he became even worse as the evening wore on. Finally, he told us he had to go home to sleep it off.

210. MCU, *as in 208: the woman crosses to Roger's mother and the camera pans with her.*

WOMAN: Oh, I *knew* I should have served dinner . . .

211. MS, *as at end of 209.*

WOMAN (*offscreen*): . . . earlier!

ROGER (*lifts his arms, drops them to his side, and steps forward into* MS): What a performance!

212. MS: *the woman on the left and the four other visitors on the right.*

JUNKET: Mrs. Townsend, does the name . . .

213. MS, *as at end of 211, with Roger taking a step forward and looking on intently.*

JUNKET (*offscreen*): . . . George Kaplan mean anything to you?

WOMAN (*offscreen*): George Kaplan?

214. MS, *as in 212.*

WOMAN: No.

JUNKET: I didn't think so.

215. MCU, *as in 213.*

ROGER: Well, where's her husband? *He's* the one you should be questioning. (*He takes a few anxious paces back toward the fireplace.*)

J U N K E T (*offscreen*): Is there any place . . .

216. M S, *as in 214.*

J U N K E T: . . . where he can be reached?

W O M A N: Why, yes. The United Nations.

217. M S, *as in 215: Roger, standing alone in the distance. He reacts by walking forward a step.*

R O G E R: United Na—

W O M A N (*offscreen*): He's addressing the General Assembly . . .

218. M S: *the four other visitors, looking askance at Roger.*

W O M A N (*offscreen*): . . . this afternoon.

219. M S, *as in 217.*

R O G E R (*after a quick double take*): All right, so he's addressing . . .

220. M S, *as in 216.*

R O G E R (*offscreen*): . . . the General Assembly.

J U N K E T (*to the woman*): Sorry we had to bother you. (*He turns and moves for the door.*)

W O M A N (*camera pans as she moves to show her visitors out*): No bother at all.

221. M S, *as in 219: Roger, who has been left behind, moves toward the departing group, hoping to make one last point. The camera pans with him, bringing his mother into the frame.*

R O G E R: Now wait a minute! I. . . . (*He pauses and looks at his mother.*) Oh. (*She takes his arm and leads him out.*)

Reception Room, interior, day

222. L S: *Roger and his mother exit the library. The camera pans as they cross toward the rest of the group.*

W O M A N (*offscreen*): Will you be wanting to get in touch with my husband, Captain?

J U N K E T (*as Roger approaches*): No, Mrs. Townsend, that won't be necessary.

R O G E R: You mean you're not going to do any more about this?

R O G E R ' S M O T H E R (*tapping him on the arm*): Roger . . . (*he turns to look at her*). *Pay* the two dollars!

Roger snorts in disgust and walks out. The camera pans as the rest of the group follows him.

Nondiegetic music begins.

Townsend Estate, exterior, day

223. L S: *Roger, his mother, and his lawyer walk down the front steps to the police car.*

224. M S: *the woman shows the two detectives out the front door.*

W O M A N (*standing at the door, smiling and waving*): Good-bye!

225. L S, *as in 223: The detectives get into the car, start the engine, and drive off. As they exit to the right, the camera pans slowly to the left, moving*

about 90° and coming to a stop on a MS of a gardener, who is trimming a hedge. The gardener is bent over, with his back to the camera.

226. CU: *out-of-focus telephoto image, showing only the ivy growing on the wall of the estate. The gardener straightens and turns to look at the departing car, his face coming into view from below the screen. It is Valerian.*
Dissolve.

Entrance to the Plaza Hotel, exterior, day

227. LS: *a taxi pulls up and Roger and his mother get out. The camera pans as they walk up the front steps to the entrance of the hotel.*
The nondiegetic music ends.

ROGER'S MOTHER: I don't see why you want me along.

ROGER: Well, you lend a certain air of respectability.

ROGER'S MOTHER: Don't be sarcastic, Roger.

Lobby of the Plaza Hotel, interior, day

228. LS: *Roger and his mother enter the hotel and walk forward past the desk. The camera pans as Roger leads his mother around a corner and then pauses by the house telephones.*

ROGER: There you are, dear.

229. MS: *Roger and his mother standing beside the telephones.*

ROGER: Park yourself there. (*He picks up a telephone.*) Well, here goes. . . . Hello, operator? Have you got a George Kaplan staying here? (*We hear the operator's voice indistinctly.*) That's right. . . . You have? Room seven ninety-six? Ring it, will you please? (*To his mother.*) You see?

ROGER'S MOTHER: I see. Well, I hope he clears up this silly business. You're ruining my. . . .

ROGER (*overlapping*): Quiet. Hush. Shhsh. Shut up! (*To operator.*) Oh. Well, did he leave word when he'd be back? Really? Oh, thank you. (*He hangs up.*) Well, that's odd. He hasn't answered his telephone in two days.

ROGER'S MOTHER: Maybe he got locked in the bathroom.

ROGER: Mother, do me a favor, will you? (*Reaches into his pocket and removes a folded packet of money.*) Put on that sweet, innocent look you do so well and go to the desk and get the key to seven ninety-six.

ROGER'S MOTHER: Don't be ridiculous. I wouldn't do such a thing.

ROGER (*removing a bill from the packet*): Ten dollars?

ROGER'S MOTHER: Not for all the money in the world!

ROGER (*removing another bill*): Fifty?

ROGER'S MOTHER: Roger, you are disgraceful! (*She snatches the money out of his hand and turns toward the desk.*)
Dissolve.

Hotel Corridor, interior, day

230. L S : *Roger and his mother walk down the corridor toward the camera, speaking in low voices.*

ROGER'S MOTHER: . . . car theft, drunk driving, assaulting an officer, lying to a judge, . . . and now, housebreaking.

R O G E R (*as he reaches the door to room 796 and starts to put the key in the lock*): Not housebreaking, dear. Hotelbreaking. There's a difference.

ROGER'S MOTHER: Of five to ten years.

M A I D (*offscreen*): Just a minute, please!

231. L S : *reverse angle. A hotel maid walks forward from a nearby room.*

232. M S : *Roger's mother, Roger, and the maid at the doorway of room 796.*

MAID: Will you be wantin' me to change your bedding, sir?

ROGER: Yes, well, uh, but not right now.

MAID: Well, I only mention it, sir, because the bed doesn't seem like it's been slept in, and I was just wonderin' if I oughta go on changin' the linens, you know?

R O G E R (*opening the door*): Thank you for your interest.

M A I D : You're welcome, sir. (*She walks away as Roger and his mother enter the room.*)

Hotel Room, interior, day

233. L S : *Roger and his mother enter, pausing near the doorway.*

ROGER: She seemed to think I'm Kaplan. (*The camera pans as he crosses the room.*) I wonder if I *look* like Kaplan? (*He pauses, walks forward toward a desk, and picks up a scrap of paper lying on the blotter.*) Oh, well, look who's here!

ROGER'S MOTHER (*turning to look*): Who? Where?

234. INSERT: *Roger holds a photo torn from a newspaper, showing six men standing in two rows on the steps of a public buiding. In the background we can see "University of" carved in stone. The next word is blocked from our view by a pillar, although half of its initial letter, which might be an M or an N, is partly visible. In the middle of the back row is the strange man who kidnapped Roger and tried to kill him. The camera zooms toward his face.*

ROGER: Our friend who's assembling the General Assembly this afternoon.

235. M S : *Roger and his mother.*

ROGER'S MOTHER: Roger, I think we should go.

ROGER: Don't be nervous.

The camera pans and then tracks forward, following him as he crosses to a bedside table.

ROGER'S MOTHER: I'm not nervous. I'll be late for the bridge club.

ROGER: Good, you'll lose less than usual.

236. INSERT: *Roger presses a message button marked "Chambermaid" on the bedside table.*

237. MS, *as at end of 235. Roger turns and walks to the bathroom. The camera pans, tracks forward, and stops, framing him in the open doorway as he examines the toilet articles above the lavatory. He picks up a comb.*
ROGER: Humph.
He turns and reenters the bedroom, the camera tracking backward as he crosses to his mother.
ROGER *(as he crosses)*: Bulletin. Kaplan has dandruff.
ROGER'S MOTHER: In that case I think we should leave.
The doorbell rings.
ROGER: Too late.
He crosses to the door, and the camera pans to follow him.

238. MS: *Roger opens the door. Standing outside is the maid from the previous sequence.*
MAID: You rang for me, sir?
ROGER: Yes. Come in a moment. *(She enters and he closes the door.)* What's your name?
MAID: Elsie, sir.
ROGER: Elsie, do you know who I am?
MAID: Sure, you're Mr. Kaplan.

239. MS: *Roger, seen from over the maid's shoulder.*
ROGER: Uh, when did . . . when did you first see me?

240. MS, reverse angle: *The maid, seen from over Roger's shoulder.*
MAID: Outside the door.

241. MS, *as in 239.*
MAID: Out in the hall, a couple of minutes ago. Don't you remember?
ROGER: And that's the first time you've laid eyes on me?

242. MS, *as in 240.*
MAID: Can I help it if you're never around, Mr. Kaplan?
ROGER: Well then, how do you know I *am* Mr. Kaplan?
MAID: What?
ROGER: How do you know I'm Mr. Kaplan?
MAID: Why, of course you are!

243. MS, *as in 241.*
MAID: This is room seven ninety-six, isn't it?
ROGER: Mmm-hum.
MAID: So, you're the gentleman in room seven ninety-six, aren't you?
ROGER: All right, Elsie, thanks. *(He turns to open the door.)*
MAID: Will that be all, sir?
ROGER: For the time being, yes.
The doorbell rings. Roger looks anxious. He opens the door, revealing a valet who is carrying a newly laundered suit.

VALET: Valet.

ROGER: Oh, yes, come in.

The maid exits and the valet steps inside as Roger closes the door.

VALET: Shall I hang it in the closet, Mr. Kaplan?

ROGER: Yes, please.

The valet crosses and Roger follows him into the room. The camera pans. Roger glances meaningfully toward his mother as he walks past her. The camera tracks forward as Roger and the valet walk to the closet.

ROGER: Tell me, I forgot. What time did I give you that suit?

VALET (*after hanging up the suit and closing the door*): Last night. Around, uh . . . around six.

ROGER: Ah. Did I give it to you personally?

VALET: Personally? Why, no, Mr. Kaplan. You called down on the phone and described the suit to me and said it would be hanging in your closet.

ROGER: Mmm-hmm.

VALET: Like you always do. Anything wrong?

ROGER (*smiling and glancing toward his mother*): Oh, no. Just curious. Here, thanks. (*He tips the valet.*)

VALET: Oh, thank you.

The camera tracks backward and pans as they recross the room.

VALET: Nice to meet you, Mr. Kaplan.

The camera pans and follows the valet's exit.

244. MS: *Roger and his mother, looking off toward the door after the valet has gone.*

ROGER (*turning to his mother*): Hmm. Isn't that the damndest thing? I'm beginning to think that no one in the hotel has actually seen Kaplan.

ROGER'S MOTHER: Maybe he has his suits mended by invisible weavers.

Roger grimaces and walks toward the closet, removing his coat. His mother follows, and the camera tracks forward. He opens the door and takes out the newly laundered suitcoat.

ROGER: Let me see something.

He slips on the dark coat. The arms are too short, leaving several inches of his shirt cuffs exposed.

ROGER'S MOTHER: I don't think that one does anything for you.

He removes the pants from the hangar and holds them up to his waist.

245. MCU: *Roger's legs, showing that the pants are too short.*

246. CU: *Roger's mother, smiling sarcastically.*

ROGER'S MOTHER: Ah, now, that's *much* better!

247. MS, *as at end of 244: Roger angrily tosses the pants on the bed and starts to remove the coat.*

ROGER: Obviously they've mistaken me for a much shorter man!
The telephone rings.

248. INSERT: *the ringing telephone on the bedside table.*

249. MS, *as at end of 247: Roger pauses with the jacket halfway off. He looks at his mother.*

ROGER: Should I?

ROGER'S MOTHER: Certainly not!

Roger slips off the jacket and hands it to his mother.

ROGER: Here, hold that, will you?

The camera pans as he crosses and sits on the edge of a bed. He answers the telephone. An unmotivated keylight (i.e., a light without an apparent source in the scene) from behind and below the camera gives his figure a slightly eerie look, casting his shadow high on the wall in the background.

ROGER: Hello?

VOICE ON TELEPHONE (*recognizable as Valerian*): It is good to find you in, Mr. Kaplan.

During the next exchange of lines, the camera tracks slowly forward, looking down at Roger and framing him in CU.

ROGER: Who is this?

VOICE: We met only last night and still you do not recognize my voice. I should feel offended.

ROGER: Yes. I know who you are. And I'm not Mr. Kaplan.

VOICE: Of course not. You answer his telephone, you live in his hotel room, and yet you are not Mr. Kaplan. (*Chuckles.*) Nevertheless, we are pleased to find you in. (*Hangs up.*)

ROGER: Now wait . . .

250. MS: *Roger and his mother, who is standing beside the bed.*

ROGER (*rattling the telephone receiver*): Hello. Operator? Operator?

OPERATOR'S VOICE: Yes.

ROGER: Operator, this is Mr. Thorn . . . Kaplan, in seven ninety-six. That call that just came through, where did that come from? Was that an outside call, or did it come from the lobby?

OPERATOR: Just a minute, sir, I'll see.

ROGER: Well, hurry, please.

ROGER'S MOTHER: Who was it?

ROGER: *Only* one of the men who tried to kill me last night.

ROGER'S MOTHER: Oh, we're back to that one, are we?

ROGER (*jiggling the telephone*): Hello, Operator?

OPERATOR: Mr. Kaplan?

ROGER: Yes.

OPERATOR: That call was made from the lobby, sir.

ROGER: It was?

He hangs up the telephone, leaps up, and starts putting on his coat.

ROGER (*to his mother*): It was from the lobby. They're probably on their way up here right now. Come on, let's get out of here.

The camera pans and tracks backward as he slips on the coat and crosses the room. He pauses at the desk and picks up the newspaper photograph.

ROGER'S MOTHER (*following along behind*): I think I'd like to meet these killers.

Nondiegetic music begins as they cross to the door.

Hotel Corridor, interior, day

251. LS: *Roger and his mother exit the room and walk quickly down the hallway and around a corner.*

252. LS: *they reach the elevators. Roger presses the down button and waits impatiently. Just as the down elevator arrives, a second elevator on the right opens. Valerian and Licht step out into the hallway. Seeing Roger and his mother, they follow them onto the down elevator.*

Elevator, interior, day

253. MCU: *Roger stands near the front of the crowded elevator and watches as Valerian and Licht squeeze in next to him. The camera pans as he turns to look meaningfully at his mother, who is standing on the left. She looks at Roger, then offscreen toward the two assailants, and then back at Roger. She closes her eyes and shakes her head in disbelief. Rodger nudges her. She looks again toward the assailants.*

254. MCU: *her POV. Valerian and Licht stand innocuously at the side of the elevator.*

255. MS: *The crowded elevator, with Roger's mother on the left, Roger in the middle, and the two assailants on the right. Roger's mother looks at the two strange men.*

The nondiegetic music ends.

ROGER'S MOTHER (*smiling*): You gentlemen aren't *really* trying to kill my son, are you?

Roger stiffens and looks forward.

256. MCU, *as in 254: Valerian and Licht smile, look at one another, and begin laughing aloud.*

257. CU: *Roger, looking grimly forward. The laughter spreads across the elevator, shared by all the other passengers.*

258. CU: *Roger's mother looks around at the laughing crowd, and then begins laughing herself. She looks toward Valerian and Licht and laughs even more broadly.*

259. MCU, *as in 256: Valerian and Licht laugh heartily.*

260. MCU: *Roger's mother and several of the other passengers continue laughing.*

261. CU, *as in 257: Roger continues to look grimly forward as everyone laughs.*

ELEVATOR OPERATOR'S VOICE (*offscreen*): Lobby, please. Watch your step.

262. MCU: *Roger and the two assailants stand near the front of the elevator. Roger eyes the two men warily. We hear the sound of the elevator grille opening. As Valerian and Licht start to exit, Roger steps in their path and shoves them back into the elevator.*

ROGER: Oh, no, gentlemen, please! Ladies first! Come along, ladies. (*He ushers several women out.*)

Hotel Lobby, interior, day

263. MS: *Roger moves out into the lobby, continuing to usher the women passengers. The camera tracks backward.*

ROGER: Come along. Good.

He turns and dashes off to the right.

264. LS: *from the doorway of the hotel, we see Roger running across the lobby toward us. In the background, his mother calls after him.*

ROGER'S MOTHER: Roger! Roger, will you be home for dinner?

Roger slips through the doorway and out into the street.

Entrance to the Plaza Hotel, exterior, day

265. LS: *the hotel doorman is opening the door of a taxi for a couple who are standing at the curb. Roger runs straight past them and jumps into the taxi.*

Taxi, interior, day

266. MCU (*process*): *Roger closes the door, slides across the seat, and looks over his shoulder out the back window.*
DRIVER (*offscreen*): Where to?
ROGER: I don't know. Just keep going.
Nondiegetic music begins.

Entrance to the Plaza Hotel, exterior, day

267. LS: *the camera pans as Valerian and Licht rush out the front doorway. The doorman is opening the door of another taxi for the same couple we saw earlier. The assailants run past them and jump into the taxi.*

268. MCU (*process*), as in 266: *Roger looks out the back window and then forward. He takes a scrap of paper from his pocket and looks at it.*

269. INSERT: *Roger holding the newspaper photo he took from the hotel room.*

270. MCU (*process*), as in 268.
ROGER: Take me to the United Nations.
DRIVER (*offscreen*): Right.
ROGER (*looking over his shoulder again*): General Assembly Building.
DRIVER: (*offscreen*): Right.
ROGER: I'm being followed. Can you do anything about it?

271. CU (*process*): *reverse angle, showing the back of the driver's head.*
DRIVER: Yes I can.

272. MCU (*process*), as in 270.
ROGER: Do it. (*He looks over his shoulder.*)
Dissolve.

United Nations, exterior, day

273. LS: *a distant view of the United Nations building as the taxi arrives.*

274. LS: *a slightly closer view as the taxi stops at the entrance.*

275. MS (*process*): *Roger gets out of the taxi.*

276. LS, as in 274: *the taxi drives off and Roger walks up the steps of the building.*

General Assembly Building, interior, day

277. LS (*matte*): *seen as a tiny figure in the distance, Roger crosses the lobby toward the information desk.*

278. MS: *Roger steps up to the desk.*
The nondiegetic music ends.
RECEPTIONIST: May I help you, sir?
ROGER: Yes, please. Where will I find Mr. Lester Townsend?
RECEPTIONIST: Mr. Lester Townsend of UNIPO? And did you have an appointment, sir?
ROGER: Well, . . . yes. Yes, he expects me.
RECEPTIONIST: Your name, please?
ROGER (*hesitates*): My name?

RECEPTIONIST: Yes, please.

ROGER: Kaplan. George Kaplan.

RECEPTIONIST: One moment, please. (*She dials a number on a telephone.*)

United Nations, exterior, day

Nondiegetic music begins.

279. LS: *the taxi bearing Roger's two assailants pulls up to the curb.*

280. MS (*process*): *Valerian gets out.*

VALERIAN (*to Licht in the cab*): Wait for me at the corner of Forty-Seventh.

281. LS: *the cab drives off as Valerian goes up the steps of the building.*

General Assembly Building, interior, day

282. MS, *as in 278: the receptionist hangs up her telephone, writes something on a piece of paper, and hands the paper to Roger.*

RECEPTIONIST: If you will give this to one of the attendants in the public lounge, she will page him for you.

ROGER: Thank you very much.

RECEPTIONIST: You're welcome, Mr. Kaplan.

Roger turns and walks off to the left.

283. LS (*matte*), *as in 277: Valerian enters and walks across the lobby, going off to the left.*

284. LS: *Roger enters the crowded public lounge. Groups of well-dressed diplomats are standing at a bar or seated on couches around the room. The camera pans as Roger crosses to another reception desk.*

VOICE ON PUBLIC ADDRESS SYSTEM: Mr. Bernotti of the Swiss Observer's office. . . . Mr. Bernotti of the Swiss Observer's office. . . .

285. MS: *Roger hands the slip of paper to the receptionist.*

ROGER: Page Mr. Lester Townsend, please.

RECEPTIONIST: Certainly, Mr. Kaplan. (*She speaks into a microphone on the desk.*) Mr. Townsend of UNIPO. . . . Mr. Townsend of UNIPO. . . .

The nondiegetic music ends.

The camera pans to the right as Roger turns away from the receptionist and looks around the room, then it halts at the entry to the lounge, where Valerian has just arrived. The camera tracks forward as he stands in the entranceway, slipping on a pair of gloves.

RECEPTIONIST (*offscreen, over the public address system*): . . . please call at the communications desk of the public lounge. Mr. Townsend of UNIPO, please call at the communications desk of the public lounge.

286. MS: *a man walks forward to the desk and stands beside Roger, who is still looking around the room.*

TOWNSEND (*to the receptionist*): You paged me?

RECEPTIONIST: Yes, Mr. Townsend. (*To Roger.*) Mr. Kaplan?

ROGER: Yes?

RECEPTIONIST: You wanted to see Mr. Townsend.

ROGER: Yes.

RECEPTIONIST: This is Mr. Townsend.

TOWNSEND (*offering his hand*): How do you do, Mr. Kaplan.

ROGER (*smiling at the receptionist as he shakes the stranger's hand*): This isn't Mr. Townsend.

TOWNSEND: Yes it is.

ROGER: Well, there must be some mistake. Mr. *Lester* Townsend?

TOWNSEND: That's me. What can I do for you? (*He gestures and leads Roger off to the right.*)

287. MS: *Valerian, observing Roger and Townsend from beside a piece of modernist statuary near the entrance to the lounge. He puts one of his gloved hands into his pocket and steps out of sight behind the archway leading into the room.*

288. MS: *the camera tracks with Roger and Townsend as they cross the lounge.*

ROGER: Are you the Townsend who lives in Glen Cove?

Townsend pauses and turns to face Roger, standing with his back to the entrance of the room.

TOWNSEND: That's right. Are we neighbors?

A photographer's flashbulb goes off somewhere in the background.

ROGER: A large red brick house with a curved, tree-lined driveway?

TOWNSEND: That's the one.

ROGER: Were you at home last night, Mr. Townsend?

TOWNSEND: You mean in Glen Cove?

ROGER: Yes.

TOWNSEND: No, I've been staying in my apartment here in town for the past month. I always do when we're in session here.

ROGER: What about Mrs. Townsend?

289. MS: *Townsend, seen from over Roger's shoulder.*

TOWNSEND: My wife has been dead for many years.

290. MS: *reverse angle. Roger, seen from over Townsend's shoulder.*

TOWNSEND: Now, Mr. Kaplan, what's this all about?

ROGER: Forgive me, but who are those people living in your house?

291. MS, *as in 289.*

TOWNSEND: What people? The house is completely closed up.

292. MS, *as in 290.*

TOWNSEND: Just the gardener and his wife living on the grounds.

293. MS, *as in 291. Townsend folds his arms across his chest.*

TOWNSEND: Now, Mr. Kaplan, suppose you tell me who you are and what you want.

294. M S : *Roger and Townsend facing one another in a 50–50 composition, with Roger on the left.*

    R O G E R : I, uh, please, just a minute. (*He reaches into his pocket and takes out the newspaper photograph, showing it to Townsend.*) Do you know this man?

    In the background, a photographer is lining up a group of dignitaries from Africa for a picture. Townsend looks down at the paper and suddenly gasps, his mouth gaping and his eyes bulging out.

    Nondiegetic music begins.

295. M S , *as in 287. Valerian is standing in the doorway. Suddenly he runs off to the left.*

296. M S , *as in 294. Townsend, his arms still folded across his chest and his mouth still open, slowly collapses forward into Roger's outstretched hands. A knife is sticking out of his back. The camera tracks backward as Townsend slowly collapses to the floor, steadied in Roger's arms. Roger grasps the handle of the knife and pulls it loose, holding it in astonishment.*

    B Y S T A N D E R : Look!

297. M S : *a group of diplomats seated around a table turn to look. Two of them stand up.*

298. M S : *viewed from a low angle, three of the women receptionists lean forward across their desk, looking anxiously toward Roger.*

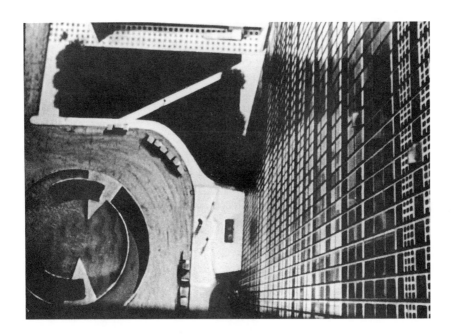

299. L S, *as at end of 296: Roger, who has been leaning over Townsend's dead body, stands up and gapes at the knife in his hand. He turns around to look at the other people in the room. The photographer in the background snaps his picture, startling him with a flashbulb. People begin gathering around the body.*

    A WOMAN'S VOICE (*offscreen*): He's got a knife! Look out!

    ROGER (*holding the knife*): Listen to me, I had nothing to do with this!

    A WOMAN'S VOICE: Call the police!

    ROGER (*crouching slightly and backing away with the knife in his hand*): Wait a minute! Don't come any nearer! Get back!

300. M S: *the camera pans as Roger drops the knife on the floor and dashes for the exit.*

    The music segues into the "fandango" theme.

United Nations, exterior, day

301. L S (*matte*): *looking straight down from the top of the glass-walled Secretariat building at the fountain and entrance drive, we see Roger's antlike figure run out the door, along the sidewalk, and into a waiting taxi. Dissolve.*

A Government Office in Washington, D.C., exterior, day

302. C U: *a portion of an engraved plaque on the exterior of the building, reading* "UNITED STATES INTELLIGENCE AGENCY." *In the shiny surface of the plaque, we can see the reflection of the Capitol dome. Dissolve.*

United States Intelligence Agency Office, interior, day
The nondiegetic music ends.

303. CU: *the front page of The* Evening Star, *with a headline reading* "DIPLO-
MAT SLAIN AT U.N." The bold type over the lead story announces, "Assassin
Eludes Police Efforts." Roger is shown in a large picture, looking straight
at the camera and holding a knife in a threatening position. A smaller
headline to the left of the picture declares, "Nixon Promises West Will Remain in Berlin."

    FIRST AGENT (*offscreen, reading from the paper*): ". . . the photograph
has been tentatively identified as Roger Thornhill, Manhattan advertising executive, indicating that the name of George Kaplan, which he
gave to an attendant in the General Assembly Building, was false."

*The camera pulls back and tilts up to a level view, revealing the profile of
the man who is reading from the paper. It continues to pull back and
slowly tracks in a circle, stopping behind an empty chair at one end of a
conference table. Seated around the table are four male intelligence
agents (unnamed) and a female agent, referred to as Mrs. Finlay.*

    FIRST AGENT (*continuing to read*): "A possible motive for the slaying
was suggested by the discovery that, earlier today, Thornhill had appeared in a Glen Cove, Long Island, police court charged with drunk
driving with a stolen car. In his defense he charged that the murder victim, Mr. Townsend, had tried to kill *him* the night before." (*He drops
the paper, and the agent next to him picks it up.*) Brother!

    SECOND AGENT: What about that!

    MRS. FINLAY: Does anyone know this Thornhill?

    FIRST AGENT: No, not me.

    SECOND AGENT: Never heard of him.

    MRS. FINLAY (*to the man at the head of the table*):   Professor?

304. MCU: *the Professor shakes his head, "no."*

    THIRD AGENT (*offscreen*): Apparently the poor sucker . . .

305. MS: *looking across the table at the two agents who have been reading
the paper.*

    THIRD AGENT (*indicating the paper*): . . . got mistaken for George
Kaplan.

    FIRST AGENT: How could he get mistaken for George Kaplan when
George Kaplan doesn't even exist?

    THIRD AGENT: Don't ask me how it happened. Obviously it happened.
Vandamm's men must have grabbed him and tried to put him away,
using Lester Townsend's house.

306. MS: *reverse angle, looking across the table at the other two agents.*

    SECOND AGENT: And the unsuspecting Mr. Townsend winds up with
a stray knife in his back.

307. MS, *as in 305.*

THIRD AGENT: *C'est la guerre.*

FIRST AGENT: If it's so horribly sad, how is it I feel like laughing?

308. MS, *as in 306.*

MRS. FINLAY: What are we going to do?

SECOND AGENT: Do?

MRS. FINLAY: About Mr. Thornhill.

309. MCU, *as in 304.*

PROFESSOR: We, uh, we do nothing.

310. MS, *as in 308.*

MRS. FINLAY: Nothing?

311. MCU: *the Professor, seen from a slightly higher angle.*

PROFESSOR: That's right, nothing.

He rises and begins to walk around the table, the camera panning to follow him until he stops behind two of the agents.

PROFESSOR: Oh, we could congratulate ourselves on a marvelous stroke of good fortune. Our nonexistent decoy, George Kaplan, created to divert suspicion from our actual agent, has fortuitously become a live decoy.

MRS. FINLAY: Yes, Professor. But how long do you think he'll stay alive?

PROFESSOR: Well, that's his problem. (*He walks offscreen to the right.*)

SECOND AGENT (*offscreen*): What Mrs. Finlay means is that. . . .

312. LS: *the Professor has moved over to a window at the end of the room, looking out at the Capitol building.*

PROFESSOR: Oh, I know what she means. (*He turns his back and looks out the window.*)

SECOND AGENT (*offscreen*): We can't sit back calmly and wait to see who kills him first, . . .

313. LS: *reverse angle, looking toward the agents sitting around the table.*

SECOND AGENT: . . . Vandamm and company or the police.

314. LS, *as in 312: the Professor turns away from the window.*

PROFESSOR: What can we do to save him, without endangering our own agent?

315. MS: *Mrs. Finlay and the second agent.*

MRS. FINLAY: Aren't we being just a wee bit callous?

PROFESSOR (*walking into the frame from offscreen right*): No, my dear woman, we're not being callous. (*The camera pans as he paces back across the room*). We didn't invent our nonexistent man, and give him the name of George Kaplan, and establish elaborate behavior patterns for him, and move his prop belongings in and out of hotel rooms for our own private amusement. (*He sits wearily in an upholstered red leather chair at the end of the room.*) We created George Kaplan and

labored successfully to convince Vandamm that this was our own agent, hot on his trail, for a desperately important reason.

316. MS, *as in 315.*

SECOND AGENT: Check. Nobody's denying that.

317. MS: *the Professor rises from his chair and walks back to the head of the table. The camera pans with him.*

PROFESSOR: Very well, then. If we make the slightest move to suggest that there is no such agent as George Kaplan, give any hint to Vandamm that he's pursuing a decoy instead of our own agent, then our agent, working right under Vandamm's very nose, will immediately face suspicion, exposure (*he sits down in his place at the head of the table*), and assassination. (*He picks up a pipe.*) Like the two others who went before.

318. LS: *a bird's-eye view, looking down on the conference table.*

MRS. FINLAY: Good-bye, Mr. Thornhill, wherever you are.
Dissolve.

Grand Central Station, interior, early evening

319. LS: *the crowded center of the station. The camera cranes down to show two uniformed policemen looking at passersby.*

PUBLIC ADDRESS ANNOUNCER (*offscreen*): Train number twenty-five, the Twentieth-Century Limited, due to leave at six P.M., for Chicago, will depart on track number. . . .

As the two policemen turn and walk away to the left, the camera pans slowly to the right, coming to rest at a closed telephone booth, in which we see Roger having an urgent conversation.

Telephone Booth, interior, early evening

320. CU: *Roger, speaking on the telephone.*

ROGER: Yes, yes, dear, I know. I know. Now, listen to me, Mother, I beg you. I *called* the Plaza. Kaplan checked out. He went to the Ambassador East in Chicago. Yes, that's why I'm— (*he listens impatiently*)— Well, I *can't* go to the police, at least not yet. *You* saw the newspapers. My fingerprints are on the knife; I'm a car thief, a drunk driver, and I murdered a man for revenge. I wouldn't have a chance, and I won't have until I find George Kaplan, who obviously knows what this is all about. (*He listens.*) No, dear, the train, it's safer. (*He listens.*) Well, because there's no place to hide on a plane if anyone should recognize me. (*He listens.*) Oh, you want me to jump off a moving plane? Yes, well, thank you so much, Mother. Yes, good-bye. (*He hangs up.*)

Terminal, interior, early evening

321. MS: *Roger exits the booth, pausing to look uneasily into the eyes of a man who is waiting to use the telephone. The camera pans left as Roger crosses the station and disappears into the crowd.*

322. MS: *a low-angle view of a man who is reading a tabloid with a giant headline:* "MANHUNT ON FOR U.N. KILLER." *Roger enters from offscreen left and pauses to look at the headline.*

323. MS: *a high-angle view of Roger, reacting to what the newspaper says. He reaches into his coat pocket and takes out a pair of sunglasses, putting them on. The camera pans right as he moves off into the crowd. Two more uniformed policemen come into view, standing by the information desk. The camera pauses to register their watchful glances around the room; then it continues to pan, picking up Roger as he walks toward the ticket counters in the distance.*

324. LS: *a high-angle view of Roger approaching one of the ticket booths.*

Ticket Booth, interior, early evening

325. MS: *the ticket agent, seen from over Roger's shoulder.*

TICKET AGENT: Yes, sir?

ROGER: Give me a bedroom on the Twentieth-Century, please.

TICKET AGENT (*looks at his watch*): Leaving in five minutes.

326. MS (*process*): *reverse angle. Roger, seen from over the agent's shoulder.*

ROGER: Yes, I know. Could you make it snappy?

327. MS: *as in 325.*

TICKET AGENT: I think they're all sold out.

328. MS (*process*), *as in 326.*

ROGER: Sold out?

TICKET AGENT: You can always go coach.

ROGER: I . . . I can't do that. What time is the next train?

329. MS, *as in 327.*

TICKET AGENT: Nothin' till ten. You're in a hurry, huh?

ROGER: Well, could you call them and see what they have?

TICKET AGENT: Somethin' wrong with your eyes?

330. MS (*process*), *as in 329.*

ROGER: Yes, they're sensitive to questions.

331. MS, *as in 328.*

ROGER: Will you call them?

TICKET AGENT: Sure, sure. (*He looks down at something on his desk.*)

332. INSERT: *the ticket agent's* POV. Propped against the cash box inside the ticket booth is the newspaper photo of Roger wielding a knife.

333. MS, *as in 331.*

TICKET AGENT: Don't go away.

334. MS (*process*), *as in 330. The ticket agent turns from the window and walks several paces to a concealed spot behind the files of tickets. The camera tracks backward and pans slightly to follow him, leaving Roger out of sight. The agent picks up a telephone and dials a number.*

TICKET AGENT (*quietly*): He's at window fifteen, upper level. Hurry. *He hangs up, turns, and retraces his steps, the camera following.*

TICKET AGENT (*loudly*): You're in luck, Mister! *Suddenly the agent stops in his tracks. Roger has disappeared. The camera zooms forward toward an empty ticket window.*

Terminal, interior, early evening

335. LS: *Roger, still wearing the sunglasses, walks beneath an archway and turns left, the camera panning to follow him. He approaches a guard at the departure gate for the Twentieth-Century Limited.*

GUARD: Ticket?

ROGER: Oh, I'm just seeing some friends off. (*He looks over his shoulder.*)

336. LS: *through the archway, we can see two uniformed policemen running toward the gate.*

337. MS: *the guard and Roger.*

GUARD: I'm sorry, I'll have to know the names and space before I can let you . . .

Roger dashes past him.

GUARD (*looking off to the left as Roger disappears*): . . . through.

338. LS, *as in 336: The policemen running forward. They begin to shout.*

339. MS, *as in 337: The guard moves off to the left, following Roger.*

POLICEMEN (*offscreen*): Hey! Come here!

Train Platform, interior, early evening

340. LS: *the camera tracks with Roger as he walks briskly along beside the train, glancing over his shoulder. He steps into the open doorway of one of the train's cars.*

Train, interior, early evening

341. L S : *Roger walks toward the camera, down the length of the narrow cor-*
ridor of a sleeping car. He pauses to look out one of the windows.

342. L S : *Roger's* P O V . *The uniformed policemen are boarding the next car.*

343. L S , *as in 341: Roger reacts, turning and jogging down the corridor in*
the opposite direction.

344. M C U : *Roger approaches the end of the car. Seen from over his shoulder,*
an attractive blond woman dressed in black turns the corner and nearly
collides with him.

R O G E R : Oh.

He steps to the left, but at the same moment she steps left also.

345. M C U : *reverse angle, looking over the woman's shoulder at Roger. He*
steps to the right, and so does she.

R O G E R : I'm sorry.

346. M C U , *as in 344: again Roger steps to the left, and again she moves in the*
same direction.

R O G E R : I'm sorry.

W O M A N (*smiling*): My fault. (*She starts to move around him, but he*
moves with her.) I'm sorry.

She looks over Roger's shoulder and sees something.

347. L S : *The woman's* P O V , *looking down the corridor. The two policemen*
have entered the car and are approaching. Their path is momentarily
impeded by a passenger and a Pullman porter who is carrying heavy
luggage.

348. M C U , *as in 346: Roger turns and looks down the car. He reacts, and the*
woman notices his anxiety. Suddenly he opens a compartment door and
ducks inside, closing the door behind him. She stands alone in the corri-
dor, looking toward the policemen.

349. L S , *as in 347: the passenger and the porter enter a compartment at the*
other end of the car, and the two policemen walk briskly forward.

350. M S : *as the policemen approach the woman, she points off to the right.*

W O M A N : He went that way. I think he got off.

C O N D U C T O R (*offscreen*): All aboard!

The policemen rush off in the direction in which the woman is pointing.

351. M S : *The woman's* P O V , *looking at the two policemen as they exit the*
corridor.

352. M S , *as in 350: The woman stands for a moment, watching to see that the*
policemen are gone. Behind her, the compartment door opens and Roger
peeks out, looking first at her, then down the corridor, then at her.

R O G E R : Thank you.

W O M A N (*seductively*): Quite all right.

R O G E R : *Seven* parking tickets.

W O M A N : Oh.

She exits to the left and Roger stands watching her, glancing down toward her ankles.

353. LS: *Roger's* POV, *looking toward the woman as she walks away. The train jolts into motion and starts to leave the station.*

354. MS: *Roger stoops to look out the train window.*

355. LS: *Roger's* POV, *looking through the window at the two policemen, who are visible from the waist down, standing on a red carpet along the station platform. The train continues moving out of the station. Dissolve.*

Countryside, exterior, evening

356. LS: *from just outside one of the cars, we can see the long train rounding the bend of a river, moving west. The sun is setting over a ridge of mountains in the distance. The camera slowly pans to the right, aiming toward the interior of the train.*

Club Car, interior, evening

357. LS: *the camera continues panning to the right, across a dark area, hiding the transition from the previous shot. It stops at an open doorway, looking into the crowded club car. A conductor and his assistant are moving up the aisle, checking tickets. They walk toward the camera, pausing in the foreground beside a door marked "*TOILET.*" After consulting a list of passengers, they exit to the left rear of the camera. The toilet door opens and Roger pokes his head out, still wearing sunglasses. Noting that the coast is clear, he closes the door and walks off through the club car.*

358. MS: *from a low angle and from behind, we see Roger approaching the end of the club car. He notices a newspaper lying on a table and quickly folds it in half, concealing it under a stack of bound magazines. Then he exits the car.*

Dining Car, interior, evening

359. LS: *from a low angle, looking past a group of diners in the foreground, we see Roger enter the dining car. Soft music is playing on the car's public address system. A steward approaches Roger.*

STEWARD: Good evening, sir. One?

ROGER: Please.

The steward and Roger move off to the right.

360. LS (*process*): *Roger follows the steward down the length of the car, moving toward the camera. The steward passes completely out of the shot. As Roger nears the foreground, the camera tilts up slightly, framing him in CU. He stops, reacting to something offscreen.*

361. MS (*process*): *reverse angle. The steward indicates an empty chair at a table already occupied by the blond woman. She looks directly into Roger's face with evident interest.*

362. MS (*process*): *the steward helps Roger take a seat.*

363. MS (*process*): *The woman is seen from over Roger's shoulder. She continues looking directly at him and smiles slightly as he adjusts his chair and consults the menu.*

STEWARD (*offscreen*): Cocktail before dinner?

ROGER: Yes, please. A Gibson.

STEWARD (*offscreen*): Right away.

The steward's arm is visible as he hands Roger a menu. The woman sips her coffee and stares at Roger over the rim of the cup.

364. MS (*process*): *reverse angle, from over the woman's shoulder. Roger feels her stare. He glances at her, then looks back at the menu.*

365. MS (*process*), *as in 363: The woman puts down her cup and looks discreetly at her plate. She glances toward the far end of the car, but her eyes quickly wander back to Roger's face.*

366. MS (*process*), *as in 364: Roger looks at the woman and smiles.*

ROGER (*glancing back at the menu*): Well, here we are again.

367. MS (*process*), *as in 365.*

WOMAN (*pregnantly*): Yes.

368. MS (*process*), *as in 366.*

ROGER (*indicating the menu*): Recommend anything?

369. MS (*process*), *as in 367.*

WOMAN: The brook trout. A little trouty, but quite good.

370. MS (*process*), *as in 368: Roger nods and closes the menu.*

ROGER: Sold.

371. MS (*process*), *as in 369: The woman watches as Roger writes down his order. From offscreen, a waiter brings him a Gibson.*
     ROGER (*writing*): Brook . . . trout.

372. MS (*process*), *as in 370: Roger hands his order to the offscreen waiter.*
     ROGER: There you are. Thank you.
     WAITER (*offscreen*): Yes, sir.

373. MS (*process*), *as in 371: The woman gazes openly at Roger as he shifts awkwardly in his seat. (Throughout this exchange of shots, he is seated with his back against a small partition, whereas she has an open area behind her.)*

374. MS (*process*), *as in 372: Roger turns slightly and looks over his shoulder, around the partition.*

375. MS (*process*), *as in 373: Roger looking over his shoulder.*

376. MS (*process*), *as in 374: Roger turns back toward the woman, who is still looking at him. He adjusts his sunglasses and smiles shyly*): I know. I look vaguely familiar.

377. MS (*process*), *as in 375.*
     WOMAN: Yes.
     ROGER: You feel you've seen me somewhere before.
     WOMAN (*nodding slowly*): Mmmm.

378. MS (*process*), *as in 376.*
     ROGER: Funny how I have that effect on people. It's something about my face.

379. MS (*process*), *as in 377.*
     WOMAN: It's a nice face.

380. MS (*process*), *as in 378.*
     ROGER: You think so?

381. MS (*process*), *as in 379.*
     WOMAN: I wouldn't say it if I didn't.
     ROGER (*sipping his Gibson*): Oh, you're *that* type. (*He removes the sunglasses.*)
     WOMAN: What type?
     ROGER: Honest.
     WOMAN: Not really.

382. MS (*process*), *as in 380: Roger cleans the lenses of the sunglasses with his napkin.*
     ROGER: Good, because honest women frighten me.
     WOMAN: Why?
     ROGER: I don't know. Somehow they seem to put me at a disadvantage.

383. MS (*process*), *as in 381.*
     WOMAN: Because you're not honest with them?
     ROGER: Exactly.
     WOMAN: Like that business about the seven parking tickets?

384. MS (*process*), *as in 382: Roger smiles slightly, folds the sunglasses, and puts them in his pocket.*

ROGER: What I mean is, the moment I meet an attractive woman, . . .

385. MS (*process*), *as in 383.*

ROGER: . . . I have to start pretending I have no desire to make love to her.

WOMAN: What makes you think you have to conceal it?

386. MS (*process*), *as in 384.*

ROGER: She might find the idea objectionable.

387. MS (*process*), *as in 385.*

WOMAN: Then again, she might not.

388. MS (*process*), *as in 386: the woman sips her coffee. Roger smiles and toasts her with his Gibson.*

ROGER: Think how lucky I am to have been seated here!

389. MS (*process*), *as in 387.*

WOMAN: Oh, luck had nothing to do with it.

390. MS (*process*), *as in 388: Roger sips the Gibson.*

ROGER: Fate?

391. MS (*process*), *as in 389.*

WOMAN (*shaking her head slowly to indicate "no"*): I tipped the steward five dollars . . .

392. CU (*process*): *Roger reacts with pleased surprise, holding his glass poised in midair.*

WOMAN: . . . to seat you here if you should come in.

393. CU (*process*): *reverse angle. The woman smiles at Roger.*

394. CU (*process*), *as in 392: Roger smiles and lowers the glass.*

ROGER: Is that a proposition?

395. CU (*process*), *as in 393.*

WOMAN (*shrugs slightly*): I never discuss love on an empty stomach.

396. CU (*process*), *as in 394.*

ROGER: You've already eaten.

397. CU (*process*), *as in 395.*

WOMAN: But you haven't.

398. CU (*process*), *as in 396: Roger pauses and reacts with a sly smile as the waiter brings him his food.*

ROGER: Don't you think it's time we were introduced?

399. CU (*process*), *as in 397.*

WOMAN: I'm Eve Kendall. I'm twenty-six and unmarried.

400. CU (*process*), *as in 398: the waiter's arm is still visible in the shot, arranging Roger's dinner.*

EVE (*offscreen*): Now you know everything.

ROGER: Tell me, what do you do, besides lure men to their doom . . .

401. CU (*process*), *as in 399.*

ROGER (*offscreen*): . . . on the Twentieth-Century Limited?

EVE (*looking down and sipping her coffee*): I'm an industrial designer.

402. CU (*process*), *as in 400.*

ROGER (*pauses*): Jack Phillips, . . .

403. CU (*process*), *as in 401.*

ROGER (*offscreen*): . . . western sales manager for Kingby Electronics.

EVE (*smiling*): No you're not. You're Roger Thornhill . . .

404. CU (*process*), *as in 402.*

Roger is taking his first bite of the trout. He straightens and stops chewing.

EVE (*offscreen*): . . . of Madison Avenue, and you're wanted for murder . . .

405. CU (*process*), *as in 403.*

EVE: . . . on every front page in America.

406. CU (*process*), *as in 404.*

EVE (*offscreen*): Don't be so modest.

ROGER (*pauses*): Oops.

407. CU (*process*), *as in 405.*

EVE (*sipping her coffee and looking seriously at Roger*): Oh, don't worry.

408. CU (*process*), *as in 406.*

EVE (*offscreen*): I won't say a word.

ROGER: How come?

409. CU (*process*), *as in 407.*

EVE: I told you. It's a nice face.

410. CU (*process*), *as in 408.*

ROGER: Is that the only reason?

411. CU (*process*), *as in 409.*

EVE (*shrugs*): It's going to be a long night.

412. CU (*process*), *as in 410.*

ROGER (*relaxes slightly*): True.

413. CU (*process*), *as in 411.*

EVE: And I don't particularly like the book I've started.

414. CU (*process*), *as in 412.*

ROGER: Ahhh.

415. CU (*process*), *as in 413.*

EVE: Do you know what I mean?

416. CU (*process*), *as in 414.*

ROGER: Now let me think. . . .

The Muzak playing in the background fades out, replaced by a throbbing nondiegetic score that is keyed to the pulsing rhythm of the train. This score modulates into the love theme.

417. CU (*process*), *as in 415: Eve looks meaningfully at Roger.*

418. CU (*process*), *as in 416.*

ROGER (*pause*): Yes, I know exactly what you mean.

419. C U (*process*), *as in 417: Eve looks down and reaches into her purse.*
420. C U (*process*), *as in 418: smiling, Roger reaches into his pocket.*
421. C U (*process*), *as in 419: Eve takes out a cigarette and looks back at Roger.*
422. C U (*process*), *as in 420: Roger opens a matchbook.*
423. C U (*process*): *Eve is shown in full profile, holding the cigarette in her hand. She glances toward the matchbook.*
424. I N S E R T : *from Eve's* P O V , *we see an* E C U *of the matchbook. On the cover are Roger's initials, "R.O.T."*
425. C U (*process*), *as in 422: Roger tears off a paper match and glances down at the cover of the matchbook.*
    R O G E R : My trademark: Rot.
426. C U (*process*), *as in 423.*
    E V E : Roger O. Thornhill. What does the O. stand for?
427. C U (*process*), *as in 425.*
    R O G E R : Nothing.
    He lights the match.
428. C U (*process*), *as in 426: Roger's hand enters the frame from the left, holding out a lighted match. Eve takes the hand in her own, leans forward, and lights the cigarette. Roger's hand starts to withdraw, but she doesn't let go.*
429. C U (*process*), *as in 427: Roger's surprised reaction as Eve pulls his hand back toward her face.*

430. CU *(process), as in 428: Eve leans toward Roger's hand and blows out the match.*

431. CU *(process), as in 429: Roger looks intently at Eve as he takes back the extinguished match.*

432. CU *(process), as in 419: Eve returns Roger's look.*

433. CU *(process), as in 431: Roger drops the match in an ashtray and smiles.*
    ROGER: I'd invite you to my bedroom . . .

434. CU *(process), as in 432.*
    ROGER: . . . if I had a bedroom.
    EVE: No roomette?

435. CU *(process), as in 433.*
    ROGER: Nothing. Not even a ticket.

436. CU *(process), as in 434: Eve puffs on the cigarette and slowly exhales smoke.*
    ROGER: I've been playing hide and seek with the Pullman conductor . . .

437. CU *(process), as in 435.*
    ROGER: . . . ever since the train left New York.

438. CU *(process), as in 436.*
    EVE: How awkward for you.

439. CU *(process), as in 437.*
    ROGER: Yes, isn't it? No place to sleep.

440. CU *(process), as in 438.*
    EVE: I have a large drawing room all to myself.

441. CU *(process), as in 439.*
    ROGER: That doesn't seem quite fair, does it?

442. CU *(process), as in 440.*
    EVE: Drawing room E. Car thirty-nine oh one.
    The nondiegetic music ends.

443. CU *(process), as in 441.*
    ROGER: Such a nice number.

444. CU *(process), as in 442.*
    EVE *(smiles slightly):* It is easy to remember.

445. CU *(process), as in 443.*
    ROGER: Thirty-nine oh one.

446. CU *(process), as in 444.*
    EVE: See?

447. CU *(process), as in 445.*
    ROGER *(glancing down at his plate):* No luggage.

448. CU *(process), as in 446: the train is slowly coming to a stop. Eve glances out the window and notices something.*
    EVE: So?

449. CU *(process), as in 447: through the window beyond Roger's right shoulder, we can see a man getting out of an automobile.*
    ROGER: Well, you wouldn't have an extra pair of pajamas, would you?

450. CU (*process*), *as in 448: Eve has turned slightly to the right, as if preparing to leave.*

EVE: Wouldn't I?

451. CU (*process*), *as in 449: through the window, we can see two men walking toward the train. Roger smiles at Eve.*

452. CU (*process*), *as in 450.*

EVE: Incidentally, I wouldn't order any dessert if I were you.

453. CU (*process*), *as in 451.*

ROGER (*nods*): I get the message.

454. CU (*process*), *as in 452.*

EVE (*putting some things into her purse*): That isn't exactly what I meant.

455. CU (*process*), *as in 453: Roger's smile fades.*

EVE: The train seems to be making an unscheduled stop.

456. CU (*process*), *as in 454.*

EVE: And I just saw two men get out of a police car . . .

457. CU (*process*), *as in 455: Roger looks worried.*

EVE (*offscreen*): . . . as we pulled into the station.

458. CU (*process*), *as in 456.*

EVE: They weren't smiling.

Suspenseful nondiegetic music begins.

Eve starts to get up from the table.

459. CU (*process*), *as in 457: Roger frowns. Eve rises in the foreground and exits to the left. Roger looks out the window.*

460. LS: *Roger's* POV, *looking out the window. Two plainclothes officers are boarding the train.*

461. LS: *Roger jumps quickly from his seat. He reaches into his pocket and tosses some money on the table. The camera pans to watch him hurry off in an opposite direction from the police. Offscreen, we hear the sound of another train passing, and a heavy jolt as the Twentieth-Century Limited starts up again.*

462. MS: *a low angle, showing the rear entrance to the dining car. Eve is on her way out. Roger follows her, pausing to look over his shoulder in the direction of the police. He exits.*

463. LS: *a reverse view, looking down the car toward the front entrance. The two policemen have entered and are walking forward. They stop to talk to the steward.*

Eve's Compartment, interior, later that evening

464. LS: *Eve is seen in profile reclining on the couch, reading a book.*

The nondiegetic music ends.

ROGER (*offscreen, muffled*): I think you'd better go out and tell those police to hurry.

EVE: Patience is a virtue.

ROGER: So is breathing.

EVE: Just lie still.

The camera tilts up to the closed upper berth over Eve's head.

ROGER: Have you got any olive oil?

EVE (*offscreen*): Olive oil?

ROGER: I want to be packed in olive oil if I'm going to be a sardine.

465. MS (*process*): *a frontal view of Eve, with the train window beyond her head. The train is passing a lake or river, with the sun setting behind low hills on the horizon. There is a knock at the door.*

EVE (*closing the book but not getting up*): Come in.

466. MS: *low reverse angle, from Eve's POV. The door opens and the two plainclothes policemen enter.*

EVE (*offscreen*): Who are you?

FIRST POLICEMAN (*showing his badge*): State police.

467. MS (*process*), *as in 465.*

SECOND POLICEMAN (*offscreen*): Your name, please.

EVE: Eve Kendall. Is anything wrong?

468. MS, *as in 466.*

FIRST POLICEMAN: There was a man at your table tonight in the dining car.

469. MS (*process*), *as in 467.*

EVE: Yes.

SECOND POLICEMAN (*offscreen*): Friend of yours?

EVE: I never saw him before.

470. MS, *as in 468: the first policeman removes a photograph from his pocket and hands it to Eve.*

FIRST POLICEMAN: Is this the man?

471. MS (*process*), *as in 469: the first policeman is partially visible as he hands the photograph to Eve.*

EVE (*looking at the photo*): Yes, I think so. (*Handing it back.*) It's not a very clear picture.

472. MS, *as in 470.*

FIRST POLICEMAN: It's a Wirephoto. We just got it from the New York police.

473. MS (*process*), *as in 471.*

EVE: Police?

474. MCU: *a closer, low-angle shot of the two policemen, seen in three-quarter profile.*

FIRST POLICEMAN: He's wanted for murder.

475. MS (*process*), *as in 473: Eve sits up.*

EVE: Good heavens, no!

476. MCU, *as in 474.*

FIRST POLICEMAN: The steward says you left the dining car together.

477. MS (*process*), *as in 475.*

 EVE: We might've happened to leave at the same time, but not together.

478. MCU, *as in 476.*

 FIRST POLICEMAN: What did you two talk about?

479. MS (*process*), *as in 477.*

 EVE: Talk about?

480. MCU, *as in 478.*

 FIRST POLICEMAN: Yeah, the waiter said that you were getting along pretty good with this Thornhill fella.

481. MS (*process*), *as in 479.*

 EVE: Is that his name? Thornhill?

482. MCU, *as in 480.*

 FIRST POLICEMAN: You mean he didn't tell you?

483. MS (*process*), *as in 481.*

 EVE: He didn't tell me anything. All we did was chat about different kinds of food, . . .

484. MCU, *as in 482.*

 EVE (*offscreen*): . . . train travel versus plane travel, that sort of thing.

485. MS (*process*), *as in 483.*

 EVE: Rather innocuous, I must say, considering he was a fugitive from justice. Who did he kill?

486. MCU, *as in 484.*

 FIRST POLICEMAN: He didn't say where he was going, did he?

487. MS (*process*), *as in 485.*

 EVE: No, I assume Chicago. You think perhaps he got off when you got on?

488. MCU, *as in 486.*

 FIRST POLICEMAN: Look, if you happen to catch sight of him again, Miss, uh . . . .

489. MS (*process*), *as in 487.*

 EVE: Kendall.

 FIRST POLICEMAN (*offscreen*): Will you let us know?

 EVE: I'm going to bed soon, and I intend to lock my door, so I doubt if I'll be seeing him or anybody else tonight.

490. MCU, *as in 488.*

 FIRST POLICEMAN: Well, just in case you do, we'll be in the observation car at the rear of the train.

491. MS (*process*), *as in 489.*

 EVE: It's comforting to know that.

492. MCU, *as in 490: the two policemen exit, looking sour and suspicious.*

 EVE (*offscreen*): Good night.

 The door closes.

493. MCU: *Eve, seen in profile. She looks up at the closed berth.*

EVE (*a loud whisper*): Still breathing?

ROGER (*offscreen, muffled*): Either hurry up, or get me a snorkel.

The camera pulls back slightly as Eve reaches for her purse.

EVE: I'm looking for the can opener I stole from the porter.

She takes out a key to the berth. The camera tilts upward as she stands on the couch and puts the key in the lock. She turns the key and the berth thuds open, revealing Roger, who is lying fully clothed on the unmade bunk.

EVE: Hello there.

ROGER (*grumpily*): Hello.

He reaches into his pocket and takes out his sunglasses.

494. MCU: *Roger inspects the sunglasses, which have broken in two. He looks down at Eve.*

ROGER: Hmmm.

495. MCU: *a reverse angle, showing Eve as she looks up at Roger and smiles slightly.*

496. MCU, *as in 494.*

ROGER: Tell me, why are you so *good* to me?

497. MCU, *as in 495.*

EVE: Shall I climb up and tell you why?

498. MCU, *as in 496: Roger reacts, smiling.*

Dissolve.

Countryside, exterior, later that evening

499. LS: *from outside one of the rear cars, we see the train rounding a bend in a river. The sun has fallen below a mountain in the distance.*

Dissolve.

500. LS: *from the same angle as in 499, we see the train moving across empty countryside. The sun has almost disappeared.*

Eve's Compartment, interior, evening

501. MS: *Roger and Eve stand and embrace, looking into one another's eyes. She is leaning slightly against a wall near the washroom door.*

Nondiegetic music begins, playing the love theme we heard earlier in the dining car.

EVE: You know, I've been thinking. It's not safe for you to roam around Chicago looking for this George Kaplan that you've been telling me about. You'll be picked up by the police the moment you show your face.

ROGER: Such a nice face, too. (*He bends forward to lightly kiss the tip of her nose.*)

502. CU: *a high angle, looking down at Eve from over Roger's shoulder. They brush their lips lightly together, and she runs her finger along the edge of his ear.*

EVE: Now don't you think it would be a better idea if you stayed in my
hotel room while I located him for you and brought him to you? (*She
moves her hand to the nape of his neck.*)

ROGER: Can't let you get involved. It's too dangerous.

EVE (*smiling*): I'm a big girl.

503. CU: *an "impossible" (owing to the wall) reverse shot from a low angle,
looking over Eve's shoulder at Roger.*

ROGER: Yeah, and in all the right places, too.

504. CU, *as in 502: they kiss.*

EVE: This is ridiculous. You know that, don't you?

ROGER: Yes.

EVE: I mean, we've hardly met.

ROGER: That's right.

EVE: How do I know you aren't a murderer?

ROGER: You don't.

EVE (*as Roger slowly raises his hands along the wall behind her head, as
if he were about to grasp her neck*): Maybe you're planning to murder
me right here, tonight.

505. CU, *as in 503: Roger gently strokes her hair with both hands.*

ROGER: Shall I?

506. CU, *as in 504.*

EVE: Please do.

Roger bends to her face.

507. C U , *as in 505: they kiss, with Roger holding the back of her head in his hands.*

508. C U , *as in 506: the kiss continues. She strokes the back of his neck.*

509. C U , *as in 507: the kiss slowly ends, with Roger starting to move back from her face.*

510. C U , *as in 508: Roger straightens, looking into Eve's half-closed eyes. Her eyes open.*

511. C U , *as in 509.*

      R O G E R : Beats flying, doesn't it?

512. C U , *as in 510.*

      E V E : We should stop.

      R O G E R : Immediately.

      E V E : I ought to know more about you.

513. C U , *as in 511.*

      R O G E R (*smiling*): Well, what more could you know?

514. C U , *as in 512: they kiss briefly.*

      E V E : You're an advertising man, that's all I know.

515. M S : *Roger and Eve in a close embrace. She is leaning more directly against the wall than in the previous establishing shot.*

      R O G E R (*lightly kissing her*): That's right.

      As they kiss again, their bodies turn slowly, until they reverse positions: he is leaning against the wall and she is bending slightly down toward his face.

      R O G E R : Oh. Train's a little unsteady.

      E V E : Who isn't?

      They kiss.

      R O G E R : What else do you know?

      E V E : You've got taste in clothes, taste in food . . .

      He kisses her neck. Her head falls back and she closes her eyes.

      R O G E R : . . . and taste in women. I like your flavor.

      Their bodies rotate again as they kiss, until she is leaning against the wall and he is looking down at her. They have moved nearer to the camera, and are now framed in C U .

      E V E (*as Roger kisses her lightly on the neck*): You're very clever with words. You can probably make them do anything for you. Sell people things they don't need, make women who don't know you fall in love with you. . . .

      R O G E R : I'm beginning to think I'm underpaid.

      They kiss. A door buzzer sounds, but they do not hear it.

516. C U : *the back of Roger's head as he kisses Eve. Her hand strokes the back of his neck. The door buzzer sounds again. Suddenly Roger becomes alert.*

      R O G E R : Look out.

*He breaks from the embrace and the camera pans as he steps into the
nearby washroom, closing the door. The camera continues to pan as Eve
crosses to the door of the compartment, switches on a light, and opens the
door to admit a porter who is carrying bed linens.*

EVE: Oh, porter. (*Bends to put on her shoes.*) Don't bother with the
washroom.

PORTER: Yes, ma'am.

The nondiegetic music ends.

EVE (*handing the porter the key to the overhead berth*): Oh, by the way,
I found this on the floor. Does it belong to you?

PORTER: Yes ma'am. I've been looking all over for it.

EVE (*exiting the compartment*): I'll wait outside.

PORTER: Thank you.

Washroom, interior, evening

517. MS: *Roger stands in the washroom. He checks himself in the mirror,
smoothing down his hair. He pauses and frowns. From the toilet articles
on the sink, he picks up a tiny shaving brush, designed for travel. After
contemplating the brush for a moment, he puts it back. Then he picks up
an equally tiny razor, taking it out of its case. Offscreen, we hear the
sound of the train whistle and the clacking of the train wheels.*

518. INSERT: *The minuscule razor, held in Roger's hand.*

EVE (*offscreen*): Thank you, porter.

PORTER (*offscreen*): Thank you, ma'am. Good night, now.

EVE (*offscreen*): Good night.

519. MS, *as in 517: Roger frowns at the razor and replaces it in its case.
Offscreen, we hear the sound of a door closing.*

EVE (*offscreen*): Come out, come out . . .

Nondiegetic music, the love theme, begins.

Eve's Compartment, interior, evening

520. MS: *Eve, standing outside the washroom door.*

EVE: . . . wherever you are.

*Roger opens the door and steps out. The camera pans slightly to the left
as Eve tosses her purse aside, sits on the newly made bed, and removes
her shoes.*

EVE: The porter.

ROGER: So I see. (*He switches off the light and crosses to sit beside Eve
on the bed.*) Now . . .

521. MS: *Roger and Eve, sitting and facing one another on the bed.*

ROGER: . . . where were we?

EVE (*taking his face in her hands and kissing him*): Here.

ROGER: Ah, yes. Nice of him to have opened the bed.

EVE (*kissing him lightly*): Yes.

ROGER: Only one bed.

E V E (*continuing to kiss him*): Yes.

R O G E R : Well, it's a good omen, don't you think?

E V E : Wonderful. (*She kisses him again.*)

R O G E R : You know what that means?

E V E : Mmm.

R O G E R : What? Tell me.

E V E : It means you're going to sleep on the floor.

She kisses him passionately, and the camera tracks slowly forward, framing their two heads in C U. *The kiss ends. Roger and Eve embrace, with her face nearest the camera. The camera tracks forward a bit more. A serious expression appears on Eve's face and her eyes glance secretly to the right, as if she were looking over her shoulder toward the corridor outside the compartment.*

The nondiegetic music ends on a somber chord.

Corridor, interior, evening

522. M S : *the porter walks down the corridor, carrying a note in his hand. He stops and presses a buzzer at a door, which opens.*

P O R T E R (*offering the note*): A message from the lady in thirty-nine-oh-one.

A hand emerges from the open door and takes the note. The porter bows and exits.

Another Compartment, interior, evening

523. C U : *the note, held in a man's hand. The man closes the door and opens the note, which reads, "What do I do with him in the morning? Eve." The camera tracks back to a* M S *and pans, following him as he crosses to sit down on the couch. He is Leonard, the sinister man Roger encountered in Glen Cove. Next to him on the couch is his employer, Vandamm. Leonard hands the note to him, and he reads it and smiles. The camera pans to the left, past the compartment window. The train whistle sounds. The camera pans through darkness.*

Countryside, exterior, evening

524. L S : *the darkness hides the cut to this shot. The camera continues to pan until it seems to reach the outside of the train. Once again the camera looks down the long row of cars as the train rounds a bend in a river. The last glow of sunset is visible over a mountain in the distance.*

Fade out.

Fade in.

Platform of La Salle Street Station, Chicago, exterior, morning

525. L S : *the engine of the Twentieth-Century Limited, stopped at the end of its run. Two uniformed policemen walk past.*

526. L S : *two policemen are watching as people exit the train. Eve steps out, followed by Roger, who is carrying her bags, disguised in the uniform of*

*a redcap. He and Eve walk forward down the platform and stop, framed
in a* MS, *looking at something in the distance.*

527. LS: *the camera tracks slowly forward. From Roger and Eve's* POV, *we
see the two plainclothes policemen who had questioned Eve on the train.
They are walking grimly toward the camera.*

528. MS, *as at end of 526: the camera tracks backward as Eve and Roger con-
tinue moving down the platform.*
   EVE (*to Roger, without looking at him*): You keep walking. I'll catch up.
   ROGER: Yes, ma'am.

529. MS (*process*): *Roger crosses in the foreground, moving off down the platform. The two policemen enter the frame from the right, seen over Eve's
shoulder. They stop.*
   FIRST POLICEMAN (*to Eve*): Anything to report, Miss Kendall?

530. MS (*process*): *a reverse angle, looking past the two policemen at Eve.*
   EVE: Why, yes. I had a fine night's sleep.

531. MS, *as in 529.*
   FIRST POLICEMAN: No, I mean . . . have you seen the man we're
   looking for?

532. MS, *as in 530.*
   EVE: Oh, Mr. Thornycroft?

533. MS, *as in 531.*
   FIRST POLICEMAN (*looking disgruntled*): Thornhill.

534. MS, *as in 532.*
   EVE: Oh, no. No, I'm awfully sorry. But good luck to you both.
   She smiles and exits. The two policemen turn to watch her go.

535. LS: *from the two policemen's* POV, *we see Eve walking off down the
platform toward Roger, who is carrying her bags.*

536. MS (*process*): *Roger and Eve, facing the camera, walk side by side down
the platform.*
   EVE: How are we doing?
   ROGER: Oh, I may collapse at any moment.
   EVE: Not yet. First we have to run the gauntlet. (*She glances off to the
   right.*) Look.

537. LS: *a reverse-angle tracking shot, from Roger and Eve's* POV. *The station platform is lined with uniformed policemen and plainclothes detectives, who are keenly watching the passengers.*

538. MS, *as in 536.*
   ROGER (*shifting one of the suitcases under his arm*): I'm accustomed to
   having a load on, but what *have* you got in these bags?
   EVE: Bowling balls, naturally.
   ROGER: Oh, naturally. Which one of these has my suit in it?
   EVE: The small one underneath your right arm.

ROGER (*looking down*): Oh, thanks. That ought to do the suit a lot of good.

EVE: I'm sure Mr. Kaplan won't mind a few wrinkles.

ROGER: If he's still there. What time is it?

EVE (*glancing at her watch*): Nine-ten.

ROGER: Nine-ten? He's probably left his hotel room by now.

EVE: I'll call him for you as soon as we get inside the station.

ROGER: I can do it.

EVE: A redcap in a phone booth? Slightly suspicious.

ROGER: Oh, yes. Well, all right. Uh, what are you going to tell him? You know what?

EVE: Mmm-hmm.

ROGER: What?

EVE: You want to see him right away. Terribly urgent. Matter of life and death. No explanations.

ROGER: Right.

EVE: While I'm calling you can change your clothes.

ROGER: Where do you propose I do that, in Marshall Field's window?

EVE: I sort of had the men's room in mind.

539. CU (*process*): *Roger looks at her.*

ROGER: Did you now? You're the smartest girl . . .

540. CU (*process*): *Eve's reaction.*

ROGER (*offscreen*): . . . I ever spent the night with on a train.
Nondiegetic music, the love theme, begins.
Eve looks down somewhat sadly, then glances over her shoulder.

541. LS: *Vandamm and Leonard, following from a distance at the far end of the platform, engaged in conversation. As they approach, the camera tracks to the right, across a pillar.*

542. CU, *as in 540: Eve looks ahead, then offscreen left toward Roger.*

543. CU, *as in 539.*

ROGER (*smiling*): I think we made it.

544. LS: *a tracking shot from Roger's POV, looking toward the entrance to the station. There are no policemen in sight.*

545. MS: *Roger and Eve cross the frame from right to left, moving down the last section of the platform.*
The love theme ends, and the nondiegetic music shifts into a chase tempo.

546. LS: *the two plainclothes detectives who questioned Eve are standing outside the train, together with a couple of uniformed policemen. Suddenly a commotion starts inside the doorway of one of the cars. A small, elderly man wearing long underwear steps into the doorway, and the police begin frantically questioning him.*

FIRST POLICEMAN: Which way did he go? . . . Which way did he go?

MAN IN UNDERWEAR: I don't know. He took my clothes and went up
that way. (*He points down the platform.*)

FIRST POLICEMAN: Come on!
He and the other police rush off.

547. MS: *the man in underwear remains behind. From inside his underwear,
he takes out a folded packet of money and begins counting it.*

Main Lobby of the Station, interior, morning

548. LS: *a high-angle, bird's-eye view of the lobby, which is filled with passengers. A group of plainclothes police run into the lobby and begin examining each of the redcaps, turning them around to look into their faces.*

549. LS: *a closer view of the same action.*

550. LS: *a still closer view. Two policemen grasp two redcaps by the shoulders and turn them around, looking into their surprised faces.*

551. LS: *a closer view, almost at ground level. A policeman seizes a middle-
aged, overweight redcap and looks him in the face.*

552. MS: *a ground-level view. Another policeman grabs a redcap and turns
him around.*

553. MS: *another policeman, turning another redcap around.*

554. CU: *the face of an elderly redcap, after being spun around and looked at
by a policeman.*
The nondiegetic music ends.

Men's Room, interior, morning

555. LS: *Roger is standing at one of the sinks, heavily lathering his face for a
shave. He has changed out of the redcap's uniform and is wearing trousers and shirtsleeves. Next to him, a fat man in an undershirt is shaving
with a straight razor. Reflected in the mirror, the two plainclothes detectives from the train enter the room and look around. They move out of the
frame and we hear the sound of doors crashing as they open all of the toilet stalls. Roger continues to lather his face, frowning and glancing over
his shoulder.*

556. MS: *in the mirror over Roger's shoulder, we see the detectives exit the
room. Roger begins to shave. He is using Eve's travel razor, which cuts a
ridiculously narrow path through the shaving cream. He does a double
take, and turns to look at the man standing next to him. The man looks
down at the razor and his face takes on a baffled expression. He and
Roger resume shaving. Roger cuts a narrow path down the middle of his
upper lip and stands back to survey the results. He looks a bit like Hitler
or Chaplin.*

Waiting Room of the Train Station, interior, morning

557. LS: *the camera looks down a row of telephone booths inside the station.
Through the window of the first booth, we can see Eve speaking on the
telephone.*
Nondiegetic music begins.

558. MS: *Eve, seen through the door of the telephone booth. She nods her head and speaks, but we cannot hear her words. The camera begins tracking slowly to the right, along the row of booths, coming to a stop four doors down. Through the fourth door we see Leonard, who is intently explaining something over the telephone.*

559. LS: *Eve, seen through the door of the first booth. She nods, as if listening to instructions.*

560. MS, *as in 558: Leonard finishes his speech and hangs up the telephone.*

561. MS, *as in 560: Eve hangs up and exits the booth. The camera pans slightly to follow her movement. In the distance, at the other end of the row of booths, Leonard also exits. He and Eve stand for a moment, not looking at one another. He walks off into the background, where Vandamm is reading a newspaper near a magazine stand. Leonard and Vandamm confer, and then exit to the left.*

562. MCU: *Eve stands outside the booth, looking off in their direction.*
PUBLIC ADDRESS ANNOUNCER (*offscreen, continuing through the next three shots*): . . . departing at ten A.M., Chicago daylight time, for Michigan City, Niles . . . , Laughton, Kalamazoo, Battle Creek, Marshall . . . , Jackson, Ann Arbor, Ypsilanti, and Detroit, now ready on Track Six.
Eve glances around the lobby, and then notices something offscreen, to the rear of the camera.

563. LS: *Eve's* POV. *Roger emerges from the men's room, dressed in his gray suit and carrying a bag.*

564. MCU, *as in 562: Eve lowers her eyes. Her mouth sets somewhat grimly. She looks up, and then exits to the right.*

565. LS: *Eve walks to the right. The camera pans, following her across the waiting room.*

566. MS: *Roger stands behind a pillar, waiting. Eve enters the frame from the left. Roger smiles.*
EVE: What took you so long?
ROGER: Big face, small razor. (*He reaches out to touch her on the arm.*) Tell me, did you get Kaplan?
EVE: Yes.
ROGER: Fine. What did he say?
EVE: He'll see you, but not at the hotel under any circumstances. He'll see you on the outside.
ROGER: Well, where? When?
EVE: I've got it all written out for you. (*She hands him a note.*)
ROGER: Thanks.
EVE: You're to take the Greyhound bus that leaves Chicago for Indianapolis at two, and ask the driver to let you off at Prairie Stop, Highway Forty-One.

R O G E R (*putting the note in his pocket*): Prairie Stop, Highway Forty-One. Good.

E V E : It's about an hour and a half's drive from Chicago.

R O G E R : Fine. I'll rent a car. (*He reaches out to touch her.*)

E V E (*uneasily, avoiding his eyes*): No car. Mr. Kaplan said bus. He wants to be sure you're alone.

R O G E R : All right. What will I do when I get there?

E V E : Just wait beside the road. He'll be there at three-thirty.

R O G E R : How will I know him?

E V E : He'll know you. You made the Chicago papers, too.

R O G E R : Ah, yes.

E V E : Have you got your watch set for Central time?

567. C U (*process*): *Roger, seen from over Eve's shoulder.*

R O G E R : Yes, I did that. Thanks. (*He looks at her.*) What's the matter?

568. C U (*process*): *Eve, from over Roger's shoulder.*

E V E : Matter?

569. C U (*process*), *as in 567.*

R O G E R : Yes. Yes, you seem . . . I don't know, you seem tense.

570. C U (*process*), *as in 568.*

E V E : You know, you better go before the police run out of redcaps.

571. C U (*process*), *as in 569.*

R O G E R : We'll see each other again, won't we?

572. C U (*process*), *as in 570.*

E V E : Sometime, I'm sure.

573. C U (*process*), *as in 571.*

R O G E R (*tenderly*): I never had a moment to thank you properly.

E V E : Please go.

R O G E R : Yes, but . . . but where will I find you?

574. C U (*process*), *as in 572.*

E V E (*turning away slightly*): I've got to pick up my bags now.

575. C U (*process*), *as in 573.*

R O G E R (*handing her the suitcase and some ticket stubs*): Oh, yes, well, these are the checks for the large cases.

576. C U : *her hand takes the suitcase. His hand touches hers.*

R O G E R (*offscreen*): Wait a minute.

577. C U (*process*), *as in 574: she is turning to go.*

R O G E R : Please.

She looks off over his shoulder, as if she sees something.

578. L S : *Eve's* P O V , *looking across the waiting room. There are no police in sight.*

579. C U (*process*), *as in 575.*

E V E : They're coming.

Roger sets his mouth in a grim line, and exits to the left.

580. C U (*process*): *Eve watches Roger go.*
Slow dissolve.
The nondiegetic music ends.
Prairie Stop, exterior, midday
581. L S : *a stationary, extremely high-angle view of flat, brown farmland,
without a tree in sight. Highway 41 cuts diagonally across the screen, running in a straight line from the horizon to the lower right of the frame.
Near the center of the composition is a sign marking a dirt road that exits
onto the highway. To the left is a plowed field, and to the right a smaller
dirt road. A Greyhound bus appears on the horizon, moving down the
highway and coming to a stop. Roger exits the bus, which drives off. He
stands there—a tiny speck on the landscape, barely distinguishable from
the fenceposts lining the left side of the highway.*
582. L S : *a ground-level view of Roger, standing beside the road to the left of
the frame. To the right is nothing but the empty sky and the flat, brown horizon. Roger looks to his right, in the direction of the departing bus.*
583. L S : *Roger's* P O V *, looking down the highway at the bus, which is disappearing over the horizon.*
584. M S : *a frontal view of Roger, standing beside the road, next to the sign
marking the bus stop. He clasps his hands in front of his body, looking off
to the left. Behind him is a flat horizon and a bare, rocky field. He turns
and looks to the right.*

585. LS: *Roger's* POV, *looking down the road in the opposite direction, at barren fields, a line of fenceposts, and the dusty shoulder of the highway.*

586. MS, *as in 584: Roger frowns and looks across the road.*

587. LS: *Roger's* POV, *looking across the road at a flat horizon and another empty field.*

588. MS, *as in 586: Roger turns and looks behind him, glancing a bit off to the left.*

589. LS: *the empty dirt road that joins the highway, running off to the horizon.*

590. MS, *as in 588: Roger turns around, his hands at his side, squinting in the sun. He looks to the left, and puts his hands in his pockets. He then glances across the road to the left.*

591. LS: *Roger's* POV, *looking across the highway. A dirt lane runs off into empty farmland, marked by a small signpost. On the horizon is a dry cornfield.*

592. MS, *as in 590: Roger looks off to the right.*

593. LS: *Roger's* POV, *looking down the highway. A car appears on the horizon.*

594. MS, *as in 592: Roger stiffens a bit, looking expectant.*

595. LS, *as in 593: the car—a white convertible with the top up—approaches and speeds past, the camera panning to follow it.*

596. MS, *as in 594: Roger's head turns, following the car as it disappears in the opposite direction.*

597. LS: *Roger's* POV, *watching the car vanish on the dusty horizon.*

598. MS, *as in 596: Roger glances down at the ground, then across the road to the right.*

599. LS, *as in 597: the flat, empty field across the road.*

600. MS, *as in 598: Roger looks to the left.*

601. LS, *as in 597: a dark car appears on the horizon.*

602. MS, *as in 600: Roger looks more intently down the road.*

603. LS, *as in 601: the car approaches slowly.*

604. MS, *as in 602: Roger straightens and starts to remove his hands from his pockets.*

605. LS, *as in 603: the car—a four-door Cadillac—drives slowly past, the camera panning to follow it.*

606. MS, *as in 604: Roger's head turns, watching the car drive off to the right. He lowers his hands into his pockets and looks down the road.*

607. LS: *Roger's* POV, *looking toward the Cadillac as it disappears over the horizon.*

608. MS, *as in 606: Roger frowns and looks off to the right.*

609. LS, *as in 607: as the Cadillac disappears, another vehicle approaches.*

610. MS, *as in 608: Roger continues to frown.*

611. LS, *as in 609: the vehicle gets closer.*

612. MS, *as in 610: Roger stiffens and looks up slightly.*
613. LS: *a low-level view from across the road, looking toward Roger, who is silhouetted against the horizon. A mammoth, ten-wheel freight truck speeds past, entering the frame from the right and kicking up a dust cloud.*
614. MS, *as in 612: Roger turns away from the passing truck and rubs dust from his eye with his left hand. He returns the hand to his pocket, shrugs, and glances across the road. He straightens, noticing something.*
615. LS: *Roger's POV, looking at the dirt trail across the road. From behind the cornfield to the right, a car appears, traveling along one of the tributaries of the dirt road.*
616. MS: *Roger stands with his hands in his pockets, looking across the road.*
617. LS, *as in 615: the car turns and heads toward the highway.*
618. MS, *as in 616: Roger watches the car.*
619. LS, *as in 617: the car—an aging green two-door—approaches the highway.*
620. MS, *as in 618: Roger continues to look across the road.*
621. LS, *as in 619: the camera pans, following the car up to the highway. The car stops and the passenger door opens.*
622. MS, *as in 620: Roger straightens and starts to remove his hands from his pockets.*
623. LS, *as in 621: a man in a brown suit and hat gets out of the car, closes the door, and waves good-bye to the driver. The car backs up.*
624. MS, *as in 622: Roger takes his hands out of his pockets.*
625. LS, *as in 623: the car turns around and drives off. The man in the brown suit walks to the roadside.*
626. MCU: *Roger stands with his hands at his side, frowning and looking intently across the road.*
627. LS, *as in 625: the camera pans slightly to follow the man to the roadside. He stands with his hands in his hip pockets, looking off to the right. Then he turns and looks across the road at Roger.*
628. MCU, *as in 626: Roger leans forward a bit.*
629. LS: *a low-level view of Roger and the man, standing across from one another on either side of the highway. In the background, a cloudless sky and a flat horizon.*
630. MCU, *as in 628: Roger unbuttons his coat and spreads it open, putting his hands on his hips. He bites his lower lip and stares at the man.*
631. LS, *as in 627: the man looks back at Roger.*
632. MS: *Roger lowers his hands to his side, glances up the empty highway, and starts to cross toward the man. The camera pans to follow him.*
633. LS: *a subjective tracking shot, showing Roger's POV as he walks across the highway. The man stands with his hands in his hip pockets, looking directly toward the camera.*
634. MS: *the camera tracks alongside Roger as he walks across the highway.*

635. LS, *as in 633: the subjective camera tracks forward, drawing nearer to the man.*

636. MS, *as in 634: reaching the other side of the highway, Roger walks up to the man, clasps his hands in front of his body, and nods "hello."*

   ROGER: Hi. (*Rubbing his hands together, he looks around.*) Hot day.

   MAN: Seen worse.

   ROGER (*after an awkward silence*): Are you supposed to be meeting someone here?

   MAN: Waitin' for the bus. (*He looks to the right, down the highway.*) Due any minute.

   ROGER: Oh.

   MAN (*looking beyond Roger's shoulder, toward the other side of the road*): Some of them crop-duster pilots get rich, . . .

637. LS: *the man's* POV, *looking at the empty field on the other side of the highway. In the distance, just above the horizon, a small plane is dusting the field, its engine barely audible.*

   MAN (*offscreen*): . . . if they live long enough.

638. MS, *as in 636: Roger rubs his hands together. He glances toward the plane and then toward the man, who is still looking off in the distance.*

   ROGER: Yeah. (*Pause.*) Then, . . . then your name isn't Kaplan?

   MAN (*still looking toward the plane*): Can't say it is, 'cause it ain't. (*Hearing the sound of another motor, he straightens and looks down the highway to the right.*) Here she comes, right on time.

639. LS: *the man's* POV, *looking down the highway at an approaching bus.*

640. MS, *as in 638: the man looks back toward the plane.*

   MAN: That's funny.

   ROGER: What?

   MAN: That plane's dustin' crops where there ain't no crops.

641. LS, *as in 637: the plane, seen in the distance.*

642. MS: *Roger and the man stand together at the right of the frame. Roger glances toward the plane and the man looks expectantly at the approaching bus.*

643. LS, *as in 639: the bus arrives and stops.*

644. MS, *as in 642: the door of the bus swings open and the man gets on. The door shuts. The bus drives off, leaving Roger alone beside the highway. Roger stands with his hands on his hips, and then he consults his watch. Placing his hands on his hips again, he looks across the road.*

645. LS, *as in 641: the plane banks and begins to fly toward the highway, its engine growing louder.*

646. MS: *a frontal view of Roger, standing beside the highway, his back to the dirt road. His hands are folded in front of his body and he is squinting slightly, looking toward the plane.*

647. L S , *as in 645: the camera tilts and pans, following the plane. It has leveled off and is flying straight toward the highway. As it approaches, we can see its outline more clearly: it is a biplane, of the sort used to spray crops.*
648. M S , *as in 646: Roger squints and watches the plane.*
649. L S , *as in 647: the plane draws nearer, diving toward the camera.*
650. C U : *Roger looks at the plane more intently, straightening slightly and lowering his arms to his side.*
651. L S , *as in 649: the plane is quite near. It dives menacingly toward the camera, the noise of its engine growing to a roar.*
652. C U , *as in 650: startled, Roger turns and ducks.*
653. M S (*process*): *A ground-level reverse angle, showing Roger as he drops to the ground, lying flat on his stomach. The plane buzzes a few feet over his head, kicking up dust and dirt. Roger lifts his head and watches the plane fly past.*
654. L S : *Roger's* P O V , *looking toward the plane as it speeds off, skimming the ground. The plane climbs and goes into a turn.*
655. L S : *Roger lifts himself from the dirt, resting on one knee and looking toward the plane.*
656. L S : *Roger's* P O V , *looking at the plane. It is circling for another pass.*
657. L S , *as in 655: Roger gets to his feet and watches the plane.*
658. L S , *as in 656: the plane completes its turn and begins another attack.*
659. M S : *a low-angle view of Roger. He is crouched, looking toward the plane. He turns his body slightly to the right, poised as if to run.*
660. L S , *as in 658: the plane dives toward the camera.*
661. M S , *as in 659: Roger spins to the left and the camera pans, following him as he dives toward a ditch beside the highway.*
662. M S (*process*): *a ground-level reverse angle, showing Roger as he dives into a shallow, rocky ditch. The plane roars a few feet overhead, but this time it strafes the ground with machine-gun fire. It swoops past, stirring up violent gusts of wind and dust. Roger lifts his head and watches it fly off.*
663. L S : *Roger's* P O V , *looking toward the plane as it banks and begins another turn. The camera pans to follow it.*
664. M S , *as in 662: still lying in the ditch, Roger lifts his head and looks behind him down the highway.*
665. L S : *Roger's* P O V , *looking at ground level down the highway. A car is approaching.*
666. M S (*process*), *as in 664: Roger reacts, jumping to his feet.*
667. L S : *Roger leaps from the ditch and runs onto the highway, where he stands and waves his arms at the approaching car.*
668. M S : *the car speeds past and Roger turns to watch it go. He sighs and looks across the highway toward the plane.*

669. LS: *Roger's* POV, *looking toward the plane as it circles and begins another dive.*

670. MS: *a low-angle view, looking over Roger's shoulder toward the approaching plane. He turns and looks desperately behind him. Then he looks back at the plane, which is drawing near. Suddenly he turns and begins to run down the dirt road leading off the highway. The camera tracks backward as he sprints down the road, the plane gaining on him. He dives for the ground and the plane roars past over his head.*

671. MS (process): *a ground-level view of Roger as he dives head first onto the dirt road. The roar of the plane is heard offscreen, and machine-gun fire kicks up dust. Roger looks up toward the plane as it passes, and then he glances offscreen to his right.*

672. LS: *a ground-level shot, showing Roger's* POV. *In the distance, across a stretch of dirt, is the field of dry corn he had noticed earlier.*

673. MS (process), *as in 671: Roger looks at the plane and then at the field of corn. He jumps up.*

674. LS: *a low-angle view of Roger getting to his feet. In the distance, the plane is circling for another pass. Roger runs off to the right.*

675. MS: *the camera tracks beside Roger as he sprints toward the cornfield.*

676. LS: *viewed from behind, Roger dashes across a bare patch of ground and plunges into the cornfield.*

677. M S : *looking over the top of the cornfield, we can see a few of the dry stalks rustling as Roger moves among them.*

678. M C U *(studio interior): a low-level view inside the cornfield. Roger drops to the ground and hides. Offcreen, the sound of the plane grows louder. Roger crouches on all fours.*

679. L S : *the camera is positioned just beyond the outside row of cornstalks, tilted up at the sky. The plane approaches from the distance and dives toward the field, swooping over it and almost touching the stalks.*

680. M C U *(studio interior), as in 678: Roger ducks and the dry stalks rustle as the plane rushes overhead. Roger looks up and smiles. Offscreen, we hear the sound of the plane circling for another dive. Roger's smile fades.*

681. L S , *as in 679: the plane banks, turns, and goes into a dive.*

682. M C U *(studio iterior), as in 680: crouching on his knees, Roger listens intently as the plane engine grows louder.*

683. L S , *as in 681: the plane dives. As it passes over the cornfield, it sprays a cloud of insecticide.*

684. M C U *(studio interior), as in 682: Roger looks up and raises his arm. White smoke engulfs him, filling the entire screen. We hear the sound of the plane and Roger's violent coughing. Gradually the smoke clears enough to make Roger visible. Shielding his eyes and nose with a pocket handkerchief, he lunges deeper into the cornfield, away from the smoke.*

685. L S *(studio interior): Roger dashes out of the smoky part of the cornfield and runs forward through the stalks, into a low-angle C U . Standing just inside the last row of corn, he parts two of the stalks and looks out toward the road.*

686. L S : *Roger's P O V , looking through the parted cornstalks at the highway. In the distance, a truck is approaching.*

687. C U , *as at end of 685: Roger glances over his shoulder in the direction of the plane, and then back at the road. Grimly setting his jaw, he runs forward, exiting the frame to the left rear of the camera.*

688. L S : *a reverse angle, showing Roger as he leaves the corn field. Running away from the camera, he sprints toward the highway and the approaching truck.*

689. L S : *in the distance, the plane circles.*

690. L S : *a low-angle view from behind Roger, as he dashes into the middle of the highway. He stops directly in the path of the oncoming truck, raising his arms and waving.*

691. L S : *the plane banks over the cornfield and prepares to dive toward the highway.*

692. M C U *(process): facing the camera, Roger waves his arms frantically. He glances over his shoulder in the directon of the plane, and then looks back toward the oncoming truck, an oil tanker. Offscreen, we hear the truck's motor and horn.*

693. L S : *Roger's* P O V , *looking directly into the nose of the oncoming truck. The truck sounds its horn.*

694. M C U *(process), as in 692: Roger holds up his hands in a "stop" signal. He looks over his shoulder in the direction of the plane, and then he looks back toward the truck. Offscreen, the horn sounds.*

695. L S , *as in 693: the truck is much closer, moving full speed toward the camera. The horn sounds again. As the truck approaches* M C U , *we hear the sounds of grinding brakes and skidding tires.*

696. M C U *(process), as in 694: Roger's mouth opens and his eyes grow wide in fear. He holds his ground and continues to signal "stop." Offscreen, the horn blares and the tires skid.*

697. M C U , *as at end of 695: traveling at high speed, the truck plunges forward into* C U , *its horn growing louder and its front grille filling the screen.*

698. C U : *Roger's face, flinching with anxiety as the truck nears. The camera zooms forward to* E C U . *Offscreen, the horn blares. Roger's hands move to shield his face, and he falls backward.*

699. M S : *a low-level view from behind Roger, as the truck skids forward and knocks him down. He falls to the pavement and the truck advances, its bumper extending partly over his body.*

700. M C U : *Roger's head strikes the pavement and the truck skids to a stop. Roger is lying beneath the front axle. He raises his head slightly and looks anxiously offscreen.*

701. L S : *Roger's* P O V , *looking past the front tire of the truck and toward the cornfield. The plane is diving straight at the truck and wobbling unsteadily, as if it were pilotless.*

702. L S : *from a reverse angle, we see the plane collide with the second of two large tanks trailers being towed behind the truck.*

703. L S : *a slightly closer view shows the tank exploding and the plane bursting into flame.*
    Nondiegetic music, the "fandango" theme, begins.

704. L S : *a still closer view at ground level, looking from the nose of the truck toward the burning plane. The driver's door opens and two men jump out. Roger scrambles from beneath the front wheels.*
    F I R S T   D R I V E R *(to Roger):* Get out of here! The other tank may blow! *The two drivers dash off to the right, but Roger lingers behind, backing slowly away from the truck and staring at the blaze.*

705. L S : *seen from behind, the two drivers run toward the cornfield.*

706. M S : *the camera tracks backward, watching Roger as he walks briskly but unsteadlily away from the burning truck. Over his shoulder, the second oil tank explodes. Roger ducks and breaks into a slow run.*

707. M S : *a reverse angle. Roger trots away from the camera into* L S , *looking back over his shoulder in the direction of the truck. Beyond him, two passing vehicles have pulled over to the side of the highway. The first of*

these is an old pickup truck with a used refrigerator standing in its bed. A farmer in a straw hat jumps out of the truck, and three passengers—a woman and two men in rural clothing—get out of the car behind it. Roger stumbles toward them.

FARMER (*to Roger*): What happened?

Roger rubs his forehead wearily and points in the direction of the burning plane. His words are inaudible.

708. LS: *a low-level view. The farmer's arm is in the foreground at the right of the frame, and we look past it toward the burning truck and plane.*

709. LS: *a low-angle shot of Roger and the four passersby, who are looking offscreen left, toward the burning wreck. Roger backs slowly away from the others, and unobtrusively exits to the right as they move forward to the left.*

710. LS: *the farmer and the three passengers from the car are seen from behind as they try to approach the flaming truck. They stop, watching the fire and unable to move closer. Hearing something, the farmer turns and looks over his shoulder.*

711. LS: *a reverse angle. The pickup truck pulls away from the roadside, makes a U-turn, and starts off down the highway.*

712. LS, *as in 710: the farmer waves and starts running toward the camera, chasing after the truck.*

FARMER: Hey!

713. LS, *as in 711: seen from behind, the farmer goes running and yelling after the truck, which speeds off toward the horizon.*

FARMER: Come back! Hey! Come back! Come back! Hey!

The farmer stops—a tiny figure in the middle of the highway, watching the truck disappear.

The nondiegetic music ends.

Dissolve.

Michigan Avenue, Chicago, exterior, sunset

714. LS: *The farmer's truck is parked at the curb, the refrigerator still sitting in its bed. Two uniformed policemen are inspecting it, apparently baffled.*

Ambassador East Hotel, exterior, early evening

715. LS: *from across the street, we observe the entrance of the hotel. The camera pans left, revealing Roger, who is concealing himself behind the corner of a nearby building. He wipes his face with his handkerchief and dusts off his suit with his hand. The camera pans right, following him as he steps out of the shadows. He crosses the street and walks toward the entrance of the hotel.*

Lobby of the Ambassador East Hotel, interior, early evening

716. LS: *Roger enters through the front door. He dusts himself off and turns to the left, crossing to the reception desk.*

717. MS: *Roger steps up to the desk, where a tuxedoed clerk is sorting mail. After a moment the clerk turns around. He glances with evident surprise at Roger's soiled clothing.*

DESK CLERK: Yes?

ROGER: Could you let me have Mr. George Kaplan's room number please?

DESK CLERK: Kaplan.

ROGER (*straightening his tie*): Yeah.

DESK CLERK (*consulting a stack of papers*): I think he checked out.

ROGER: He checked out?

DESK CLERK: That's right. Checked out at seven-ten this morning.

ROGER: Seven-ten? Are you sure?

DESK CLERK (*showing Roger a paper in his hand*): Yes. Left a forwarding address. Hotel Sheraton-Johnson, Rapid City, South Dakota.

ROGER (*removing a slip of paper from his pocket and glancing at it*): Seven-ten? Well then, how come I got a message from him at nine. . . . (*He pauses, realizing something.*)

DESK CLERK: What's that?

ROGER (*frowning angrily at his private thoughts*): Nothing. Nothing. *Roger continues to stew, while the clerk goes back to sorting mail. Then Roger notices something offscreen right.*

718. LS: *Roger's* POV. *In the distance, Eve crosses the lobby, wearing a red and black evening dress. She pauses at the concierge's desk, her back to the camera.*

719. CU: *Roger looks grimly toward Eve.*

720. LS, *as in 718: Eve picks up a newspaper at the desk and turns around, reading something on the front page. She moves toward the hotel's two elevators.*

721. CU, *as in 719: Roger continues to watch her.*

722. LS, *as in 720: Eve gets into the first elevator.*

723. CU, *as in 721: Roger glances slightly upward.*

724. CU: *the numbers above the elevator door light up, indicating that Eve has traveled to the fourth floor.*

725. MS, *as in 717: Roger turns to the desk clerk, who is still sorting mail.*

ROGER: Sorry to bother you again. . . .

DESK CLERK (*turning to face Roger*): Uh-huh?

ROGER: Er, Miss Eve Kendall is expecting me. She's in room four something or another. I've forgotten the number. Would you mind? *The clerk checks his listings, and then the mailbox where Eve's room key is stored.*

DESK CLERK: She's in four sixty-three.

ROGER: Oh yes, that's right. Thanks.

Roger walks off toward the elevators.

726. LS: *a reverse angle, showing Roger from behind as he walks over to the second elevator and gets in.*
Dissolve.

Hotel Corridor, interior, early evening

727. MS: *Roger turns a corner and walks toward the camera, searching for Eve's room. Offscreen, there is the faint sound of automobile horns passing on the street. The camera pans slightly to the right as he steps up to her door and stands outside, listening for voices. Hearing nothing, he rings the doorbell.*

728. MCU: *from over Roger's shoulder, we see Eve open the door. She gazes at Roger without speaking.*
ROGER: Hello.
Nondiegetic music, the love theme, begins.

Eve's Hotel Room, interior, early evening

729. MCU: *a reverse angle. Roger steps into the room, a grim, angry expression on his face. He moves forward out of the frame and Eve closes the door, turning to look at him. She registers surprise and relief.*

730. MS: *Roger turns and looks at Eve, and as he does so, his angry expression gives way to a slightly forced smile.*
ROGER: Surprised?

731. MCU, *as at end of 729.*
EVE: Yes.

732. MS, *as in 730.*
ROGER: No getting rid of me, is there?

733. MS: *Eve rushes across the room into Roger's arms. The camera pans to follow her, framing the couple in MCU. She embraces Roger tearfully and passionately, burying her head in his chest. He frowns, holding his hands in midair behind her head. The camera dollies right in a half circle, stopping to look directly into Roger's face.*
ROGER: I could use a drink.
Eve steps back from the embrace and crosses upstage to the left. The camera pans to follow her.
EVE: We have some scotch.
ROGER (*offscreen*): With water, no ice.
Her back to the camera, Eve mixes the drink. The camera pans right, returning to Roger. He looks at Eve, and then glances down to the right.

734. INSERT: *from Roger's POV, we see the front page of the* Chicago Daily Sun-Times, *lying on a table. The leading headline reads, "Two Die As Crop-Duster Plane Crashes And Burns: Low Flying Craft Hits Oil Tanker; Truck Drivers Escape Holocaust." At the lower left of the page is a smaller item, headlined "Diary Tells How Russians 'Hired' German Rocketmen."*

735. M S : *on the opposite side of the room, Eve mixes Roger's drink. We look past her at Roger, who is standing in the distance.*

E V E : How did it go today?

Roger pauses and turns toward her, putting his hands in his pockets.

R O G E R : The meeting with Kaplan?

E V E : Uh-huh.

R O G E R : He didn't show up.

The nondiegetic music ends.

E V E : Oh?

R O G E R : It's funny, isn't it?

E V E : Why funny?

736. M C U : *Roger, looking at Eve.*

R O G E R : Oh, after all those involved and explicit directions . . .

737. M S , *as in 735.*

R O G E R : . . . he gave you on the phone.

E V E : Maybe I copied them down wrong.

738. M C U , *as in 736.*

R O G E R : I don't think you got them wrong. I think you sent me to the right place, all right.

739. M S , *as in 737.*

E V E (*stirring the drinks*): Well, why don't you call him back again, and see what happened?.

R O G E R : I did. He checked out. Went to South Dakota.

E V E : South Dakota?

R O G E R : Mmm-hmmm. Rapid City.

E V E : Well, what are you going to do next?

740. M C U , *as in 738.*

R O G E R : Oh, I haven't made my mind up yet.

741. M S : *Eve is viewed in three-quarter profile as she completes the drinks.*

R O G E R (*offscreen*): It may depend on you.

Eve turns and crosses to Roger, holding the two drinks in her hands. The camera pans to follow her.

E V E : On me?

R O G E R : Sure. You're my little helper, aren't you? (*He takes his drink from Eve.*) Thank you. (*Toasting her.*) To us. To a long and lasting friendship. Meaning, from now on, I'm not going to let you out of my sight, sweetheart. (*He takes a sip of his drink.*)

E V E : I'm afraid you'll have to.

R O G E R : Oh, no.

E V E : I do have plans of my own, you know. And you do have problems.

R O G E R : Well, wouldn't it be nice if my problems and your plans were somehow connected? Then we could always stay close to each other and not have to go off in separate directions. Togetherness. You know what I mean?

They each take a sip of their drinks. The telephone rings. Eve doesn't move. The telephone keeps ringing.

ROGER: Go ahead, it can't be for me.

Eve turns and moves upstage, where she sits on the edge of the bed and picks up the telephone. In the foreground, Roger sips his drink.

EVE: Hello. (*Listening to an indistinct voice.*) Yes.

Roger slowly crosses to the right, not looking at Eve. The camera tracks with him, keeping her in view in the background.

EVE: No, not yet. I'm not ready. (*Listening.*) What time? (*Listening.*) I'll meet you. (*Listening.*) What's the address? (*Listening.*)

As Eve picks up a pencil to write down the address, Roger stops and glances over his shoulder in her direction.

742. MS: *Eve, seated on the bed.*

EVE: Yes. Good-bye.

She hangs up the telephone, tears the sheet with the address from a pad, and rises. The camera tilts up slightly to frame her movement. Holding the paper in front of her body, she folds it and crosses toward the camera. As she moves forward, the camera centers on the slip of paper, allowing it to come into ECU.

ROGER (*offscreen*): Business?

EVE: Yes.

ROGER (*offscreen*): Industrial designing business?

The camera tilts down as Eve opens a purse on the desk and slips the paper inside. The purse also contains a gun.

EVE: Mmm-hmmm.

ROGER (*offscreen*): All work and no play?

743. MS: *Eve is in the foreground, facing the camera. Roger stands behind her in the distance. He walks slowly toward her.*

ROGER: A girl like you should be enjoying herself this evening instead of taking phone calls from clients.

He places his drink on the table near her purse, and she turns to face him.

ROGER: What about having dinner with me? (*He reaches out and takes her by the waist.*)

EVE: You can't afford to be seen anyplace.

ROGER: Well, let's have it up here. Nice and cozy. (*He pulls her close.*)

EVE (*resisting the embrace*): No, I . . . I can't.

She breaks from the embrace and crosses upstage right, the camera panning to follow her.

ROGER (*offscreen*): I insist.

EVE (*pausing at the table where she mixed the drinks, and keeping her back turned to Roger*): I want you to do a favor for me.

744. MS: *Roger, standing with his empty arms slightly outstretched.*
    EVE (*offscreen*): A big, big favor.
    Nondiegetic music, the love theme, begins.
    ROGER: Name it.
745. CU: *Eve, standing at the table, in profile.*
    EVE: I want you to leave, right now.
746. MS, *as in 744.*
    EVE (*offscreen*): Stay far away from me and don't come near me again.
747. CU, *as in 745: Eve turns to look over her shoulder toward Roger.*
    EVE: We're not going to get involved.
748. MS, *as in 746.*
    EVE (*offscreen*): Last night was last night, and that's all there was.
749. CU, *as in 747.*
    EVE: And that's all there is, there isn't going to be anything more be-
    tween us.
750. MS, *as in 748.*
    EVE (*offscreen*): So please, good-bye . . .
751. CU, *as in 749.*
    EVE: . . . good luck. No conversation, just leave.
752. MS, *as in 750.*
    ROGER: Right away?
753. CU, *as in 751.*
    EVE: Yes.
754. MS, *as in 752.*
    ROGER: No questions asked?
755. CU, *as in 753.*
    EVE: Yes.
756. MS, *as in 754.*
    ROGER (*hesitating*): No, I can't do that.
757. CU, *as in 755.*
    EVE: Please.
758. MS, *as in 756.*
    ROGER: After dinner.
759. CU, *as in 757.*
    EVE: Now.
760. MS, *as in 758.*
    ROGER: After dinner. Fair is fair.
761. MCU: *Eve, seen from a slightly different angle. She pauses to consider.*
    EVE: All right. On one condition.
    She smiles slightly and crosses left toward Roger, the camera panning to follow her.
    EVE: That you let the hotel valet do something with this suit first.
    The nondiegetic music ends.

EVE (*reaching out and touching Roger's lapels*): You belong in the stockyards looking like that.

ROGER: Okay.

Reaching down, Eve picks up her purse from the table beside Roger. Then she indicates the telephone beside the bed in the distance.

EVE: There's the phone.

She crosses to the right, returning to the mirrored dressing table. The camera pans to follow her. Reflected in the mirror, Roger approaches the telephone.

762. MS: *a low-angle shot, looking across a lamp on the bedside table at Roger, who sits on the bed, crosses his legs, and picks up the telephone.*

ROGER: Hello. Valet service, please.

As he waits, he picks up the notepad Eve had used to write down the address of her appointment. He studies the top page under the light of the lamp. An indistinct voice is heard at the other end of the telephone line.

ROGER: Valet? This is. . . . (*turning over his shoulder toward Eve*) Oh, where are we?

EVE (*offscreen*): Four sixty-three.

ROGER (*into the telephone*): Four-six-three. How quickly can you get a suit sponged and pressed? Yes, fast. (*An indistinct answer on the phone.*) Twenty minutes. Fine. OK, four-six-three. (*He hangs up.*)

763. LS: *Roger rises from the bed and begins removing articles from his pockets, placing them on the table.*

ROGER (*to Eve*): He'll be right up.

EVE (*offscreen*): Better take your things off.

Roger turns and crosses right to Eve, who is standing with her back turned at the mirrored table. The camera pans, framing him and Eve in MS.

ROGER: Now. . . . (*Reaching out to touch Eve, whose back is still turned.*) Now, what can a man do with his clothes off for twenty minutes? (*He takes Eve by the shoulders and turns her around to face him.*) Couldn't he have taken an hour?

EVE: You could always take a cold shower.

Eve reaches up and begins helping Roger remove his coat.

ROGER (*turning around as she removes the coat*): That's right. You know, when I was a little boy, I wouldn't even let my mother undress me. (*He turns and faces her in his shirtsleeves, smiling.*)

EVE (*tossing the coat on the bed*): You're a big boy now.

ROGER: Yes.

Eve starts to unbutton his trousers.

764. MCU: *another angle, looking slightly up at Roger from over Eve's shoulder. He stops her, clasping both of her hands in his.*

ROGER: Tell me, how does a girl like you get to be a girl like you?

765. MCU: *reverse angle, looking down toward Eve from over Roger's shoulder.*

EVE (*smiling*): Lucky, I guess.

766. MCU, *as in 764.*

ROGER: Oh, not lucky. Naughty. Wicked. Up to no good. Ever *kill* anyone?

767. MCU, *as in 765: Eve's smile fades.*

Nondiegetic music, a brooding variation of the love theme, begins.

ROGER: Because I bet you could tease a man to death without half trying. (*He lightly pinches her cheek.*) So stop trying, huh?

768. MCU, *as in 766: Roger turns from Eve and walks off toward the bathroom, unfastening his trousers.*

769. MCU: *Eve watches Roger, controlling a hurt expression. As he moves toward the bathroom, he is reflected in the mirror beyond her head. He enters the bathroom and closes the door. The door buzzer sounds. Eve crosses left to the bed and picks up Roger's jacket, the camera panning to follow her.*

EVE (*calling out*): Be with you in a minute. (*Holding the jacket, she crosses left to the bathroom door. The camera pans to follow. She knocks on the door. From inside, Roger says something indistinctly.*) Trousers, please. (*The door opens partway and Roger hands her the trousers.*)

ROGER: Here you are.

The camera pans with Eve as she crosses right to the entrance, opens the door, and hands the suit to the valet.

EVE (*to the valet*): Thank you. (*She closes the door and turns toward the camera.*)

ROGER (*offscreen*): I think I'll take that cold shower, after all.

EVE: Good.

The nondiegetic music ends.

She moves hastily into the room, the camera tracking backward. She picks up her coat from a chair. The camera pans as she crosses right to the mirrored dressing table for her purse. Offscreen, we hear the shower running, and Roger whistling "Singin' in the Rain." Eve looks over her shoulder toward the bathroom. She turns back to the table, opens a drawer, and removes a sheet of folded paper; glancing at the paper, she slides it into her purse as she recrosses left to the bedside table. The camera pans to follow her. She pauses and picks up something Roger has placed on the table.

770. INSERT: *Eve's hand, holding the group photograph Roger found in "George Kaplan's" room at the Plaza in New York. Offscreen, Roger continues to whistle.*

771. MS: *inside the bathroom, Roger is hiding behind the half-open door and peeking through a crack in the doorjamb. He stands with his back to the camera, loudly whistling "Singin' in the Rain," still wearing his shirt and tie. In the right foreground, we can see the spray of the running shower.*

772. LS, *as at end of 769: Eve glances cautiously over her shoulder toward the bathroom, replaces the photograph on the table, and tiptoes out of the room. The camera pans as she crosses left and exits, closing the door behind her. Offscreen, we hear the running shower and Roger's whistling.*

773. MS, *as in 771: Roger watches Eve go. Still whistling, he moves toward the opening in the door.*
    Nondiegetic music, a chase theme, begins.

774. MS: *Roger steps out of the bathroom, crosses to the bed, and sits down beside the telephone. The camera pans and tilts down to follow his movements. Crossing his bare legs, he studies the blank notepad on the bedside table. He picks up a pencil and begins lightly shading a spot in the center of the pad. Offscreen, the shower continues to run.*

775. INSERT: *The shaded notepad reveals the imprint of an address: "1212 N. Michigan." Offscreen, the sound of the shower.*
    Dissolve.

Michigan Avenue, exterior, night

776. LS: *a taxi pulls up to the curb and Roger gets out. The taxi exits and he walks to the left.*

777. LS: *a low-angle view from the curbside, showing Roger as he walks into an art gallery marked 1212. A plaque beside the door reads "Shaw & Oppenheim Galleries."*

Art Gallery, interior, night

The chase theme ends, replaced by the dark variation of the love theme.

778. CU: *a high-angle view of the back of Eve's blond head. She is seated in a chair, reading an auction catalogue. A man is standing offscreen behind her, and his hand is caressing her bare shoulders. The hand glides upward, lightly squeezing the back of her neck.*
    AUCTIONEER (*offscreen*): . . . this magnificent pair of Louis Seize fauteuils. Original gilt finish. Upholstered in pure silk damask. How much may I say to start? What am I bid?
    The camera tracks backward and tilts level, revealing that the man holding Eve's neck is Vandamm. He moves his hand to her shoulder. Next to him is Leonard, lounging against a table and studying another catalogue. The camera continues to drift back to a LS, and then slowly pans right, across the crowded auction room, moving past the auctioneer.
    WOMAN'S VOICE (*offscreen*): One hundred.
    AUCTIONEER: One hundred is bid. Thank you. One-fifty is bid here. Say the two hundred. Thank you. Two hundred is bid. Say the three

hundred. I have three hundred. Four hundred by the little lady. Thank you, sir.

The nondiegetic music ends.

AUCTIONEER: Four-fifty is bid for the pair. Can I hear five hundred? Will you say five hundred? Can I say the five hundred? Fair warning and last call—sold to Mr. Stone, second row. Four hundred and fifty dollars.

The camera has now panned completely around the room to the rear entrance, where Roger is standing. He looks toward Eve and scowls. The camera tracks forward, framing him in MS.

AUCTIONEER (*offscreen*): And now, lot number one-oh-three.

779. LS: *Roger's* POV, *looking across the heads of the people attending the auction, toward Vandamm and Eve.*

AUCTIONEER (*offscreen*): Ah, this lovely Aubusson settee!

780. MS, *as at end of 778: the camera tracks backward as Roger moves into the room. Keeping his eyes fixed on Eve, he crosses left. The camera pans to follow him. He reaches the aisle at the far side of the room, and walks slowly down it toward Eve and Vandamm. The camera tracks forward, watching him from behind.*

AUCTIONEER (*offscreen*): In excellent condition! Please start the bidding. How much? Eight hundred is offered, thank you. Eight hundred is bid, say the nine, go nine hundred. Nine hundred is bid, now who'll say one thousand?

781. MS: *a reverse angle. Vandamm is resting his hand on Eve's shoulder, and we see Roger approaching in the distance. He walks up and stands behind Eve, smiling grimly and appraising the scene. Vandamm and Leonard notice him.*

AUCTIONEER (*offscreen*): One thousand, thank you. One thousand, at one thousand, say eleven hundred. Can I hear eleven hundred? Selling at one thousand. . . .

ROGER: The three of you together.

782. CU: *Eve hears Roger's voice and looks up in surprise. Then she looks forward, saying nothing.*

ROGER: Now that's a picture only Charles Addams could draw.

AUCTIONEER (*offscreen, heard dimly under Roger*): One thousand once, twice. . . .

VANDAMM (*offscreen*): Good evening, Mr. Kaplan.

783. MS: *Vandamm, Eve, and Leonard, seen from over Roger's shoulder. During this and the next several shots, the auctioneer's voice can be heard offscreen, although his words are indistinct.*

ROGER: Before we start calling each other names, perhaps you'd better tell me yours. I haven't had the pleasure.

VANDAMM: You disappoint me, sir.

784. MS, *as in 781.*

ROGER (*looking down at Eve*): I was just going to say that to her.

VANDAMM: I've always understood you were a pretty shrewd fellow at your job.

785. MS, *as in 783.*

VANDAMM: What possessed you to come blundering in here like this? Could it be an overpowering interest in art?

786. MS, *as in 784.*

ROGER: Yes, the art of survival. (*He looks toward Leonard.*)

787. MS, *as in 785.*

ROGER (*to Leonard*): Well, have you poured any good drunks lately?

788. MS, *as in 786: Vandamm is still resting his hand on Eve's shoulder. She lowers her eyes, but does not turn to face Roger.*

EVE (*to Vandamm, without turning her head*): He followed me here from the hotel.

789. MS, *as in 787.*

LEONARD: He was in your room?

790. MS, *as in 788: Eve nods.*

ROGER: Sure, isn't everybody?

791. CU: *Vandamm looks down at Eve, unsmiling.*

AUCTIONEER (*offscreen*): One hundred fifty, thank you. Now say the two.

792. CU: *Eve, looking forward. Vandamm's hand slowly withdraws from her shoulder. Her eyes glance to the right, conscious of his movement.*
AUCTIONEER (*offscreen*): Do I hear two? Two hundred, thank you.

793. MS: *Vandamm and Leonard. Vandamm continues to withdraw his hand, looking down at Eve. Leonard glances at Vandamm, and then looks off to the right.*
AUCTIONEER (*offscreen*): Now the three? Do I hear three? Three? Three hundred, anyone?

794. LS: *near the front row of the audience, a uniformed guard is holding up a piece of pre-Columbian statuary. The auctioneer and his assistant are standing at a rostrum in the distance.*
AUCTIONEER: Three hundred, thank you, now the four. Do I hear four? Four hundred, anyone?

795. MS, *as in 793: Leonard nudges Vandamm, who looks from Eve to the auction.*
AUCTIONEER (*offscreen*): Four hundred is bid.

796. LS, *as in 794.*
AUCTIONEER: Say the five? I have four hundred.

797. MS, *as in 795: Vandamm nods toward the auctioneer, whose voice becomes indistinct through the next several shots.*

798. CU: *Roger, looking toward Vandamm.*
ROGER: I didn't realize you were an art collector. I thought you just collected corpses.

799. MS, *as in 797: Vandamm glances over his shoulder to the left, as if looking for a way to be rid of Roger. Then he gestures toward Leonard with his right hand, in which he holds a pair of reading glasses.*
VANDAMM (*to Leonard*): Five hundred.

800. *Leonard signals to the auctioneer.* CU, *as in 798: Roger looks down toward Eve.*
AUCTIONEER (*offscreen*): Five hundred. Thank you.
ROGER: I'll bet you paid plenty . . .

801. CU: *Eve, looking ahead uncomfortably.*
ROGER (*offscreen*): . . . for this little piece of sculpture.

802. CU: *Vandamm looks down toward Eve, noting her reaction.*
VANDAMM (*signaling to Leonard with the reading glasses*): Seven hundred.

803. CU, *as in 800.*
ROGER: She's worth every dollar of it, take it from me.

804. CU, *as in 801.*
ROGER (*offscreen*): She puts her heart into her work.

805. CU, *as in 802.*
ROGER (*offscreen*): In fact her whole body.

806. LS, *as in 796.*

AUCTIONEER: Sold, then, to Mr. Vandamm, at seven hundred.

807. CU, *as in 805: Vandamm sighs.*

AUCTIONEER (*offscreen*): Number one hundred six, for your pleasure, is. . . .

808. CU, *as in 807.*

The auctioneer's voice becomes indistinct.

ROGER: Oh, Mr. Vandamm!

809. MS: *looking over Roger's shoulder at Vandamm.*

VANDAMM: Has anyone ever told you that you overplay your various roles rather severely, Mr. Kaplan? First you're the outraged Madison Avenue man who claims he's been mistaken for someone else.

810. MS: *reverse angle, looking over Vandamm's shoulder at Roger.*

VANDAMM: Then you play the fugitive from justice, supposedly trying to clear his name of a crime he knows he didn't commit.

811. CU: *Leonard, looking offscreen toward Roger.*

VANDAMM (*offscreen*): Now you play the peevish lover . . .

812. CU, *as in 804: Eve looks down uneasily.*

VANDAMM (*offscreen*): . . . stung by jealousy and betrayal.

813. MS, *as in 809.*

VANDAMM: Seems to me you fellows could stand a little less training from the FBI and a little more from the Actors Studio.

814. MS, *as in 810.*

ROGER: Apparently the only performance that will satisfy you is when I play dead.

815. MS, *as in 813.*

VANDAMM: Your very next role. You'll be quite convincing, I assure you.

As Vandamm speaks, Leonard crosses behind him to the left, looking toward Roger. Leonard moves around Vandamm and walks forward, almost brushing Roger's shoulder; then he turns and walks off toward the back of the room. The camera pans to follow him.

AUCTIONEER (*offscreen*): . . . twenty five dollars, thank you. Three seventy-five is bid. I have three seventy-five, go the four hundred.

816. MS: *Roger, Eve, and Vandamm.*

The auctioneer's voice becomes indistinct.

ROGER (*watching Leonard go, then turning to Vandamm*): I wonder what subtle form of manslaughter is next on the program? Am I to be dropped into a vat of molten steel and become part of a new skyscraper?

The camera dollies in an arc to the left. Roger looks down at Eve.

ROGER: Or are you going to ask this *female* to kiss me again and poison me to death?

Eve jumps up from her seat and tries to strike Roger with her purse. He catches her by the arm.

R O G E R (*pausing, a bit surprised by Eve's outburst*): Who are you kidding? You have no feelings to hurt.

Without speaking, Eve sits down again, staring at the auction and trying to compose herself. The camera tracks forward toward Vandamm, framing him in C U. *He is looking down at Eve with evident suspicion. He glances up at Roger.*

A U C T I O N E E R (*offscreen*): How much to start the bidding on the collector's porcelain?

817. M C U: *seated in the audience and looking offscreen right toward Vandamm is the Professor, from the United States Intelligence Agency.*

A U C T I O N E E R (*offscreen*): Please start the bidding.

818. M C U: *Vandamm, viewed from over Roger's shoulder. The auctioneer's voice becomes indistinct.*

V A N D A M M: Mr. Kaplan, we've had just about enough of you.

R O G E R: Then why don't you send for the police?

Vandamm glances offscreen left.

819. L S: *Vandamm's* P O V, *looking across the audience at the auction. Standing alone in the doorway at the back of the room is Valerian, whom we last saw at the United Nations.*

A U C T I O N E E R (*offscreen*): . . . six, six hundred. . . .

820. MCU, *as in 818.*
The auctioneer becomes indistinct.
ROGER: That's the last thing you'd want, isn't it? Me in the hands of the police.

821. MCU: *reverse angle, looking at Roger from over Vandamm's shoulder.*
ROGER: There's something I might tell them. And that's the reason you had this one here (*indicating Eve*) hustle me on the train last night.

822. MCU, *as in 820.*
ROGER: Something seems to tell me I've got a much better chance of survival if I go to the police.

823. MCU, *as in 821: Roger glances down toward Eve.*

824. CU: *Eve, staring forward toward the auction.*
ROGER (*offscreen*) Good night, sweetheart. Don't think it wasn't nice.
AUCTIONEER (*offscreen*): Say the twelve. Twelve hundred dollars there. Twelve hundred is bid. Say thirteen hundred.
Behind Eve, we can see Roger as he turns and walks off down the aisle. Eve's eyes brim with tears.
Nondiegetic music, the somber variation of the love theme, begins.

825. MS: *The camera pans, following Roger as he reaches the end of the aisle and turns, walking forward toward the exit. The camera tracks backward. Suddenly Roger stops, looking ahead with alarm. The camera continues moving back.*
AUCTIONEER (*offscreen*): May I hear thirteen hundred? They're selling at twelve hundred. Do I hear thirteen hundreed, please?

826. MS: *Roger's POV, looking at Licht, who is standing at the exit. Licht reaches into his pocket.*
AUCTIONEER (*offscreen*): Last call.

827. MS, *as in 825: Roger turns and looks left, then right.*
AUCTIONEER (*offscreen*): Sold. Twelve hundred dollars, thank you.
The nondiegetic music changes to the chase theme.

828. LS: *Roger's POV, looking toward the front of the auction room. Two uniformed men are pushing a large painting onto the stage.*

829. MS: *a frontal view of Roger as he walks forward into the room. The camera tracks backward as he advances. He glances up at the stage.*
AUCTIONEER (*offscreen*): And now, catalogue number one-oh-nine.

830. LS, *Roger's POV: at the corner of the stage, Leonard steps from behind a curtain, signaling to someone backstage. The camera tracks forward.*

831. MS, *as at end of 829: Roger stops and looks off toward Leonard.*
AUCTIONEER (*offscreen*): This superb example of this . . .

832. LS, *as in 830: Leonard moves to the right edge of the stage, and the camera pans to follow him.*
AUCTIONEER (*offscreen*): . . . early seventeenth-century master.

833. M S , *as in 831: frustrated, Roger begins to move back slightly.*
     A U C T I O N E E R (*offscreen*): It will enhance any collection of fine art.
834. L S , *as in 832: the camera pans, following Leonard as he steps off the*
     stage and stands just below it. He gazes toward Roger, blocking his way.
     A U C T I O N E E R (*offscreen*): What is your pleasure? How much to start?
835. M S , *as in 833: Roger turns to the right and looks for a seat on the aisle.*
     The camera tilts down as he forces his way into the row, making two
     women who occupy the chairs scrunch together.
     W O M A N ' S V O I C E (*offscreen*): One thousand dollars.
     A U C T I O N E E R (*offscreen*): One thousand is bid. Twelve-fifty I have . . .
836. L S : *At the back of the room, Valerian moves forward to block the aisle.*
     A U C T I O N E E R (*offscreen*): . . . now fifteen hundred.
837. M C U : *Roger sits uncomfortably on the outer edge of a chair he is shar-*
     ing with a well-dressed woman. His feet are in the aisle. He looks around
     the room and notices something to his right.
     A U C T I O N E E R (*offscreen*): Fifteen hundred is bid, thank you, now seven-
     teen-fifty.
838. L S : *Roger's* P O V , *looking across the crowd. Vandamm and Eve are*
     making a quick departure from the auction. The camera pans left, follow-
     ing them up the aisle.
839. M C U : *Roger looks over his shoulder as Eve and Vandamm head for the*
     exit. He looks forward, reacting to this development. Then he turns and
     looks over his other shoulder, watching the two figures leave the room.
     He looks forward, toward the edge of the stage.
     A U C T I O N E E R (*offscreen*): I have seventeen-fifty.
     M A N ' S V O I C E (*offscreen*): Two thousand.
     A U C T I O N E E R (*offscreen*): Two thousand is bid. Do I hear twenty-five?
     Twenty-five hundred, anyone. Twenty-two fifty once. . . .
840. M S : *Roger's* P O V . *Leonard stands beside the stage, glancing directly*
     into the camera.
841. M C U , *as in 839: Roger frowns, glancing at the auction in progress.*
     A U C T I O N E E R (*offscreen*): Twenty-two fifty twice. . . . Last call.
     The nondiegetic music ends.
     R O G E R (*calling out to the auctioneer*): Fifteen hundred!
842. L S : *Roger's* P O V , *looking toward the auctioneer. The audience in the*
     foreground murmurs and turns to look back at Roger.
     A U C T I O N E E R (*smiling*): The bid is already up to twenty-two fifty, sir.
843. M C U , *as in 841.*
     R O G E R : I . . . I still say fifteen hundred. (*He glances toward Leonard.*)
844. M S : *Leonard frowns and looks toward Roger. Offscreen, the audience*
     murmurs. Leonard glances left toward the auctioneer.
845. L S , *as in 842.*
     A U C T I O N E E R (*ignoring Roger*): I have twenty-two fifty.

846. MCU, *as in 843.*
    AUCTIONEER (*offscreen*): Do I hear twenty-five? Twenty-two fifty once. Twenty-two fifty twice.
    ROGER: Twelve hundred!
847. LS, *as in 845: the audience murmurs and turns to look at Roger.*
    AUCTIONEER: Sold! For twenty-two fifty. And now. . . .
848. LS: *a more distant view of Roger.*
    ROGER (*loudly*): Twenty-two fifty? For that chromo?
849. MS, *as in 844: Leonard looks uneasy. Offscreen, the audience buzzes. Their noise continues through the next few shots.*
850. MS: *The auctioneer looks shocked.*
851. LS, *as in 848: Roger turns to look at the back of the room.*
852. MS, *as in 850: the auctioneer looks down at his catalogue.*
    AUCTIONEER: Number one hundred ten in the catalogue.
853. LS, *as in 836: at the back of the room, Valerian edges forward.*
854. LS, *as in 851: Roger turns and looks at the catalogue held by the woman seated next to him.*
    AUCTIONEER (*offscreen*): A Louis Quinze carved and gilded. . . . Would somebody start the bidding at seven hundred and fifty dollars, please?
    ROGER (*loudly*): How do we know it's not a fake? It looks like a fake.
855. MS, *as in 852: the auctioneer reacts with a shocked expression. The audience buzzes loudly.*
856. MCU: *Leonard, standing at the edge of the stage, seems alarmed.*
857. LS, *as in 854: the audience continues to buzz.*
858. MCU: *Roger is seen in profile, looking to the right. A society matron seated in front of him turns around.*
    MATRON (*to Roger*): Well, one thing we know. *You're* no fake. You're a genuine idiot!
    ROGER: Thank you.
859. MS, *as in 855.*
    AUCTIONEER (*to Roger*): I wonder if I could—respectfully—ask the gentleman to get into the spirit of the proceedings here?
860. MCU, *as in 846.*
    ROGER: All right. I'll start it at eight.
861. MS, *as in 859.*
    AUCTIONEER (*smiling in relief*): Eight hundred. Thank you. Nine hundred?
862. MCU, *as in 860.*
    AUCTIONEER (*offscreen*): Nine hundred. One thousand is bid. Go twelve?
    ROGER: Eleven!
863. MS, *as in 861.*
    AUCTIONEER: Eleven is bid. Thank you. Go twelve. I have eleven.

864. MCU, *as in 862.*
 AUCTIONEER (*offscreen*): Go twelve. Who'll say twelve? Eleven once. Who'll say twelve? Eleven twice. . . .
 Roger looks over his shoulder at the back of the room. A man in the last row raises his hand.
 AUCTIONEER (*offscreen*): Twelve, thank you. Twelve is bid. I have twelve. Go thirteen. Who'll say thirteen?
 ROGER: Thirteen dollars!
 The audience bursts into laughter.
865. MCU: *The auctioneer and his assistant frown at Roger.*
 AUCTIONEER: You mean thirteen *hundred,* sir.
866. MCU, *as in 864.*
 ROGER: No, I . . . I mean thirteen dollars. That's more than it's worth!
867. MCU, *as in 865: the auctioneer's assistant leaves his place and crosses to the right, passing in front of the auctioneer. The camera pans slightly to center on the auctioneer.*
 AUCTIONEER: I . . . I have twelve hundred.
868. LS: *Roger's* POV. *The auctioneer's assistant confers with a stenographer. In the foreground, several people are staring toward Roger.*
869. CU: *a high-angle view of Roger, who is looking toward the auctioneer's assistant.*
870. LS, *as in 868: the assistant whispers something to the stenographer, who picks up a telephone on her desk.*
 AUCTIONEER (*offscreen*): Go thirteen. Who'll say thirteen? Who'll say twelve fifty?
871. CU, *as in 869: Roger smiles to himself, looking forward.*
 AUCTIONEER (*offscreen*): Twelve hundred once. . . .
872. MCU, *as in 867.*
 AUCTIONEER: Twelve hundred twice . . .
873. MCU, *as in 866.*
 AUCTIONEER (*offscreen*): Last call. Twelve hundred.
 ROGER: Two thousand!
 The crowd murmurs.
874. MCU, *as in 872, except that the assistant is now standing to the right of the auctioneer. Both characters look dumbfounded.*
875. MCU, *as in 856: Leonard looks anxiously around.*
876. MCU, *as in 874.*
 AUCTIONEER (*to Roger*): Two thousand?
877. MCU, *as in 878: Roger pauses, does a take, and glances at the auctioneer.*
 ROGER: Twenty-one hundred!
878. MCU, *as in 876.*
 AUCTIONEER: I'm sorry sir, but we can't. . . .

879. MCU, *as in 877.*
ROGER: Make it twenty-five hundred!

880. LS, *as in 853: the audience grows noisy, and Valerian, standing in the aisle at the back of the room looks frustrated.*

881. MCU, *as in 879.*
AUCTIONEER (*to Roger*): Would the gentleman *please* cooperate?
ASSISTANT (*loudly*): The last bid was twelve hundred!

882. MCU, *as in 879.*
ROGER: Twenty-five hundred! My money is as good as anybody's.

883. MCU, *as in 881: the auctioneer looks confused.*
AUCTIONEER: I have.... (*turning to assistant*) What was it?
ASSISTANT: Twelve hundred.

884. MCU, *as in 882.*
AUCTIONEER (offscreen): I have twelve hundred once. Twelve hundred twice....
ROGER: Three thousand!
The crowd noise grows.
AUCTIONEER (*offscreen*): Sold! For twelve hundred!

885. LS: *A large, well-dressed man at the far end of the room starts to move toward Roger's seat. The camera pans to follow him as he walks up the aisle to confront Roger, who has risen to his feet. The two figures are framed in* MS.
ROGER (*loudly*): Now, I'm not going to let you get away with that! That's not fair!
MAN (*taking Roger by the arm*): I think you'd better leave, sir.
ROGER (*to man*): You take your hands off me, or I'll sue you!
Roger turns and glances behind, toward the exit.

886. LS: *the back of the room. Valerian is nowhere in sight, and two uniformed policemen, Sergeant Flamm and a second officer, are being ushered in.*

887. MS, *as at end of 885.*
ROGER: Uh-oh. (*He turns and punches the man in the jaw.*)
Several women in the audience scream.

888. LS: *another angle, looking toward Roger as he completes the punch. The man falls to the floor. Roger turns and looks up the aisle at the policemen, who are approaching fast. The man gets to his feet, and Roger motions for him to wait. The man ignores Roger's signal and tries to return the punch.*

889. MS, *as in 887: Roger blocks the punch and hits the man in the stomach. As the man falls, Roger hugs him and falls to the floor alongside him. The camera tilts down. The policemen arrive.*

890. MCU: *the Professor is standing amid the noisy crowd. He notes the arrival of the policemen, and makes a quick exit.*

891. MCU, *as in 875: Leonard takes a step forward, then hesitates.*
892. MS, *as in 889: the policemen try to separate Roger and the man.*
893. MCU, *as in 883: the auctioneer, agitated, bites his pencil.*
894. MS: *the two policemen grasp Roger by the arms, turn him around to-*
     ward the camera, and walk him up the aisle. The camera tracks backward.

     ROGER: What took you so long?
     FLAMM: Let's take a little walk.
     ROGER: Oh, now, wait a minute. . . .
     FLAMM: Get moving!
     ROGER: I'm haven't finished bidding yet. (*He turns over his shoulder,*
     looking back at the auctioneer, and tries to raise his hand.) Three thou-
     sand! I bid three thousand!
     Roger and the policemen have reached the end of the aisle. The camera
     pans as they turn right and move toward the exit. On the way, they en-
     counter Valerian. They pause.
     ROGER (*to Valerian*): Sorry, old man. Too bad, keep trying.
     Nondiegetic music, the chase theme, begins.
     Roger and the policemen exit to the right, and the killer turns to watch
     them go.
895. MS: *the policemen drag Roger through the hallway, and the camera*
     pans right, following them.
     ROGER: Not so rough!

They pass a telephone booth. The camera stops, and they move on, exiting the frame to the right. Inside the booth is the Professor, who is making a call. He leans out to watch Roger being led off. Then he closes the door, sits down, and drops a coin in the slot.

Michigan Avenue, exterior, night

896. L S : *the policemen lead Roger out of the gallery toward their car, which is parked in the foreground. The camera pans as they put Roger in the back seat of the car. Sergeant Flamm walks around to the driver's seat, and the second policeman gets in beside Roger.*

R O G E R : Handle with care, fellas!

S E C O N D P O L I C E M A N : In there.

R O G E R : I'm valuable property!

S E C O N D P O L I C E M A N : In.

Police Car, interior, night

897. M S (*process*): *the camera looks from the front seat toward the rear of the car. The second policeman and Roger sit in the back. In the right foreground, the Sergeant Flamm gets behind the steering wheel and drives off.*

R O G E R : I want to thank you gentlemen for saving my life. Thank you, my friend, thank you. (*He reaches forward and pats the driver on the shoulder.*)

The nondiegetic music ends.

S E C O N D P O L I C E M A N : Save it for the station house.

R O G E R (*pauses, looking around*): Well, let's have some smiles and good cheer! You're about to become heroes. Don't you know who I am?

898. M S : *a closer view of the second policeman and Roger, seated side by side.*

S E C O N D P O L I C E M A N : We'll find out as soon as we book you for being drunk and disorderly.

R O G E R : Drunk and disorderly? That's chickenfeed. You've hit the jackpot! (*He quotes an imaginary headline, measuring the height of the words with his left hand.*) "Chicago Police Capture United Nations Killer."

The second policeman looks openmouthed at Roger.

R O G E R (*reaching for his wallet*): My name is Roger Thornhill.

899. M C U (*process*): *Roger's* P O V, *looking toward Sergeant Flamm. He turns around and looks into the camera. Then he checks a newspaper lying on the seat beside him.*

R O G E R (*offscreen*): Here.

F L A M M : It's him!

900. M S , *as in 898.*

R O G E R : That's right. Congratulations, men.

S E C O N D P O L I C E M A N (*leaning over the front seat to look at the newspaper photograph, and then glancing into Roger's face*): Yeah!

FLAMM (*offscreen, speaking into the police radiotelephone*): This is one-oh-five-five, Sergeant Flamm.

901. MCU, *as in 899.*

FLAMM: We've got a man here answering to the description of Thornhill, Roger.

902. MS, *as in 900: the second policeman looks at Roger's wallet and returns it, staring openmouthed at his captive.*

FLAMM (*offscreen*): Code seventy-six. Wanted by NYPD. Positive ID.

903. MCU, *as in 901.*

FLAMM (*pauses, listening to indistinct voice on the radiotelephone*): Absolutely. No question.

904. MS, *as in 902: the second policeman and Roger frown, listening to the indistinct voice at the other end of the line.*

FLAMM (*offscreen*): Michigan Avenue, proceeding north to Forty-second Precinct.

905. MCU, *as in 903.*

FLAMM (*listening*): What? (*Pause.*) Come again?

906. MS, *as in 897: the second policeman and Roger exchange glances, while Sergeant Flamm looks puzzled by what he hears on the radiotelephone.*

FLAMM: You're sure? (*Pause.*) Okay. (*Pause.*) Right. (*Pause.*) Yeah, I got it. One-oh-five-five, off and clear. (*Hangs up radiotelephone.*)

Sergeant Flamm turns the steering wheel and the tires squeal as the car makes a U-turn. Roger and the second policeman tilt to the right.

SECOND POLICEMAN: Where are we goin'?

FLAMM: The airport.

SECOND POLICEMAN: For what?

FLAMM: Orders.

ROGER: Airport? I don't want to be taken to an airport! I want to be taken to police headquarters!

FLAMM: You do, huh?

ROGER (*leaning forward*): Well, why do you think I sent for you fellows?

FLAMM (*to his fellow officer*): What about this guy, Charlie? *He* sent for *us!*

SECOND POLICEMAN (*pulling Roger by the shoulder*): Sit back.

ROGER: Didn't you hear what I said? I want to be taken to police headquarters! I'm a dangerous assassin! I'm a mad killer on the loose!

FLAMM: You ought to be ashamed of yourself!

Dissolve.

Northwest Orient Airlines Terminal, exterior, night

Nondiegetic music, the chase theme, begins.

907. LS: *the police car pulls up to the terminal. The camera pans as the two policemen escort Roger inside.*

Northwest Orient Airlines Terminal, interior, night

908. LS: *Roger and the policemen enter the crowded terminal at the far end of the room. They walk forward into* MS, *where they stop.*

PUBLIC ADDRESS ANNOUNCER (*offscreen*): Flight twenty-nine, arriving gate twelve. . . . Mr. Williams, please check station two.

FLAMM: He said right here.

ROGER: Does anyone mind if I sit down? I've been running all day.

Sergeant Flamm looks off to the right.

909. LS: *the Professor rushes in from the far end of the room, carrying a bag and holding onto his hat. The camera pans as he dashes up to the ticket counter. Roger and the two policemen stare at him. After checking with the ticket agent, he steps over to them. The group is framed in* MS.

PUBLIC ADDRESS ANNOUNCER (*offscreen*): Final call, American Airlines flight number four ninety-three, now boarding at American concourse, gate number fourteen.

PROFESSOR (*showing the police his identification*): Ah! Thought I'd never make it. Getting too old for this kind of work.

910. CU: *Roger, looking down toward the Professor, and frowning in bafflement.*

PROFESSOR (*offscreen*): All right, men. Thank you.

911. MS, *as at end of 909: the camera pans as the Professor hurries Roger off toward the departure gate.*

PROFESSOR: This way, Mr. Thornhill.

ROGER: Wait a minute. . . .

PROFESSOR: We haven't much time. This way is more private.

Departure Gate, exterior, night

912. LS: *Roger and the Professor exit the terminal, walking toward the camera.*

ROGER: I don't think I caught your name.

The nondiegetic music ends.

913. MS (*process*): *Roger and the Professor walk forward. Offscreen, we hear the sound of airplane engines.*

PROFESSOR: I don't think I pitched it.

ROGER: You're police, aren't you, or is it FBI?

PROFESSOR: FBI, CIA, ONI. . . . We're all in the same alphabet soup.

ROGER: Really? Well, you can stick this in your alphabet soup: I had nothing to do with that United Nations killing.

PROFESSOR: Oh, we know that.

ROGER: You know it? Then why did you let the police chase *me* all over the map?

PROFESSOR: We never interfere with the police. Unless absolutely necessary. It's become necessary.

ROGER (*putting his hands in his pockets*): Oh, I see. I take it I'm going to be cleared.

PROFESSOR (*taking Roger's arm*): I do wish you'd walk faster, Mr. Thornhill; we'll miss the plane.

ROGER: Where are we going? New York or Washington?

PROFESSOR: Rapid City, South Dakota.

ROGER: Rapid City? What for?

PROFESSOR: It's near Mount Rushmore.

ROGER: Well, thank you, I've seen Mount Rushmore.

PROFESSOR: So's your friend, Mr. Vandamm.

They stop.

ROGER: Vandamm?

PROFESSOR: A rather formidable kind of gentleman, eh?

914. MCU (*process*): *Roger is viewed from over the Professor's shoulder. A passenger plane is sitting on the runway behind Roger.*

ROGER: Yeah. And what about that treacherous little tramp with him?

PROFESSOR: Miss Kendall?

ROGER: Yeah.

PROFESSOR: His mistress. We know all about her.

ROGER (*pauses*): Tell me, what's Vandamm up to?

915. MCU (*process*): *reverse angle, viewing the Professor from over Roger's shoulder.*

PROFESSOR: Oh, you could say he's a sort of importer-exporter.

ROGER: Of what?

PROFESSOR: Oh, government secrets, perhaps.

916. MCU (*process*), *as in 914.*

ROGER: Why don't you grab him?

PROFESSOR: Still too much we don't know about his organization.

ROGER: Oh, I see. Well, what's all this got to do with Mount Rushmore?

917. MCU (*process*), *as in 915.*

PROFESSOR: Vandamm has a place near there. We think it's his jumping-off point to leave the country tomorrow night.

918. MCU (*process*), *as in 916.*

ROGER: Hmm. You going to stop him?

PROFESSOR: No.

ROGER: Well then, what are we going there for?

919. MCU (*process*), *as in 917.*

PROFESSOR: To set his mind at ease about George Kaplan.

920. MCU (*process*), *as in 918.*

ROGER: Oh, you, huh? You're George Kaplan; aren't you?

921. MCU (*process*), *as in 919.*

PROFESSOR: Oh, no, Mr. Thornhill. There is no such person as George Kaplan.

922. MCU (*process*), *as in 920.*

    ROGER: What do you mean, there's no such person? I've been in his hotel room. I've tried on his clothes. He's got short sleeves and dandruff!

923. MCU (*process*), *as in 921.*

    PROFESSOR: Believe me, Mr. Thornhill. He doesn't exist.

924. MCU (*process*), *as in 922.*

    PROFESSOR: Which is why I'm going to have to ask you to go on being him for the next twenty-four hours.

    ROGER: What?

925. MCU (*process*), *as in 923.*

    PROFESSOR: Come on, we'll discuss it on the plane.

    Offscreen, an airplane engine starts. Roger and the Professor are buffeted by noise and wind.

926. MS (*process*): *Roger and the Professor walk forward. The Professor holds onto his hat. Roger continues to ask questions. The Professor answers, but both of their voices are drowned out by the noise of the engine. Roger glances to the left.*

927. LS: *Roger's* POV. *An airliner is taxiing for takeoff, its engines roaring.*

928. MS (*process*), *as in 926: Roger and the Professor continue their conversation, but their voices are inaudible. Offscreen, we can hear the plane departing. Gradually, Roger's voice can be heard.*

    ROGER: Now look: You started this decoy business without me. You finish it without me!

    PROFESSOR: And well we might have, if you hadn't stumbled into it.

    ROGER: I think you ought to give me a medal and a very long vacation, instead of asking me to go on being a target just so your special agent or whatever you call him doesn't get shot at!

    PROFESSOR: Oh, not shot at, Mr. Thornhill. Found out. Once found out they're as good as dead. And thanks to you, clouds of suspicion are already forming.

    Roger stops and looks at the Professor.

    ROGER: Thanks to *me?*

    PROFESSOR: If you'll get on the plane. . . .

929. MCU (*process*): *Roger, seen from over the Professor's shoulder.*

    ROGER: Now wait a minute, you listen to me! I'm an advertising man, not a red herring. I've got a job, a secretary, a mother, two ex-wives, and several bartenders dependent upon me, and I don't intend to disappoint them all by getting myself slightly killed.

930. MCU (*process*): *reverse angle, with the Professor seen from over Roger's shoulder.*

    ROGER: The answer is no!

    PROFESSOR: Is that final?

ROGER: Yes!

PROFESSOR (*holding out his hand*): Well, good-bye, then.

ROGER (shaking hands): Good-bye.

PROFESSOR: If I thought there was any chance of changing your mind, I'd talk about Miss Kendall, . . .

931. MCU (*process*), *as in 929.*

PROFESSOR: . . . of whom you so obviously disapprove.

ROGER: Yes. For using sex like some people use a flyswatter.

932. MCU (*process*), *as in 930.*

PROFESSOR: I don't suppose it would matter to you that she was proba- bly forced to do whatever she did . . .

933. MCU (*process*), *as in 931.*

PROFESSOR: . . . in order to protect herself?

ROGER: To protect herself? From what?

PROFESSOR: Exposure. And assassination.

934. MCU (*process*), *as in 932.*

PROFESSOR: You see, Mr. Thornhill, she . . .

935. MCU (*process*), *as in 933.*

PROFESSOR (*pauses*): . . . she's one of our agents.

The camera zooms slowly toward Roger, framing him in CU.

ROGER: Oh, no!

PROFESSOR: I know you didn't mean it, but I'm afraid you have put her in an extremely dangerous situation. Much more than her life is at stake.

Roger has turned slightly away from the Professor, and is almost looking into the camera lens. Offscreen, the roar of an airplane engine can be heard. The light from a departing plane glares in Roger's face. Dissolve.

Mount Rushmore, exterior, day

936. LS: *Roger's face from the previous shot is momentarily superimposed over the carved heads atop the Mount Rushmore monument. As his face disappears, the camera zooms slightly toward the presidential carvings, and an iris encircles them.*

Observation Deck, exterior, day

937. CU: *Roger is seen in right profile, looking through a tourist's telescope mounted on a pedestal. He turns and glances down to his right.*

ROGER: Suppose they don't come?

938. MS (*process*): *Roger is seen from behind as he looks through the tele- scope. At the right, the Professor sits reading a newspaper. In the dis- tance is the presidential monument.*

PROFESSOR: They'll come.

ROGER: I don't like the way Teddy Roosevelt is looking at me.

PROFESSOR: Perhaps he's trying to give you one last word of caution, Mr. Kaplan: Speak soft and carry a big stick.

939. CU, *as in 937.*

ROGER: I think he's trying to tell me not to go through with this hare-brained scheme.

940. MCU (*process*): *the Professor is seen from a closer angle. To the left, Roger is partly visible.*

PROFESSOR: Perhaps he doesn't know to what extent you are the cause of our present trouble.

941. CU, *as in 939.*

ROGER: I don't know that I care to accept that charge, Professor. (*He adjusts the telescope.*)

942. MCU (*process*), *as in 940.*

PROFESSOR: Dear fellow, if you hadn't made yourself so damnably attractive . . .

943. CU, *as in 941.*

PROFESSOR (*offscreen*): . . . to Miss Kendall that she fell for you, . . .

ROGER: And vice versa.

944. MCU (*process*), *as in 942.*

PROFESSOR: . . . our friend Vandamm wouldn't be losing faith in her loyalty now.

945. CU, *as in 943.*

PROFESSOR (*offscreen*): It was quite obvious to him last night that she'd become emotionally involved.

946. MCU (*process*), *as in 944.*

PROFESSOR: Worst of all, with a man he thinks is a government agent.

947. CU, *as in 945.*

ROGER (*smiling as he looks through the telescope*): Are you trying to tell me that I'm irresistible?

948. MCU (*process*), *as in 946.*

PROFESSOR: I'm trying to remind you that it's your responsibility . . .

949. CU, *as in 947: Roger looks serious.*

PROFESSOR (*offscreen*): . . . to help us restore her to Vandamm's good graces . . .

950. MCU (*process*), *as in 948.*

PROFESSOR: . . . right up to the point he leaves the country tonight.

951. CU, *as in 949.*

ROGER: All right, all right.

952. MS (*process*), *as in 938: Roger turns and looks down at the Professor.*

ROGER: But after tonight?

PROFESSOR (*folding the newspaper to a new page*): My blessings on you both.

Nondiegetic music begins, with a sinister theme.
Roger crosses the frame and exits to the right. The Professor continues to read.

953. L S : *viewed from behind, Roger walks to the other side of the observation deck, passing several tourists.*

954. M C U (*process*): *Roger is seen in profile. He stops, looking off to the right.*

955. L S : *Roger's* P O V , *looking toward the parking lot outside the observation post. Vandamm, Leonard, and Eve are getting out of a white convertible.*

956. M C U (*process*), *as in 954.*

R O G E R (*looking toward the parking lot, but speaking to the Professor*):
  Here they are.

957. L S : *the Professor rises and walks left, briskly crossing the observation deck and entering the tourist shop.*

958. M C U (*process*), *as in 956: Roger turns and walks off to the left.*

959. L S : *seen from behind, Roger walks across the deck toward the cafeteria.*

Cafeteria, interior, day

960. L S : *Roger enters the cafeteria at the right and crosses left to the serving line. The camera pans to follow him. He buys a cup of coffee and crosses right to an empty table. The camera pans again. Looking off to the right, Roger starts to sit down.*

961. L S : *Eve, Vandamm, and Leonard enter the cafeteria through the same door Roger had used. Leonard stands near the door as Eve and Vandamm walk forward to Roger's table. The camera dollies to the right and pans left, framing Roger, Eve, and Vandamm.*

V A N D A M M : Good afternoon, Mr. Kaplan.

R O G E R (*indicating Eve*): Not her.

The nondiegetic music ends.
Vandamm glances at Eve, who walks off to the right without speaking.

962. L S : *Eve crosses from left to right. She passes Leonard, who takes a seat near the door.*

963. M S : *Roger and Vandamm sit down at the table.*

V A N D A M M : Did I misunderstand you about bringing her here?

R O G E R : We'll get to that later. I suppose you were surprised to get my call?

V A N D A M M : Not at all. I knew the police would release you, Mr. Kaplan. By the way, I want to compliment you on your colorful exit from the auction gallery.

R O G E R : Thank you.

V A N D A M M : And now, what little drama are we here for today? I really don't for a moment believe that you've invited me to these gay surroundings to come to a business arrangement.

R O G E R : Suppose I tell you I not only know the exact time you're leaving the country tonight, but the latitude and longitude of your rendezvous, and your ultimate destination.

VANDAMM (*pauses*): You wouldn't care to carry my bags for me, would you?

ROGER: Perhaps you'd be interested in the price, just the same.

VANDAMM: The price?

ROGER: For doing nothing to stop you.

VANDAMM (*pauses and smiles*): How much did you have in mind?

ROGER (*looking grimly down at the table*): I want the girl.

964. MCU: *Vandamm, seen from over Roger's shoulder. His smile fades. Roger turns his profile toward the camera.*

ROGER: I want the girl to get what's coming to her.

965. MCU: *Roger, seen from over Vandamm's shoulder.*

ROGER: You turn her over to me ... (*He glances forward to the left.*)

966. LS: *Roger's POV, looking toward the gift shop. Eve is browsing among the souvenirs. Standing near her, also apparently browsing, is the Professor.*

ROGER (*offscreen*): ... and I'll see there's enough pinned on her to keep her ...

967. MCU, *as in 965.*

ROGER: ... uncomfortable for the rest of her life.

968. MCU, *as in 964.*

ROGER: You do that and I'll look the other way tonight.

VANDAMM (*pauses*): She really *did* get under your skin, didn't she?

969. MCU, *as in 967.*

ROGER: We're not talking about *my* skin. We're talking about yours. I'm offering you a chance to save it.

VANDAMM: To exchange it.

ROGER: Put it any way you like.

970. MCU, *as in 968.*

VANDAMM: I'm curious, Mr. Kaplan. What made you arrive at the deduction that my feelings for Miss Kendall might have deteriorated to the point where I would trade her in for a little piece of mind?

971. MCU, *as in 969.*

ROGER (*starting to sip his coffee*): I don't deduce, I observe.

Offscreen, the sound of approaching footsteps.

972. MCU, *as in 970: Roger and Vandamm look upward to the right. The camera pulls back and tilts up slightly as Eve enters the frame. She looks down at Vandamm.*

EVE: Phillip, if you don't mind, I'm going back to the house now.

She turns and starts to exit at the right. Vandamm jumps up from his chair and stops her. The camera pans right, framing him and Eve in the middle distance as they confer. Their words cannot be heard. Vandamm signals for Leonard.

973. MCU: *Roger stands and watches from the table. He glances off toward the tourist shop.*

974. LS: *after speaking together for a moment, Vandamm, Eve, and Leonard move off toward the exit.*

975. MS: *Roger crosses the room to stop them. The camera pans right, following him.*

976. MS: *Roger seizes Eve by the arm and turns her around.*

    ROGER: Just a second, you.

    EVE (*in a firm whisper*): Stay away from me!

    Roger pulls her off to the left.

    EVE: You let go! Let go of me!

    Vandamm starts to intervene, but Leonard takes him by the arm, holding him back.

977. MS: *Roger pulls Eve by the arm and she tries to resist. They move left, and the camera pans to follow them. They stop near a pillar.*

    EVE: Stay away from me! Let go! Let go of me!

    ROGER: Save the phony tears.

    With her free hand, Eve reaches into her purse and pulls out a gun.

    EVE (*pointing the gun at Roger*): Just get back!

    Roger releases her arm and steps back.

    ROGER: Why, you little fool!

    EVE (*backing away*): You just stay away from me.

    Roger steps forward, and Eve fires the gun.

978. LS: *as Eve fires, Roger crumples to his knees. Several tourists scream.*

979. MS: *a low-angle view from behind Roger, looking up at Eve. She fires again, and Roger spins around. He falls to the floor and she runs out. A woman screams.*

    Nondiegetic music begins.

980. MS: *Vandamm starts after Eve, but Leonard restrains him.*

    LEONARD: No good, sir. You can't get involved in this.

981. LS: *a crowd rushes from the tourist shop toward Roger's fallen body. Among them is the Professor.*

982. LS: *viewed through the glass door of the cafeteria, Eve goes running off across the observation deck.*

983. LS: *a group of tourists has gathered around Roger's body. The Professor pulls a man away and stoops to examine Roger.*

    PROFESSOR: Don't touch anything!

    Parking Lot, exterior, day

984. LS: *a low-angle view, looking up from the white convertible toward the Mount Rushmore monument. Eve jumps into the car and drives off. Two figures run toward the car, but are too late to stop it.*

Cafeteria, interior, day

985. CU: *Leonard pokes his head between two tourists, looking down toward
Roger's fallen body.*

986. MS: *Leonard's* POV. *From a high angle, we see the Professor bending
over Roger. He wipes blood from his hand with a handkerchief and
shakes his head grimly.*
Dissolve.

Parking Lot, exterior, day

987. LS: *a low-angle view, looking up toward the presidential monument. In
the foreground, two rangers are loading a stretcher containing Roger's
shrouded body into the back of a government station wagon. The Professor steps through the noisy crowd and walks toward the front of the car.
The camera pans right, following him. He gets into the passenger seat
and closes the door. A ranger gets behind the wheel of the station wagon
and drives off.*
Dissolve.

Forest in the Black Hills, exterior, day

988. LS (*studio interior*): *the station wagon drives down a small dirt path and
stops. The Professor gets out, walks around to the rear, and begins to
open the doors.*

989. MS (*studio interior*): *the Professor opens the rear of the station wagon.*
PROFESSOR: Mr. Thornhill?
The nondiegetic music ends.
Roger gets up from the stretcher and crawls out.
PROFESSOR: Don't be long.
*The Professor walks around to the other side of the car, and the camera
tracks back to* LS. *Roger stands beside the green station wagon and
looks off to the right. Opposite him, Eve is standing beside her white con-
vertible. The two figures look at one another across the slender trunks of
evergreen trees.*
EVE: Hello.
ROGER: Hello.
EVE: Are you all right?
ROGER: Yes, I think so.
EVE: I asked the Professor if I could see you again.
ROGER: Oh.
EVE: There's not much time.
ROGER: Isn't there?
EVE: I wanted to tell you . . . I mean apologize.

990. LS (*studio interior*): *a slightly closer view of Roger. He is standing
alone near the left of the screen, next to the station wagon. His hands are
in his pockets.*
ROGER: Oh, no need.

He begins walking slowly to the right, through the trees and toward Eve.
The camera pans to follow him. He stops.

ROGER: I understand. All in the line of duty.

991. LS (*studio interior*): *Eve approaches Roger, walking slowly through the*
trees to the left. The camera pans with her, framing both figures in LS *as*
they meet.

EVE: I did treat you miserably.

ROGER: Ah yes. I hated you for it.

992. MS (*studio interior*): *Eve, viewed from over Roger's shoulder.*

EVE: I didn't want you to go on thinking that I. . . .

993. MS (*studio interior*): *Roger, viewed from over Eve's shoulder.*

ROGER: Well, I used some pretty harsh words. I'm sorry.

EVE: They hurt deeply.

ROGER: Naturally, if I'd known. . . .

994. MS (*studio interior*), *as in 992.*

EVE: I couldn't tell you.

ROGER: Of course not.

EVE: Could I?

995. MS (*studio interior*), *as in 993.*

ROGER (*smiling slightly and stepping forward to Eve's right, keeping his*
hands in his pockets): No, I guess not.

996. MS (*studio interior*), *as in 994: Eve turns and strolls with Roger deeper*
into the woods. The camera follows for a moment and then stops, watch-
ing the couple from behind as they move slowly off into LS.

EVE: You didn't get hurt. I'm so relieved.

ROGER: Of course I was hurt. How would you have felt?

EVE: I mean in the cafeteria, when you fell. When I shot you with the
blanks.

ROGER: Oh, that. No.

EVE: You did it rather well, I thought.

ROGER: Yes! I thought I was quite graceful.

997. MS (*studio interior*): *a closer view of Roger and Eve, seen from behind*
as they walk a few more paces.

EVE (*stopping*): Considering it's not really your kind of work.

ROGER (*stopping and turning to face her*): Well, I got into it by accident. What's your excuse?

EVE (*pauses and leans slightly against a tree*): I met Phillip Vandamm at
a party one night and saw only his charm.

ROGER: Oh.

Eve turns, grasps the tree trunk in her hand, and walks around it. Roger
moves toward her, and the camera tracks slightly forward, framing them
in MCU. *Roger and Eve stand looking at one another, on either side of*
the tree trunk.

EVE: I guess I had nothing to do that weekend, so I . . . I decided to fall in love.

ROGER: That's nice.

998. CU (*studio interior*): *Eve, seen from over Roger's shoulder.*

EVE: Eventually, the Professor and his Washington colleagues approached me with . . . (*sighs and looks down to the left*) a few sordid details about Phillip, and they told me that my relationship with him made me uniquely valuable to them.

999. CU (*studio interior*): *Roger, seen from a slightly low angle, over Eve's shoulder.*

ROGER (*half smiling*): Mmm-hmmm. So you became a girl scout, huh?

1000. CU (*studio interior*), *as in 998.*

EVE: Maybe it was the first time anyone ever asked me to do anything worthwhile.

1001. CU (*studio interior*), *as in 999.*

ROGER (*pausing looking surprised but vaguely amused by the melodrama*): Has life been like that?

1002. CU, *as in 1000.*

EVE: Mmm-hmmm.

1003. CU, *as in 1001.*

ROGER (*sympathetically*): How come?

1004. CU, *as in 1002.*

EVE (*pausing, looking longingly at Roger, and reaching out to touch him*): Men like you.

ROGER: What's wrong with men like me?

EVE (*moving closer*): They don't believe in marriage.

ROGER: I've been married twice.

EVE: See what I mean?

1005. CU, *as in 1003: Roger smiles and embraces Eve.*

ROGER: Well, I may go back to hating you. (*He kisses her gently on the cheek.*) It was more fun.

1006. CU, *as in 1004: Eve slides her arm around Roger's neck and kisses him passionately.*

Nondiegetic music, the love theme, begins.

EVE (*ending the kiss*): Good-bye, darling.

1007. CU, *as in 1005: Eve plays nervously with the knot in Roger's tie.*

ROGER: Wait a minute, not so soon.

1008. CU, *as in 1006.*

EVE (*sighs*): I've got to get back to the house and convince them that I took the long way around so nobody followed me.

1009. CU, *as in 1007: Roger embraces Eve.*

ROGER: Couldn't we stand like this for just a few hours?

1010. CU, *as in 1008: Eve steps back.*

EVE: There just isn't time; you're supposed to be critically wounded.

ROGER: I never felt more alive.

EVE: Well, whose side are you on?

1011. CU, *as in 1009.*

ROGER: Yours, always, darling.

1012. CU, *as in 1010: Eve embraces Roger.*

EVE: Please, don't undermine my resolve just when I need it most. *Offscreen, a car horn sounds. Roger turns, and he and Eve both look offscreen over his shoulder.*

1013. LS *(studio interior): The Professor, standing near the parked station wagon.*

1014. MCU *(studio interior): Roger turns to Eve. They look at one another, framed in profile. Roger puts his arm arond Eve's shoulder and they begin walking dejectedly to the left, back toward their cars. The camera tracks with them.*

ROGER: Oh, well, I guess it's off to hospital for me and back to danger for you. I don't like it a bit.

EVE: It's much safer now, thanks to you, my darling decoy.

ROGER: Don't thank me, I couldn't stand it.

EVE: All right, I won't.

They stop. Roger turns and faces Eve.

ROGER: After your malevolent friend Vandamm takes off tonight, you and I are going to get together and do a lot of apologizing to each other, in private.

EVE: You know that can't be.

ROGER: Of course it can be!

Eve looks offscreen left toward the Professor. She frowns and steps back from Roger.

EVE: Well, he *has* told you, hasn't he?

ROGER: Told me what?

1015. MS *(studio interior): the Professor crosses right, walking over to Roger and Eve. The camera pans, following him.*

PROFESSOR: Miss Kendall, you've got to get moving.

ROGER: Wait a minute.

1016. MCU *(studio interior), as in 1014: the Professor stands in the left foreground, his back to the camera. Nondiegetic music ends.*

ROGER *(to the Professor)*: What didn't you tell me?

EVE: Why didn't you?

1017. MCU *(studio interior): reverse angle, looking across Eve's shoulder toward the Professor.*

PROFESSOR *(hesitating)*: She's going off with Vandamm . . .

1018. MCU *(studio interior), as in 1016.*

PROFESSOR: . . . tonight on the plane.

ROGER (*after a shocked pause*): She's going off with Vandamm?!

1019. MCU (*studio interior*), *as in 1017.*

PROFESSOR: Well, that's why we went to such lengths to make her a fugitive from justice.

1020. MCU (*studio interior*), *as in 1018.*

PROFESSOR: So that Vandamm couldn't very well decline to take her along.

ROGER: But you said . . .

1021. MCU (*studio interior*), *as in 1019.*

PROFESSOR: I needn't tell you how valuable she can be to us over there.

1022. CU (*studio interior*): *a closer view of Roger and Eve, with the Professor no longer visible in the shot.*

ROGER: You lied to me! You said that after tonight. . . .

1023. CU (*studio interior*): *reverse angle, showing the Professor.*

PROFESSOR: I needed your help.

1024. CU (*studio interior*), *as in 1022.*

ROGER: Well, you've got it all right!

EVE (*to Roger*): Don't be angry.

ROGER: You think I'm going to let you . . .

1025. CU (*studio interior*), *as in 1023.*

ROGER: . . . go through with this dirty business?

PROFESSOR: She has to.

1026. CU (*studio interior*), *as in 1024.*

ROGER: Nobody has to do anything! I don't like the games you play, Professor.

1027. CU (*studio interior*), *as in 1025.*

PROFESSOR: War is hell, Mr. Thornhill, even when it's a cold one.

1028. CU (*studio interior*): *Roger.*

ROGER: If you fellows can't lick the Vandamms of this world . . .

1029. CU (*studio interior*): *Eve.*

ROGER (*offscreen*): . . . without asking girls like her to bed down with them and fly away with them . . .

1030. CU (*studio interior*), *as in 1028.*

ROGER: . . . and probably never come back, perhaps you ought to start learning . . .

1031. CU (*studio interior*), *as in 1029.*

ROGER (*offscreen*): . . . how to lose a few cold wars.

1032. CU (*studio interior*), *as in 1027.*

PROFESSOR (*sighs*): I'm afraid we're already doing that.

1033. CU (*studio interior*), *as in 1031: Eve turns to the right and runs toward her car. The camera pans to follow her into a LS. Nondiegetic music begins.*

1035. M S (*studio interior*): *The Professor and Roger turn to the right, looking offscreen toward Eve.*

933. L S (*studio interior*), *as at end of 1033: Eve jumps into the car, holding back her tears.*

1036. M S (*studio interior*), *as in 1034: Roger dashes off to the right, after Eve. The Professor turns and looks offscreen left, signaling to the ranger who had driven the station wagon.*

1037. M S (*studio interior*): *Eve is starting the car. Roger runs up and tries to open the door.*

R O G E R : I'm not going to let you do this.

E V E : Now, please don't spoil everything now, please!

R O G E R (*overlapping*): Now, come on, get out.

Roger opens the door. From offscreen left, a hand enters the frame and taps him on the shoulder. He turns.

1038. C U (*studio interior*): *Roger's* P O V . *The park ranger punches Roger, aiming his fist directly into the camera.*

1039. M S (*studio interior*): *a high-angle shot, showing Roger as he falls to the ground beside Eve's car. The car drives off.*
Dissolve.

A Rapid City Hospital Room, interior, night
The nondiegetic music ends.

1040. L S : *an empty hospital bed. On a bedside table to the right, a radio is broadcasting the evening news. In the foreground, Roger paces back and forth, nervously tapping a plastic comb against his hand. He wears only a bath towel, which is wrapped around his waist.*

R A D I O A N N O U N C E R (*offscreen*): . . . and shoot Mr. Kaplan twice, in full view of scores of horrified men, women, and children, who had come to the park to see the famed Mount Rushmore monument. Witnesses to the shooting described Kaplan's assailant as an attractive blonde in her late twenties.

The camera tracks back and begins panning to follow Roger as he paces back and forth.

R A D I O A N N O U N C E R (*offscreen*): Kaplan, who was removed to the Rapid City Hospital in critical condition (*Roger tries to open the door of the room, and finds it locked from the outside*), has been tentatively identified as an employee of the federal government. The tragedy developed with startling suddenness. (*Roger crosses to the right and opens the window to look down. He closes the window.*) Chris Swenson, a busboy in the Mount Rushmore cafeteria, stated that he heard voices raised in. . . .

Roger clicks off the radio. He hears the sound of a key in the door, and he quickly flops down on the bed, reclining on his elbow.

1041. L S :   *the door opens and the Professor enters, carrying two paper boxes.*
The camera pans with him as he crosses to the foot of Roger's bed.

PROFESSOR: Here we are.

ROGER (*sourly*): Hello.

PROFESSOR: (*tossing a box on the bed*): Slacks. A shirt. And these.
(*He indicates a shoe box.*)

ROGER: Thanks. (*He stands up and begins running the comb through
his hair.*)

PROFESSOR: They'll do for you around here for the next couple of
days.

ROGER: For the next couple of days? (*He smiles.*)

PROFESSOR: Hey.

ROGER: What?

PROFESSOR (*pointing to a bruise on Roger's right side*): What's this?

ROGER (*looking down at his side*): Oh, that's where I hit the chair
doing that phony fall in the cafeteria. You and your dopey schemes!
Shootings!

PROFESSOR: Otherwise feeling all right? (*He sits in a chair in the foreground, his back to the camera.*)

ROGER: Oh, yeah, fine. (*He tosses the comb aside and takes the shirt
out of the box.*) Considering your driver has a sledgehammer for a
hand. (*He feels his jaw.*)

PROFESSOR (*tilting his hat back*): I'm sorry about that.

ROGER (*unwrapping the shirt*): Oh, that's all right. I guess I deserved it. I guess I deserve that locked door, too.

1042. MS: *a reverse angle, looking slightly downward at the Professor.*

PROFESSOR: Well, if you were seen wandering about in good health, it could've proved fatal to Miss Kendall.

1043. MS: *Roger unwraps and puts on the shirt.*

ROGER: I've begun to forget her already.

PROFESSOR (*offscreen*): Good.

1044. MS, *as in 1042.*

PROFESSOR: Better that way.

ROGER (*offscreen*): Yeah. Much.

1045. MS, *as in 1043: Roger buttons the shirt.*

PROFESSOR (*offscreen*): Inside of an hour she'll be gone.

ROGER: Oh. (*He turns right and looks offscreen toward the window.*) Well, how's everything out in Rapid City?

1046. MS, *as in 1044.*

PROFESSOR: Oh, everything's fine. Mr. Kaplan's untimely shooting has now acquired the authority of the printed word.

1047. MS, *as in 1045: Roger slips on the pants.*

PROFESSOR (*offscreen*): Everyone's been cooperating beautifully.

ROGER: Well, now you can include me.

1048. MS, *as in 1046.*

ROGER (*offscreen*): I'm a cooperator.

PROFESSOR: I'm most grateful.

1049. LS, *as at end of 1041: Roger puts a belt through the loops of his trousers.*

ROGER: Care to do me a favor in return?

PROFESSOR: Anything.

ROGER: I'd like a drink. Can you get me a, can you get me some bourbon? A pint will do.

PROFESSOR (*standing*): Can I join you?

ROGER: All right. If you're going to join me, better make it a quart.

The camera pans left as the Professor crosses to the door.

PROFESSOR: See you in a few minutes. (*He exits.*)

ROGER: Yeah.

Nondiegetic music, the chase theme, begins.

1050. LS: *Roger quickly opens the shoe box and stamps on a pair of loafers. He puts a handkerchief and various belongings from the bedside table into his pocket. He crosses left, and the camera pans to follow him. He pauses, listens at the door, smiles, and tries to exit. He frowns when he discovers that the door is locked. He pulls frantically at the door, mutters "What the?" and consults his watch. He crosses right to the window, and*

*the camera pans to follow him. He looks outside, opens the window, and
pulls a chair underneath it to help him climb out.*

Hospital, exterior, night

1051.   L S :   *Roger steps out of the window, onto a ledge running along the building. Offscreen, traffic noises can be heard. Gripping the brick wall, Roger
inches along to the right. The camera follows him. He stops at the darkened window of the next room, peers inside, and opens the window.*

Hospital Room, interior, night

1052.   M S :   *Roger enters the dark room and starts to cross toward the left. The
camera pans with him. Suddenly a light switches on, and a young woman
sits up in the bed.*

The nondiegetic music ends.

W O M A N (*alarmed*): Stop!

R O G E R (*gesturing apologetically*): Oh, excuse me, I. . . .

*He moves across to the left side of the room. The camera pans slightly,
keeping him in the frame. Meanwhile, the woman slips on a pair of
glasses.*

W O M A N (*ardently, after getting a good look at Roger*): Stop!

R O G E R (*shaking his finger at the woman*): Ahh-ahh-ah! (*He exits to the
left.*)

The nondiegetic music begins again.

Dissolve.

A Road Leading to Mount Rushmore, exterior, night

1053.   L S (*matte*): *A taxi drives up a moonlit road. In the distance, we can see
the presidential monument.*

Vandamm's House, exterior, night

1054.   L S (*studio interior*): *The taxi drives up a dirt road in the forest and
parks outside the walled grounds of Vandamm's house.*

1055.   M S (*studio interior*): *Roger gets out of the taxi.*

D R I V E R :   Sure you don't want me to take you up there?

R O G E R (*paying the driver*): No thanks, never mind. This is fine.

D R I V E R :   Oh, thanks.

*As the taxi drives off, Roger crosses to the right, looking slightly upward
offscreen. He stops near a gate, and the camera tracks in to a* M C U *of his
profile.*

1056.   L S (*matte*): *Roger's* P O V , *looking up a dirt road toward a modernistic
house perched on the edge of a cliff. Lights are burning inside.*

955.   M C U (*studio interior*), *as at end of 1055: Roger considers the situation,
and moves off toward the right.*

1056.   L S (*matte*), *same angle as in 1056: Roger walks up the road. He pauses,
looks over his shoulder, and makes a stealthy run toward the house. Then
he turns off the road, circling around toward a balcony that juts over the
cliff.*

1059. MS (*studio interior*): *Roger sneaks through a rocky area and peers over a boulder.*

1060. LS (*matte*): *Roger's* POV, *showing a slightly closer view of the house. Inside, someone draws the drapes closed across the windows of the living area.*

1061. MS (*studio interior*), *as in 1059: Roger moves forward, exiting the shot at the left foreground.*

1062. LS (*studio interior*): *the two vast steel beams supporting the side of the house that extends over the cliff. Roger appears in the distance, making his way toward the nearest of them. He pauses and looks around in the darkness. Then he climbs up to the edge of the beam. The camera pans slightly and tracks forward, approaching him and finishing in a* MS. *He pauses again, looking offscreen right.*

1063. LS (*matte*): *Roger's* POV, *showing a landing field atop the mountain, its runway lights blinking in the darkness.*

1064. MS (*studio interior*), *as at end of 1062: Roger begins to climb up the rocky ground alongside the house. The camera tracks backward, framing him in* LS. *He moves up to a stone wall, and the camera pans to follow him.*

1065. CU (*studio interior*): *Roger grasps the edge of the wall and peers over the top, looking offscreen right.*

1066. LS (*studio interior*): *Roger's* POV, *looking over the edge of the wall into a driveway at the back of the house. A dark car pulls up and stops.*

1067. CU (*studio interior*), *as in 1065: Roger ducks slightly.*

1068. LS (*studio interior*), *as in 1066: Valerian gets out of the car and walks toward the house, carrying a folded newspaper. The camera pans to follow him. At the door, he is met by Anna, the housekeeper we saw at the Townsend estate on Long Island.*

1069. CU (*studio interior*): *Roger is seen from behind as he peeks over the wall. He turns around and looks offscreen left.*

1070. LS (*studio interior*): *Roger's* POV, *looking toward the living area of the house. The drapes on this side are open, revealing Vandamm and Eve, who are standing in the midst of the room. Valerian enters, gives Vandamm the newspaper, and exits.*

1071. CU (*studio interior*), *as in 1069: Roger moves toward the living area, easing his way along the edge of the house. The camera pans and then tracks to the left, following him.*

1072. LS (*studio interior*): *Roger reaches the large beam that helps to support the house. He pauses and looks up to the left.*

1073. LS (*studio interior*): *Roger's* POV, *looking along the beam up to a ledge along the outside of the house.*

1074. LS (*studio interior*), *as in 1072: Roger steps up to the beam and begins inching along it, moving up toward the living area.*

1075. L S , *as in 1073: Roger grasps the ledge with his hands and pulls himself up.*
The nondiegetic music ends on a dramatic and extended base chord.

1076. M C U (*studio interior*): *Roger pulls himself to the edge of a balcony running along the side of the house. He peers over the edge. Offscreen, voices can be heard.*
VANDAMM (*offscreen*): There's nothing to worry about.
E V E (*offscreen*): I just lost my head.

1077. M C U (*studio interior*): *a frontal view of Roger's head, peeking over the edge of the balcony.*
VANDAMM (*offscreen*): I'm not just saying this to make you feel better. I mean it.

1078. L S : *Roger's* P O V , *looking through the glass wall and into the house. Vandamm and Eve are pacing about. She is wearing a bright orange dress, and he has an arm around her shoulder. She seems distraught. The camera pans right, following them.*
E V E : I . . . I just didn't know what I was doing.
VANDAMM : He wanted to destroy you. You had to protect yourself.
From offscreen right, Leonard enters the room and walks over to a fireplace in the distance.
E V E : But not endanger you.
VANDAMM (*embracing her*): Rubbish!

1079. MCU (*studio interior*), *as in 1077.*
   VANDAMM (*offscreen*): Soon we'll be off together and I shall dedicate
   myself to your happiness.
1080. LS: *a slightly closer view of Eve and Vandamm. Leonard is lounging*
   against the fireplace, smoking a cigarette and looking at them.
   VANDAMM (*turning slightly over his shoulder toward Leonard*): What's
   the situation, Leonard?
   LEONARD: About the plane, you mean?
   VANDAMM: Of course. What was the last report?
   LEONARD: Over Whitestone on the hour. Six thousand. Descending.
   VANDAMM (*consults his watch*): About ten minutes, huh?
1081. CU (*studio interior*), *as in 1079: Roger looks off to the left, and then back*
   into the room.
   LEONARD (*offscreen*): At the most.
1082. MS: *a closer view of the three characters in the living room. Vandamm*
   holds Eve's shoulder and looks at her fondly. Leonard steps forward.
   LEONARD: And now, uh, I wonder if I might have a few words of part-
   ing with you, sir?
   VANDAMM: Certainly.
   LEONARD: In private?
   EVE (*exchanging glances with Vandamm*): I'll go up and get my things.
   (*She exits to the right.*)

1083. CU (*studio interior*), *as in 1081.*
VANDAMM (*offscreen*): Well, Leonard, how does one say good-bye . . .

1084. MLS, *as in 1082: Leonard is looking up at Eve, who is moving across*
a second-floor balcony toward her room. Vandamm crosses toward
Leonard, and the camera pans to follow him.
VANDAMM: . . . to one's right arm?
Leonard pauses, waiting for Eve to get beyond earshot. Vandamm follows
Leonard's gaze up at Eve's room, and then looks back to Leonard.
Offscreen, the sound of Eve's door closing.
LEONARD: In your case, sir, I'm afraid you're going to wish you had
cut it off sooner.

1085. CU (*studio interior*), *as in 1083.*

1086. MLS, *as in 1084: Vandamm nods, turns, and paces deeper into the room,*
his hands in his pockets.
VANDAMM: Umm.
Leonard follows Vandamm. Both figures move beyond view to the right,
their voices fading.
LEONARD: I know how terribly fond you are of Miss Kendall. . . .

1087. MS (*studio interior*): *Roger, seen in profile, leaning forward and trying*
to hear. Suddenly a light comes on to his right, and he glances up toward
the source.
Nondiegetic music begins.

1088. LS (*studio interior*): *Roger's* POV, *looking up to a lighted window on*
the second floor. Eve is inside, gathering her things for the trip.

1089. MS (*studio interior*), *as in 1087: Roger takes a coin from his pocket and*
tosses it at Eve's window. Offscreen, the sound of the coin. Roger ducks
and peeks up again.

1090. LS (*studio interior*), *as in 1088: Eve hears the sound and pauses, looking*
around.

1091. MS (*studio interior*), *as in 1089: Roger takes out another coin and tosses*
it at the window.

1092. LS (*studio interior*), *as in 1090: offscreen, the sound of the coin and the*
return of muffled voices from the living room.

1093. MS (*studio interior*), *as in 1091: Roger looks up.*

1094. LS (*studio interior*), *as in 1092: Eve goes to a door and opens it, stepping*
out on her balcony to look around.

1095. MS (*studio interior*), *as in 1093: Roger waves, desperately trying to catch*
Eve's attention. Hearing something, he looks to the right.

1096. LS: *Roger's* POV, *through the living room windows. Leonard has heard*
something, and is walking forward.

1097. CU (*studio interior*), *as in 1085: Roger ducks below the ledge.*

1098. LS (*studio interior*), *as in 1094: Eve steps back inside, closing her door.*

1099. MS: *a low-angle view of Leonard as he crosses left, looking through the window. The camera pans to follow him. He stands beside a partly open sliding glass door and looks around for a moment. Then he turns and glances offscreen right, toward Vandamm.*

LEONARD: It couldn't have been anything.

The nondiegetic music ends.

Leonard turns and crosses right, the camera panning to follow him. He stops in front of a coffee table and sits on it, his back to the camera; he is looking toward Vandamm, who is standing in the distance. Next to him on the table is the piece of pre-Columbian statuary from the art auction. As he sits, he removes Eve's gun from his coat pocket and puts it on the table behind him, hidden from Vandamm's sight.

LEONARD: You must've had some doubts about her yourself. And still do.

1100. CU *(studio interior), as in 1097: Roger peeks over the ledge, his eyes narrowing at the sight of the gun.*

VANDAMM *(offscreen)*: Rubbish.

1101. MS, *as at end of 1099.*

LEONARD: Why else would you have decided not to tell her . . .

1102. CU *(studio interior), as in 1100.*

LEONARD *(offscreen)*: . . . that our little treasure here . . .

1103. CU: *Leonard's hand, indicating the pre-Columbian statuette.*

LEONARD: . . . has a belly full of microfilm?

1104. CU *(studio interior), as in 1102.*

VANDAMM *(offscreen)*: You seem to be trying to fill mine . . .

1105. MS, *as in 1101.*

VANDAMM: . . . with rotten apples.

LEONARD: Sometimes the truth does taste like a mouthful of worms, sir.

VANDAMM: Truth?

1106. CU *(studio interior), as in 1104: Roger's eyes widen in alarm.*

VANDAMM *(offscreen)*: I've heard nothing but innuendo.

1107. MS, *as in 1105.*

LEONARD: Call it my woman's intuition, if you will, but I've never trusted neatness. Neatness is always the result of deliberate planning.

VANDAMM *(pointing over his shoulder toward Eve's room)*: She shot him in a moment of fear and anger.

1108. CU *(studio interior), as in 1106.*

VANDAMM *(offscreen)*: You were there yourself, you saw it.

1109. MS, *as in 1107: Leonard reaches behind his back for the gun.*

LEONARD: Yes.

1110. CU *(studio interior), as in 1108: Roger's eyes focus on the gun.*

1111. MS, *as in 1109: Leonard grasps the gun and rises slowly, crossing toward Vandamm and moving into* LS.

LEONARD: And thereby wrapped everything up into one neat and tidy bundle.

1112. CU *(studio interior), as in 1110: Roger looks concerned.*

1113. LS, *as at end of 1111: Leonard turns and faces Vandamm in profile.*

LEONARD *(enumerating points with his left hand, and holding his right hand behind his back)*: A, she removed any doubts you may have had about her . . . her what did you call it, her "devotion"? And B, she gave herself a new and urgent reason to be taken over to the other side with you . . .

1114. CU *(studio interior), as in 1112: Roger glances anxiously up toward Eve's room.*

LEONARD *(offscreen)*: . . . just in case you decided to change your mind.

1115. LS, *as in 1113.*

VANDAMM: You know what I think? *(He chuckles.)* I think you're jealous. *(Leonard scowls at him.)* No, I mean it! I'm very touched. Very. *Vandamm starts to turn away. Leonard suddenly pulls the gun from behind his back and points it at Vandamm.*

1116. CU *(studio interior), as in 1114: Roger's eyes widen still more.*

1117. LS, *as in 1115.*

VANDAMM *(pauses)*: Leonard? *Leonard fires the gun at Vandamm, who flinches in shock and fear.*

1118. CU *(studio interior), as in 1116.*

1119. CU: *Leonard's POV. Openmouthed, Vandamm looks down toward the gun, and then at Leonard. (His gaze is directly into the camera lens.)*

1120. CU: *Vandamm's POV. Leonard smiles in satisfaction, looking into the camera lens.*

1121. CU, *as in 1119: speechless, Vandamm gestures toward the gun.*

LEONARD *(offscreen)*: The gun she shot Kaplan with.

1122. CU *(studio interior), as in 1118.*

LEONARD *(offscreen)*: I found it in her luggage.

1021. CU, *as in 1121.*

LEONARD *(offscreen)*: It's an old Gestapo trick. Shoot one of your own people to show that you're not one of them.

1124. CU, *as in 1120.*

LEONARD: They've just freshened it up a bit . . .

1125. CU *(studio interior), as in 1122.*

LEONARD *(offscreen)*: . . . with blank cartridges.

1126. CU, *as in 1123: Vandamm pauses, and then swings a punch at Leonard, his fist aimed directly at the camera. We hear the sound of the blow.*

1127. CU: *Vandamm's POV. Leonard flies back from the camera and falls into a seated position in a chair.*

1128. CU *(studio interior), as in 1125: Roger glances toward Eve's room.*

1129. MCU: *seen from a low angle, Vandamm pulls at the fingers of his right hand and winces. Offscreen, the sound of a door opening.*
1130. CU *(studio interior), as in 1128: Roger looks up slightly.*
1131. MS: *a low-angle view of Eve, who walks forward to the edge of the second-floor balcony and looks down into the room.*
    EVE: What was that noise?
1132. LS: *Eve's POV, looking down at Vandamm and Leonard. Vandamm turns around calmly, and Leonard straightens his hair.*
    VANDAMM: Yes, we wondered what it was, too, didn't we, Leonard? Hurry on down, darling. It's almost time to leave.
1133. MS *(studio interior), as in 1131: Eve nods and turns back toward her room.*
    EVE: In a moment.
1134. CU *(studio interior), as in 1130.*
1135. MS: *Vandamm stands and looks up toward the balcony, watching Eve go. Behind him in the distance, Leonard sits in the chair. Still gazing up, Vandamm walks forward into CU. He stops, and the camera cranes slightly, looking down at him. Leonard gets up from the chair and walks forward to stand at Vandamm's shoulder.*
    LEONARD: You're not taking her on that plane with you?
    VANDAMM: Of course I am.
1136. CU *(studio interior), as in 1134. Roger watches intently.*
1137. CU *(studio interior), as in 1135.*
    VANDAMM: Like our friends, I, too, believe in neatness, Leonard. *The camera cranes up and tilts, looking sharply down on Vandamm and Leonard.*
    VANDAMM: This matter is best disposed of from a great height. Over water.
1138. CU *(studio interior), as in 1136: Roger ducks below the ledge. Nondiegetic music begins.*
1139. MS *(studio interior): Roger crouches and works his way forward along the ledge.*
1140. LS *(studio interior): a reverse angle, showing Roger as he moves along the ledge toward Eve's side of the house. Upstairs, Eve can be seen as she completes her packing. Roger grasps the ragged stones on the side of the house, and begins slowly climbing toward her window. Eve closes her suitcase, and slips on an orange jacket that matches her dress.*
1141. LS *(studio interior): a closer view of Roger from just outside Eve's window. At the left of the screen, Roger inches toward the balcony. The camera pans right, following him. Just as he puts a foot on the balcony, Eve leaves her room, turning out the light and closing the door. Roger moves quickly across the balcony and enters the room.*

Eve's Bedroom in Vandamm's House, interior, night

1142. L S : *Roger moves through the balcony door and tiptoes quickly across the darkened room, the camera panning right to follow him. He opens the inner door and stands there, listening to voices from below.*

VANDAMM (*offscreen*): How about a little champagne before we go?

EVE (*offscreen*): I'd love it.

VANDAMM (*offscreen*): It may not be cold enough.

EVE: (*offscreen*): Over the rocks will be all right.

VANDAMM (*offscreen*): Sure?

EVE (*offscreen*): Mmm.

Roger stands inside the open door and looks down at his left hand.

1143. C U : *Roger's hand. His palm is scraped and bloody from climbing the stone wall.*

1144. M S , *as at end of 1142: Roger takes a handkerchief from his pocket to wipe off the blood. He pauses and looks down at he handkerchief. Offscreen, we hear the sound of ice dropping into glasses.*

1145. C U , *as in 1143: Roger holds a handkerchief bearing his monogram: "R.O.T."*

1146. M S , *as in 1144: Roger reaches into his pocket and takes out a matchbook. From his other pocket, he takes out a small pencil.*

1147. I N S E R T : *A monogrammed matchbook. Roger opens it and writes, "They're on to you."*

1148. MCU: *Roger, writing the note.*

1149. INSERT: *Roger writes, "I'm in your room," and closes the matchbook.*

1150. MCU, *as in 1148: Roger smiles slightly, replaces the pencil in his pocket, and steps off to the right, through the door.*

Balcony, interior, night

1151. MS: *Roger slowly steps onto the balcony overlooking the living room. The camera pans right as he tiptoes down a couple of steps and onto a landing. He peers around the corner of a stone column, looking downstairs. The nondiegetic music ends.*

1152. MCU: *Roger, seen in three-quarter profile as he looks down to the right.*

1153. LS: *Roger's* POV. *A high-angle shot looking down into the living room. Vandamm turns away from a bar, holding a champagne bottle and two glasses, and crosses to the right. The camera pans to follow him, tilting down to a sharper angle. Leonard enters from below and crosses diagonally, exiting at the top of the frame. Vandamm walks to a couch where Eve is seated, and puts the bottle on the marble table behind her head. He steps to the front of the couch and hands her a glass of champagne.*

EVE: Thank you.

VANDAMM: To you, my dear . . .

1154. MCU, *as in 1152.*

VANDAMM: . . . and all the lovely moments we've had together.

1155. LS, *as at end of 1153: Vandamm touches his glass to Eve's.*

EVE: Thank you, Phillip.

1156. LS: *a high-angle view of Leonard, who is looking out the windows to the left.*

LEONARD: There he is.

1157. LS, *as in 1155: Vandamm turns and crosses to Leonard, the camera panning left and tilting up to follow him. Offscreen, we hear the distant sound of an airplane engine.*

1158. LS, *as in 1154: Roger steps forward, takes careful aim, and tosses the matchbook down and to the right, in Eve's direction.*

VANDAMM (*offscreen*): Jump in, Leonard. The champagne's fine.

LEONARD (*offscreen*): There isn't time.

VANDAMM (*offscreen*): You always were a spoilsport, weren't you?

LEONARD (*offscreen*): One of my most valuable attributes, as it now turns out.

1159. LS: *a closer view of Eve, maintaining the high-angle perspective of Roger's* POV. *Eve turns to put her champagne glass on the table behind the couch, and the matchbook drops on the carpet in front of her.*

1160. MCU: *Roger ducks behind the stone column.*

1161. LS, *as in 1157: Leonard crosses to stand in front of Eve. The camera pans and tilts down to follow him.*

LEONARD (*to Eve*): It would please me if you would think of me as being along on this journey . . .

1162. CU: *Roger, looking down and to the right from behind the column.*
LEONARD (*offscreen*): . . . if only in spirit.
1163. LS, *as in 1161.*
EVE: I shall, Leonard.
Leonard notices the matchbook at his feet.
1164. CU, *as in 1162.*
1165. LS, *as in 1163: Leonard bends, picks up the matchbook, and tosses it into an ashtray on the table in front of Eve. He turns and walks back toward his place by the window.*
Nondiegetic music begins.
1166. MCU, *as in 1160: Roger leans forward expectantly.*
LEONARD (*offscreen*): He's heading pretty far out . . .
1167. MCU: *Roger's POV, looking down on Eve, who sits with her back to the camera. She notices the matchbook bearing Roger's monogram in the ashtray to her left. She sits up suddenly.*
LEONARD (*offscreen*): . . . on the north leg, and awfully high. Well, I . . .
1168. CU, *as in 1164.*
LEONARD (*offscreen*): . . . I guess he's going to play it safe . . .
1169. MCU: *Eve slowly reaches out and picks up the matchbook. She opens it and reads the message. Suddenly she turns and glances over her shoulder.*
LEONARD (*offscreen*): . . . with a long, slow descent. Mmmm. Couldn't ask for a better night than this. Ceiling and possibilities unlimited. Ah, there he goes, starting his turn. Well, we'd better get moving!
Startled, Eve quickly closes the matchbook and reaches for her purse.
LEONARD (*offscreen*): He should have his wheels on the ground . . .
1170. CU, *as in 1168: Roger turns and tiptoes back to Eve's room. The camera pans left to follow him.*
LEONARD (*offscreen*): . . . inside of three minutes.
1171. LS, *as at beginning of 1161: Vandamm and Leonard cross partway toward Eve. The camera tilts down slightly.*
VANDAMM: Come on, Eve. (*He looks at his watch.*)
EVE (*standing up*): All right. (*She touches her right earlobe.*) Oh, I think I left my earrings upstairs. I'll be right down.
She moves off to the left, at the bottom of the frame. Vandamm and Leonard stand waiting for her, exchanging glances.
1172. LS: *Eve walks forward and left into CU, crossing the second floor balcony and entering her room. The camera pans slightly to follow her.*
Eve's Bedroom, interior, night
1173. MCU: *Roger stands behind the door in the darkened bedroom. Eve enters, turns on the light, and registers surprise. Roger closes the door and moves to face her, taking her by the arms.*
The nondiegetic music ends.

ROGER (*quietly*): Darling, we can get out through the window. There's a car downstairs.

EVE (*whispering*): What are you doing here, Roger? You'll ruin everything!

ROGER: Now, listen to me! They know all about the fake shooting. They're going to do away with you.

EVE: What are you talking about?

ROGER: Leonard found the gun with the blanks in it in your luggage! And the figure that they got at the auction sale last night is filled with microfilm!

EVE: That's how he's been getting it!

LEONARD (*offscreen, from outside the room*): Miss Kendall!

Roger and Eve pause, listening. Eve quickly opens the door and steps out.

ROGER (*whispering*): Whatever you do, don't get on that plane!

Balcony, interior, night

1174. CU, *as at end of 1172: Eve exits her room and walks into* LS *along the balcony. The camera pans slightly, following her. At the end of the balcony, Leonard is waiting. Offscreen, we hear the sound of the approaching airplane. Eve and Leonard exit to the right, going down the stairs.*

1175. LS: *a high-angle view of Vandamm and Anna, the housekeeper, standing near the window of the living room. Vandamm picks up the pre-Columbian statuette and begins to cross downscreen, toward the exit.*

VANDAMM: Don't worry, Anna, arrangements have been made. You and your husband will be over the Canadian border by tomorrow morning.

ANNA: Thank you very much, sir.

1176. CU, *as in beginning of 1170: Roger tiptoes to the stone column and looks down.*

VANDAMM (*offscreen*): Be careful.

ANNA (*offscreen*): We will, sir. And God bless you.

1177. LS, *as in 1175: the camera pans and tilts as Vandamm crosses down toward the couch. Leonard passes him, moving off at the top of the frame. Holding the statuette, Vandamm pauses beside Eve, who is standing near the couch and putting on her wrap. The camera frames them in* MCU, *looking down on the tops of their heads. Vandamm looks upscreen toward Leonard and Anna, who reenter the shot from the top of the frame. All four characters exit at the bottom.*

1178. CU, *as in 1176: Roger listens to indistinct offscreen voices. Out of his sight, Vandamm and Eve are saying good-byes to Anna at the door. The sound of the airplane grows louder. After a moment, we hear the offscreen sound of a door closing.*
Nondiegetic music begins.
Roger steps out of the shot to the left.

Living Room, interior, night

1179. L S :   *Anna enters from a distance at the right. She crosses left and picks up the two empty champagne glasses on the table. Then she crosses forward and to the right. The camera pans to follow her as she moves forward into* M S. *She stops, looking down to the right.*

1180. I N S E R T :   *a turned-off televison set. Reflected in its screen, Roger can be seen as he crosses the second-floor balcony. The camera tracks in toward the reflection.*

1181. M S :   *Anna steps to the right and puts the champagne glasses on a counter. The camera pans to follow her. She turns and walks quickly off toward the background, exiting behind the corner of a stone wall.*

1182. L S :   *a low-angle view of Roger as he sneaks along the balcony. He turns onto the stairway and begins to come down.*

1183. L S :   *Roger, seen from the first floor, steps quietly down the stairs.*
A N N A (*offscreen*): Stay where you are!
The nondiegetic music ends.
Roger stops and looks offscreen to the right rear of the camera.

1184. L S :   *a reverse angle, showing Anna as she steps out of the shadows behind a wall. She is pointing a gun at Roger.*

1185. L S :   *Roger stands on the stairway at the right of the screen, his hands by his side. Anna enters from the left foreground and walks to a chair near the foot of the stairs. She sits, still pointing the gun at Roger.*
A N N A : Sit down.
Roger pauses, then sits down slowly on the stairs. Offscreen, we hear the sound of the airplane approaching.
A N N A : As soon as the plane leaves, my husband and Mr. Leonard will be back.

Landing Field, exterior, night

1186. M S (*process*): *Eve, Vandamm, and Leonard are facing the camera, walking forward to meet the airplane. The two men glance at Eve, who looks uneasy.*
Nondiegetic music begins.

1187. L S (*matte*): *Eve's P O V, looking toward the landing field. Its lights are blinking. In the distance, the light from the arriving airplane can be seen. We can hear its landing gear strike the ground.*

1188. C U (*process*): *Eve walks forward. She turns suddenly and looks over her shoulder. In this and the next several shots, the airplane engine can be heard offscreen.*

1189. L S (*matte*): *Eve's P O V, looking back toward the house. The camera tracks back.*

1190. C U , *as in 1188: Eve looks forward.*

1191. C U (*process*): *Vandamm, walking forward and holding the statuette in his hand, glances sidelong left toward Eve.*

1192. CU (*process*), *as in 1190: Eve glances right toward Vandamm, and then turns to look over her shoulder again.*

1193. CU (*process*), *as in 1191 Vandamm is aware of Eve's nervousness.*

1092. CU (*process*), *as in 1192.*

VANDAMM (*offscreen*): What is it?

EVE: I was wondering about my earrings. (*She indicates her ear.*)

VANDAMM: Oh, they'll turn up.

1195. LS: *the plane has landed and is waiting. From behind, we see Leonard, Vandamm, and Eve walking toward it.*

1196. MS: *the three characters enter from the right and cross to the plane's open passenger door. The pilot is visible inside.*

VANDAMM (*to Leonard*): When you return to New York, . . .

1095. CU: *Eve looks off to the left, toward the house.*

VANDAMM (*offscreen*): . . . say good-bye to my sister for me.

1198. LS (*matte*): *Eve's* POV, *looking beyond the wing of the plane toward the lighted windows of the house.*

1199. CU, *as in 1197: Eve looks down and to the right.*

VANDAMM (*offscreen*): And thank her for a superb performance as Mrs. Townsend.

1200. CU: *Eve's* POV, *looking toward the luggage on the ground. Valerian, visible from the waist down, picks up two bags and walks forward toward the plane.*

LEONARD (*offscreen*): I'll do that.

1201. CU, *as in 1197.*

VANDAMM (*offscreen*): And tell your knife-throwing chum that I've re-assured his wife.

LEONARD (*offscreen*): Right.

1202. CU: *Vandamm and Leonard.*

VANDAMM: That's about all, Leonard.

1203. CU, *as in 1201: the camera pans with Eve as Vandamm leads her to the doorway of the plane. She stops and looks anxiously over her shoulder. Offscreen, two gunshots are heard.*
The nondiegetic music ends.

1204. LS (*matte*): *Eve's* POV. *Roger rushes out of the house and into the dark sedan parked near the door.*

1205. MS: *Vandamm and Eve look toward the house. She is openmouthed. Suddenly she reaches for the statuette under Vandamm's arm.*

1206. ECU: *Eve's hand snatches the statuette.*

1207. MS, *as in 1205: Eve snatches the statuette from Vandamm and runs off to the left. Vandamm, Leonard, and Valerian react with surprise, watching her go.*

1208. LS (*matte*): *Eve rushes toward the car, which stops for her.*

VANDAMM (*offscreen*): Get that figure back from her!

1209. M S , *as in 1207: Leonard and Valerian rush off to the left. Vandamm remains behind.*

1210. L S *(matte), as in 1208: Leonard and Valerian run toward the car. They arrive just as Eve climbs in and slams the door. The car speeds off.*
Nondiegetic music begins and continues to the end of the film.

1211. M S : *Vandamm looks offscreen left at the departing car.*

Car, interior, night

1212. M C U : *a low-angle view of Roger and Eve, seen from below the steering column. Eve holds the statuette in her lap.*

> R O G E R :   The housekeeper had me pinned down for five minutes before I realized it was that same silly gun of yours. (*Looking down to the statuette in Eve's lap.*) I see you've got the pumpkin.

> E V E :   Yes.

Gate, exterior, night

1213. L S   *(studio interior): moving away from the camera, the car arrives at the gate at the end of the driveway, where the doors are closed. Roger stops the car and runs out to open them.*

1214. M C U   *(studio interior): in the left foreground, Eve turns and looks behind her out the car window. In the distance, Roger bends to examine the locked gate.*

1215. L S   *(matte): Eve's P O V , looking up the road at the house. Leonard and Valerian are running down the road toward the camera.*

1216. M C U   *(studio interior), as in 1214: Eve gets out of the car and runs over to the gate, carrying the statuette. The camera tilts up slightly to follow her. She stops Roger and points down the road behind the camera. Roger takes her hand and together they run off to the left, leaving the car behind.*

Forest, exterior, night

1217. M S   *(studio interior): the camera tracks left as Roger and Eve run through a forest of slender trees.*

1218. L S   *(studio interior): Leonard and Valerian, bearing flashlights, run through the forest toward the camera.*

1219. M S   *(studio interior): Roger and Eve run forward. Her wrap snags on a tree, and Roger tries to free her.*

1220. L S   *(studio interior): Leonard and Valerian run into a small clearing. They pause, looking around.*

1221. M S   *(studio interior), as in 1217: Roger and Eve abandon the wrap. They run forward, exiting at the left of the frame.*

1222. L S   *(studio interior), as in 1218: Leonard and Valerian split up; Valerian exits at the left, and Leonard moves forward through the trees, exiting at the right.*

Mount Rushmore, exterior, night

1223. L S (*studio interior*): *Roger and Eve reach the edge of the woods, where several trees have been cut. They run forward across a bare space, into* M S. *Suddenly they stop, looking offscreen to the right rear of the camera.*

1224. E L S (*matte*): *Roger and Eve's* P O V. *In the distance are the tops of three gigantic stone heads, perched on the edge of a mountain.*

1225. M S (*studio interior*), *as at end of 1223.*
R O G E R : This is no good, we're on top of the monument!
They turn and look off to the left.

1226. L S (*studio interior*): *Roger and Eve's* P O V. *In the distance, a flashlight is moving toward them through the woods.*

1227. M S (*studio interior*), *as in 1223: Eve turns and looks over her shoulder to the right. She signals Roger, who also turns.*

1228. L S (*studio interior*): *Roger and Eve's* P O V. *Another flashlight is approaching through another part of the woods.*

1229. M S (*studio interior*), *as in 1225: Roger looks around in frustration; then he takes Eve by the hand and leads her forward. They exit to the right rear of the camera.*

1230. M S (*process*): *Roger and Eve are viewed in profile, running along as if they were hanging in space. In the background, we see nothing but sky and a distant line of hills.*

1231. E L S (*matte*): *a low-angle view, looking up at the carved faces of Mount Rushmore. Eve and Roger are visible as tiny figures atop Thomas Jefferson's head.*

1232. M S (*process*), *as in 1230: Roger and Eve stop, unsure of their footing. They look straight down.*

1233. L S (*matte*): *Roger and Eve's* P O V, *looking down the cliff, toward Jefferson's nose and Abraham Lincoln's face.*
E V E : What do we do?
R O G E R : Climb down.
E V E : We can't!

1234. L S (*process*): *Roger and Eve are viewed from behind as they clasp hands and start down the rocky edge of the monument. Roger holds the pre-Colombian statuette. In the background is Lincoln's face.*
R O G E R : Here they come. We have no choice!

1235. E L S (*matte*): *a low-angle view, looking up at the monument. Roger and Eve are visible as tiny figures moving down the rocky space between George Washington and Jefferson.*

1236. M S (*process*): *at the left of the screen, Roger and Eve cling to a small stone ledge. They turn and look down.*

1237. L S : *Roger and Eve's* P O V, *looking down the pale mountainside toward the rocky ground.*

1238. ELS (*matte*): *a high-angle view above the monument. Valerian runs to the edge of the cliff and looks down.*

1239. MS, *as in 1236: Roger and Eve move down the side of the mountain, holding onto a narrow stone ledge.*

1240. LS (*process*): *Valerian tries to work his way down another section of the monument. Behind him is the huge profile of Washington.*

1241. LS (*process*): *from another spot on the monument, Leonard also begins to climb down.*

1242. ELS (*matte*): *a high-angle shot of Washington's profile, jutting out from the side of the mountain. At the extreme left is the small figure of Valerian, climbing down the sheer rocks.*

1243. ELS (*matte*): *an extremely low-angle shot, looking up toward Jefferson's left nostril. At the left of the frame, Roger and Eve are seen as tiny figures, climbing down.*

1244. MS (*process*): *a high-angle shot, looking down at Roger and Eve, who are holding onto a corrugated stone ledge. They both look up, facing the camera. Eve struggles to catch her breath.*

　　ROGER:　Well, if we ever get out of this alive, let's go back to New York on the train together. All right?

　　EVE (*breathing heavily and trying to smile*):　Is that a proposition?

　　ROGER (*smiling*):　It's a proposal, sweetie.

　　EVE:　What happened to the first two marriages?

　　ROGER:　My wives divorced me.

　　EVE:　Why?

　　ROGER:　Oh, I think they said I led too dull a life. (*Eve struggles to laugh.*) Come on. (*Roger turns and starts to move down.*)

1245. INSERT: *Roger's right foot and Eve's left foot, standing on the narrow ledge. The heel of Eve's high-heeled shoe breaks.*

1246. MS (*process*), *as in 1244: Eve loses her hold and starts to fall. She screams.*

1247. LS (*process*): *as Eve slides down, she reaches up to grab at Roger. In the distance, we can see Jefferson's nose and Lincoln's face.*

1248. INSERT: *Eve's hand grasps Roger's hip pocket, but the pocket tears loose and she continues to fall.*

1249. LS (*process*), *as in 1247: Eve slides out of sight. Roger, still clinging to the rocks, turns and looks down.*

1250. CU (*studio interior*): *Roger looks down, holding tight to the pre-Columbian statuette with his free arm.*

1251. LS (*process*): *Eve slides farther down the monument, but manages to stop herself near a rocky outcrop. Grimacing in pain, she holds fast to the stone. Beyond her, we can see Jefferson's mouth and Lincoln's head.*

1252. CU (*studio interior*), *as in 1250: looking down, Roger moves toward Eve. He exits the shot at the bottom of the frame.*

1253. L S (*process*), *as in 1251: Eve rubs her elbow and crouches against the mountain. Roger makes his way down beside her.*
1254. M C U (*studio interior*): *still holding the statuette, Roger kneels beside Eve.*
    ROGER: You all right?
    They embrace.
1255. E L S (*matte*), *as in 1242: Valerian is still inching his way down the monument.*
1256. M C U (*studio interior*), *as in 1254: Roger helps Eve remove her jacket. They embrace again, and Roger momentarily comforts her. Then they begin to move downward again.*
    ROGER: Okay. Okay, come on.
    EVE (*gasping*): I'm out of breath.
    ROGER: I'll help. Okay, come on. Come on.
1257. E L S (*matte*): *a low-angle shot, looking up at Washington's head. To the left, Valerian is climbing down the mountain. To the right, on the opposite side of Washington, Roger and Eve are also climbing down.*
1258. L S (*process*): *Valerian makes his way down the rocks.*
1259. E L S (*m a t t e*) : *on the opposite side of the monument, Leonard is climbing down. He defies gravity by hanging on to a rock wall that tilts out over the abyss. Beyond him to the left are the profiles of Lincoln and Jefferson; in the extreme distance, barely visible as dark specks on the far*

side of Jefferson's nose, are Roger and Eve. Leonard loses his footing on
the narrow ledge, and his flashlight slides from his pocket.

1260. MCU *(studio interior)*: *a reverse angle, showing Leonard as he grimaces*
and hangs from the stone ledge.

1261. MCU *(studio interior)*: *Leonard's feet, dangling from the rock.*

1262. ELS *(matte)*, *as in 1257: Leonard loses his grip and falls.*

1263. ELS *(matte)*: *a low-angle view, looking up at the side of Lincoln's face.*
In the foreground at the right, Leonard tumbles down the rocks, landing
hard but safely on a stone outcrop. He gets slowly to his knees.

1264. LS *(studio interior)*: *Roger and Eve climb down the monument, balanc-*
ing on the narrow ledges that have been cut into the mountainside. She
has abandoned her shoes. They pause to catch their breath, looking down
to the right. The camera tracks forward to view them in MS.

1265. ELS *(matte)*: *Roger and Eve's* POV, *looking toward the stone heads of*
Theodore Roosevelt and Lincoln.

1266. MS *(studio interior)*, *as at end of 1262: Roger turns and looks off to the*
left.

1267. ELS *(matte)*: *an extremely low-angle shot, looking up the profile of*
Washington.

1268. MS *(studio interior)*, *as in 1266: Roger looks forward and slightly down.*

1269. ELS *(matte)*: *Roger's* POV, *looking beyond the stone rim of the monument*
toward the ground far below. In the distance, the treetops are quite small.

1270. MS *(process)*: *Roger clasps Eve's hand, motions to the right, and moves*
off with her.

1271. LS *(matte)*: *Roger and Eve move to the right and pause beside a sheer*
cliff edge. Standing with their backs to the camera, they look down. Be-
yond them are the gigantic heads of Jefferson, Roosevelt, and Lincoln.

1272. MS *(process)*: *Roger and Eve stand in profile at the left of the screen.*
She looks down and he looks off to the right. Behind them is Jefferson's
chin and Roosevelt's right eye.

1273. ELS *(matte)*: *Roger's* POV. *In the distance, just to the right of Lincoln's*
beard, is the small figure of Leonard.

1274. MS *(process)*, *as in 1272: Roger points toward Leonard with the pre-*
Columbian statuette. He and Eve turn and run off to the left.

1275. ELS *(matte)*: *Roger and Eve scurry across the edge of a cliff, moving to-*
ward the camera. In the distance is Jefferson's chin; behind it are the
heads of Roosevelt and Lincoln. Slowly, Roger and Eve begin to climb
over a large rock.

1276. LS *(matte)*: *a closer view of Roger and Eve as they climb up the rock.*
Parts of Jefferson, Roosevelt, and Lincoln are visible in the background.

1277. LS *(matte)*: *Leonard is gaining on Roger and Eve. He has traversed the*
space below Lincoln, Roosevelt, and Jefferson, and is climbing up a bare
rock, moving toward the camera.

1278. L S (*matte*): *Roger and Eve slide carefully down the smooth rocks beneath Washington's chin. Roger jumps down to a small ledge, and
reaches up to help Eve.*

1279. L S (*matte*): *A slightly closer view of Roger and Eve from the opposite
side. At the left of the frame, she jumps down to stand with Roger on the
ledge. In the distance is Lincoln's head. Roger and Eve turn to the left
and begin moving quickly along the side of the mountain. The camera
tracks left, following them.*

1280. M S (*matte*): *Leonard moves toward the camera. Behind him we can see
Jefferson's chin and Roosevelt's face. He advances farther, passing out of
sight at the bottom of the frame.*

1281. M S (*studio interior*): *their backs to the mountain, Roger and Eve hold
hands, moving to the left along a stone ledge. As they pass a large boulder, the camera tracks back to L S. At the upper left of the screen is
Valerian, crouched and ready to pounce on Roger.*

1282. C U (*studio interior*): *a slightly high-angle view of Eve, following
behind Roger. As she passes the boulder, she looks up to the left and
screams.*

1283. M S (*process*): *a low-angle view from behind Roger and Eve, looking between their shoulders toward Valerian. He dives forward onto Roger, and
both men go flying offscreen at the left. The camera pans slightly to the
right, framing Eve in C U as she catches the pre-Columbian statuette,
turns, and screams.*

1284. LS (*process*): *Eve's* POV, *looking down the mountain. Roger and Valerian, locked in a struggle, are tumbling over a rocky ledge. In the extreme distance we can see the ground.*

1285. CU (*process*), *as at end of 1283: Eve screams.*

1286. LS (*process*), *as in 1284: Roger and Valerian tumble to the edge of a precipice.*

1287. CU (*process*), *as in 1285: Eve bites her knuckles.*

1288. MS (*process*): *at the edge of the cliff, Valerian is crouched over Roger with a knife. Roger holds Valerian by the wrist, struggling to avoid being stabbed. Then, summoning all his strength, he shoves Valerian away, pushing him over the cliff. Roger turns slightly to the left and looks down.*

1289. LS (*matte*): *Roger's* POV. *Valerian goes falling head over heels away from the camera, straight down the side of the mountain. We hear his scream as he falls.*

1290. MS (*process*), *as in 1288: leaning on his elbow, Roger watches Valerian fall. Offscreen, Eve cries out. Roger turns, looking to the right.*

1291. LS (*studio interior*): *Roger's* POV. *A low-angle shot looking up toward Eve, who is struggling with Leonard for possession of the pre-Columbian statuette.*

1292. MS (*process*), *as in 1290: Roger jumps to his feet, moving up toward Eve.*

1293. LS (*studio interior*), *as in 1291: Leonard seizes the statuette, knocks Eve to the ground, and shoves her over the edge of the cliff.*

1294. M S *(process), as at end of 1292: the camera tracks up the sloping mountainside with Roger as he scrambles toward Eve. He stops beside a large rock and leans forward, looking down.*

1295. L S *(process): Roger's* P O V *. An extremely high-angle shot, looking down the side of the mountain. Eve is clinging by her hands to the very edge of the rocks. She looks up at the camera in terror. In the extreme distance, on the ground below, we can see a large forest and the lighted windows of the Mount Rushmore observatory.*

1296. L S *(process): a level view along the side of the mountain. At the bottom of the screen, Eve clings to the rocks; at the top, Roger reaches down for her. They try to join hands, but they are too far apart. Roger inches down a bit farther, balancing precariously on a narrow foothold.*

1297. L S *(studio interior): a low-angle view of Leonard, who stands holding the pre-Columbian statuette, looking down toward Roger and Eve.*

1298. M S *(process): an extremely high-angle view of Eve, who grasps the rocks with her fingertips and faces the camera. In the foreground, Roger reaches down to try to grasp her hand.*

1299. E C U *(studio interior): Eve's hand reaches upward from the bottom of the screen, and Roger's hand reaches down from the top. They struggle to meet. In the background, we can see that Roger's foot has a narrow toe-hold on the mountain.*

1300. C U *(process): Eve's stockinged feet slip from under her, and she starts to drop.*

1301. E C U *(studio interior), as in 1299: Roger's hand reaches down and catches Eve's hand just as she begins to fall.*

1302. M S *(process), as in 1298: Roger holds Eve in his right hand and grasps the edge of the cliff with his left.*

1303. L S *(process), as in 1296: Eve dangles from the mountainside, held by Roger.*

1304. M S *(process), as in 1302: Roger holds onto Eve.*

1305. I N S E R T *(studio interior): Roger's left hand begins to slip.*

1306. M S *(process), as in 1304: Roger strains to hold on. He turns and looks up toward the camera.*

1307. L S *, as in 1297: Leonard looks down.*

1308. M S *, as in 1306: Roger looks up at Leonard.*
R O G E R *(to Leonard):* Help!

1309. L S *(studio interior), as in 1307: Leonard steps forward and down into* M S *.*
R O G E R *(offscreen):* Help me!

1310. C U *(studio interior): straining to hold Eve, Roger looks toward the camera, aiming his gaze just beyond the upper right of the frame.*

1311. M S *(studio interior), as in 1309: Leonard is approaching the camera, stepping down to the edge of the cliff. He stops, and the camera tracks in to* C U *, showing Roger's left hand clinging to the rock ledge beside*

Leonard's foot. The camera tracks farther, moving to ECU *as Leonard lifts his foot and steps on Roger's fingers.*

1312. CU (*studio interior*), *as in 1310: Roger winces in pain.*

1313. MCU (*studio interior*): *a low-angle view, looking up at Leonard, who grasps the pre-Columbian statuette and gazes down with a sadistic expression.*

1314. CU (*process*): *Eve looks offscreen slightly to the right of the camera, toward Leonard.*

1315. INSERT (*studio interior*): *Leonard's foot mashes down on Roger's fingers. Suddenly, from offscreen, we hear a shot. The foot turns sideways and falls off to the right, leaving Roger's hand free.*

1316. INSERT (*studio interior*): *The pre-Columbian statuette falls to the rocks and breaks open, spilling out a roll of film.*

1317. MCU (*studio interior*), *as in 1313: his mouth open and his eyes rolling back, Leonard pitches forward and falls slowly out of the frame to the lower right.*

1318. LS (*process*): *a low-angle view looking up at Eve and Roger, who are hanging onto the mountainside. Leonard falls past them and out of the frame at the bottom right.*

1319. ELS (*matte*): *a low-angle view of a group of men standing atop the monument in the far distance.*

1320. LS (*process*): *a closer view of the group atop the monument. We see the Professor, three state troopers, and a plainclothes agent. To the left of the screen, guarded by one of the troopers, is Vandamm. To the right, a trooper is returning his gun to its holster.*

   PROFESSOR: Thank you, Sergeant.

   VANDAMM: That wasn't very sporting, using real bullets!

1321. CU (*process*): *Roger faces the camera, looking offscreen to the lower left. He struggles to grasp Eve.*

   ROGER: Here, reach. Now. . . .

1322. CU (*process*), *as in 1314.*

   EVE: I'm trying!

1323. ECU (*process*): *the same angle as in 1321, but a closer view of Roger.*

   ROGER: Come on, I've got you!

1324. ECU (*process*): *Eve's face, looking slightly to the right of the camera. She struggles to reach up.*

   ROGER (*offscreen*): Up!

   EVE: I can't make it!

1325. ECU (*studio interior*), *as in 1323.*

   ROGER: Yes you can.

1326. ECU (*process*), *as in 1324: Eve struggles, moving toward the camera.*

   ROGER (*offscreen*): Come on.

   The nondiegetic music modulates from the suspense theme to the love theme.

   EVE (*desperately*): Pull harder!

1327. ECU (*studio interior*), *as in 1325.*

   ROGER (*his eyes smiling*): Come along, Mrs. Thornhill!

1328. ECU (*process*), *as in 1326: Eve grimaces and struggles forward.*

   A Sleeping Compartment on the Twentieth-Century Limited, interior, night

1329. CU: *Roger smiles and pulls Eve up beside him. The camera moves back to a low-angle* MS, *revealing that Roger and Eve are sitting on the top berth of a sleeping compartment aboard the Twentieth-Century Limited. The camera continues to move back and Roger and Eve embrace, dangling their feet over the edge of the berth. She is wearing white pajamas, and he is dressed as he was on the mountainside.*

   EVE (*laughing*): Oh, Roger, this is silly!

   ROGER: I know, but I'm sentimental.

   They kiss. As Roger's arm encircles Eve, we see bandages on the fingers of his left hand.

Countryside, exterior, night

1330. L s : *a high-angle view of the train, which is speeding away from the cam* *era and entering a tunnel in a mountainside.* "THE END" appears at the center of the screen, with "NORTH BY NORTHWEST" at the lower left and the MGM logo at the lower right.

Interviews, Reviews, and Commentaries

Interviews

A brilliant self-publicist, Hitchcock was a willing subject for interviewers, and he never seemed to tire of recounting the same anecdotes over and over. Of the scores of interviews he granted, some of the best were with the French critics at *Cahiers du Cinéma,* who were serious students of his work. The example reprinted here is from a conversation with Jean Domarchi and Jean Douchet (the latter a particularly intelligent analyst of Hitchcock's major films of the 1950s and 1960s) on the occasion of the French premiere of *North by Northwest*. It appears in English for the first time, translated by Lahcen Hassad and Darlene Sadlier.

Screenwriter Ernest Lehman was interviewed about *North by Northwest* on several occasions, and he sometimes wrote fondly about his experiences with Hitchcock in a column for *American Film* magazine. He was a major figure in Hollywood during the 1950s and 1960s, whose other screen credits include *Executive Suite* (1954), *Sabrina* (1954), *Sweet Smell of Success* (1957), *West Side Story* (1961), and *Who's Afraid of Virginia Woolf?* (1966). In *The Prize* (1963, directed by Mark Robson), he enlivened his adaptation of an Irving Wallace novel by borrowing some of his own ideas from *North by Northwest*. He also worked for Hitchcock on another occasion, writing the screenplay for the director's last film, *Family Plot* (1976). He is interviewed here by John Brady.

An Interview with Alfred Hitchcock

Jean Domarchi and Jean Douchet

O n his way through Paris for the opening of *North by Northwest,* Alfred
Hitchcock was kind enough to give us a long interview. Avoiding the
questions dealt with by Claude Chabrol and François Truffaut,[1] we asked
him, this time, to respond to certain critical points and to make us privy to some of
his professional secrets.

A Big Mistake

Which of your last two films do you like better?

Vertigo and *North by Northwest* don't have much in common and weren't
produced in the same spirit. *Vertigo* is a psychological fairy tale, close to necro-
philia. The hero wants to make love to a dead woman. But *North by Northwest* is
an adventure film, treated with a certain levity of spirit. *Vertigo* is much more
important to me than *North by Northwest,* which is nevertheless a very entertaining film.

*Your film seems to be made up of a series of brilliant scenes that don't always have
a specific relationship to the general theme of the story. Thus, when Cary Grant
comes in through the window. . . .*

Yes, it doesn't have any relationship to the story. It's a joke. That's because,
when someone enters by the door, it doesn't give the scene its proper movement.
It's always necessary to have something that really fills things up.

North by Northwest *takes up the themes of most of your films. For example, the
innocent and unjustly accused man in* The Wrong Man.

Don't think I'm just repeating myself over and over again. Painters always paint
the same flower; they begin painting it when they have no experience, and then
they paint it anew based on all the experience they've acquired. There's a very big
difference. Yes, the theme is that of *The Wrong Man:* the innocent man. If I use this
theme, it's because it helps me to resolve an important part of my artistic and

1. "Entretien avec Alfred Hitchcock," *Cahiers du Cinéma* 44 (February 1955): 19–31.

Translated by Lahcen Hassad and Darlene Sadlier from "Entretien avec Alfred Hitchcock," *Cahiers du
Cinéma* 102 (December 1959), 17–28. Reprinted by permission.

technical work. I have strong feelings about the art of cinema, but I don't believe in dialogue. I create suspense, and I'm trying to play with the audience like a cat with a mouse. In order, therefore, to make the audience feel anxiety, suspense, etc., one has to have a hero with whom they can identify. I believe it's useless to try to make them understand the feelings of a gangster. It's impossible because they don't know that kind of individual. But the man on the street, the ordinary man, is someone they understand. It's as if they had become an integral part of the adventures told by the film.

In North by Northwest *you appear to be remaking* Saboteur. *Why?*
Because I wasn't satisfied with *Saboteur.* The heroes weren't interesting; the actors weren't good enough. And it wasn't a true film. It had a lot of bad things, many huge mistakes in the Statue of Liberty scene, for example. . . .

Yes!
Well! Tell me what those mistakes are.

The scene was implausible.
No, that's not it at all. The villain was in danger, not the hero. This is very important for the spectator. If it's good, he goes away happy. If not, he feels that it isn't good without knowing why.

Art before Democracy

Did you choose Mount Rushmore and the Statue of Liberty because of their moral significance for the American spectator or as dramatic décor?
As dramatic décor. For me, art comes before democracy. In the case of Mount Rushmore, I managed to strike a compromise with the authorities. They didn't want any gunshots or violent scenes on the monument or with the monument in the background. I said "very well" and I honored the terms of our agreement. I showed the heroes on the rocks *beside* the monument. You may have noticed there is no violence *on* the monument. I kept my promise. But later on, the authorities decided to suppress all mention of themselves in the credits. They said, "Even if nothing was shot on the monument, the public will still think it was shot there." I think they were unhappy because in the course of the film one of their forest rangers knocks down Cary Grant. That scene bothered them.

During the first two hours the physical action in your film seems perfectly suited to the expression of certain emotions, but in the end the picture suffers from a separation of its elements. The photography and colors in the climactic scene aren't as beautiful as in the other scenes.

That's because I had to respect the terms of the agreement. As it is, the scene is the best we could do under those conditions. It was difficult to do. We had to make sure that everyone could see all the tiny figures in the image. And we had a lot of difficulty getting the right balance of colors.

The Moving-Around Principle

Was it Mount Rushmore itself that prompted you to make the film or was it the idea of a chase film that came first?

The idea of the cinematographic chase fascinated me twenty-five years ago. In those days, I understood that the chase film was ideal from a cinematic point of view, not only because it allowed a lot of action, but mostly because the idea of a chase makes possible lots of changes in background scenery. I don't know why. That's the way it is. But just as the film—be it in preparation, in the camera, or in the projection booth—has to move around, so in the same way I think the story has to move around also. This may well be a foolish association of ideas. In fact, whenever I have the business of the story to consider, the first question I ask myself is: "In what direction are we going?"

Example: in 1936 I adapted Somerset Maugham's "Ashenden." Do you know Maugham? He was a spy in Geneva during World War I. He wrote "Ashenden" and he chose Switzerland as its setting. I wondered: since it's set in Switzerland, let's see what they have there. It would be interesting to show that they have chocolate, lakes, the Alps, and also their special Swiss dances. Having set a film in a particular place, one has to use that place in a dramatic way. In other words, when there is movement, one has to ask whether there is anything in that particular setting that contributes to it. If there are scenes of movement in a particular setting, one has to use the setting in a dramatic way, and not just show it simply to make a pretty picture.

For example, in the film *The Secret Agent,* the spectator knows that a man intends to kill another man. On a battlefield, we kill people, but we don't know whom we kill. If you're told, "You're ordered to kill him, that specific guy over there," that seems against the rules of war. In my film, where does this very important event take place? In Switzerland. The hero, John Gielgud, for whom a similar problem of conscience arises, climbs up the mountain accompanied by Peter Lorre, the killer, and Percy Marmont, the intended victim. At a certain moment, Gielgud gets scared. He doesn't want to climb any further. He stops at an observation point and watches the other two climb through a telescope. Thus I've used the Alps in a dramatic way. In the telescope, he clearly sees the two men, who are very far away. He shouts, "Watch out!" but of course that doesn't do any good, for, although they're close by in the telescope, in reality they're far away and can't hear him.

Likewise, in *North by Northwest,* a particular setting is used dramatically on the two occasions when Cary Grant manages to escape. First, in Chicago, he succeeds in evading the police disguised as a porter in a red cap. Porters in red caps are one of the characteristic features of Chicago. Then, at the auction, he manages to escape from Mason. He kicks up a row to get the police to come. He takes advantage of the setting. This kind of scene is very difficult to find. Twice as difficult as in an ordinary story; it's very different. One can constantly say: "I want things like this or that." The script writer will answer: "Impossible." Me, I tell him: "This must be in the film."

The theme of the chase gives me the chance to develop original ideas, but I must insist upon very strict rules of composition.

A Piece of Cake, Not a Slice of Life

The credits and opening shot in your films have always been of great importance. Hence in North by Northwest. . . .

The graphic designs correspond to a genuine architecture. At the beginning I shot various scenes in New York, and the shots inspired the credits by Saul Bass. He made drawings that perfectly matched the image. As for the opening shot, it's important for me because most of the time it sets the mood. I don't know, however, if it's good to have a very important shot in the beginning. Often, in the movie house, people are still prattling, getting a seat, or finishing their peanuts at the end of the first reel. It's good, if possible, to shock the spectator. We must struggle in our own way against the prattlers and those who take five minutes to get seated. That's why, after the credits, I sometimes put in some very dramatic shots. Like in *Vertigo.* But notice that a lot of my good films have very ordinary credits. Often, once the film is over, the audience has completely forgotten the beginning.

In North by Northwest, *Cary Grant must constantly struggle with the outside world and the objects that surround him and conflict with his desire.*

For me, this opposition between persons and things is absolutely fundamental; it shows the problems ordinary people have to deal with when they are placed in extraordinary situations. Conflict is the basis of all drama. That's why humor is so important. Humor is the loss of dignity, it's the loss of the normal, it's therefore the abnormal. Spectators who go to movies lead normal lives. But they go there to see extraordinary things, to see nightmares. For me, the cinema is not a slice of life but a piece of cake.

So that the spectator can fully appreciate the value of the abnormal, it should be presented in the most realistic way possible. The spectator can always tell whether what is represented is true or not. He gets uneasy if he has doubts about the accuracy of certain details. If he didn't, I wouldn't be able to create suspense. It's very important to have real suspense. It's important that nothing be left in the mind of the spectator except suspense.

Nothing in the World Is as Dull as Logic

But Mr. Hitchcock, you say that you give great importance to the exactness of details. Yet your films often seem illogical. At the beginning of North by Northwest, *what happens to Cary Grant seems unbelievable. What were his friends doing at this time?*

But you forget that he disappears for only two or three hours. It's the time factor that's in play. Have you ever come home late in the evening? Your family wouldn't be as worried as you might think. Someone once asked me how in the first scene in *Vertigo* Stewart got down from the roof of the house. The answer is: he went down the fire escape. I didn't film this scene because it would've been very tedious.

The Confession of a Mormon

How can the hands of the hero stand the pressure of the foot which stamps on them in North by Northwest *and* Strangers on a Train?

I'll show you. Come here. Put out your hands. I'll put my foot on them. But mind you, I weigh a hundred kilos.

When I have to deal with this kind of question, I resort to an old maxim of mine: nothing in the world is as dull as logic. I use the same logic as the Mormons. Do you know the Mormons? When kids ask them difficult questions, they tell them: "Get lost."

There's something more important than logic, and that's imagination. If we insist on always thinking in logical terms, we will never use our imagination. Sometimes, when I'm working with my scriptwriter, I suggest something to him. "Not possible!" he says. But the idea is good, even if the logic isn't. Logic, we should pitch out the window!

If logic is less important than imagination, does it mean that those films of yours that are based on logic are less important for you?

Yes, less important, especially *The Wrong Man*. Everything in *The Wrong Man* is true. The judge is the same one as in the real story. We shot the film in the same prison, in the real prison. But I don't like the way the film is constructed. In the first part, the man is the star; in the second part, it's the woman. You cast off the man and then you say: "Here's the woman." For me, that's not good; it's an error. *The Wrong Man,* that was me. I was unable to change the film because it was based entirely on reality. It was a failure.

What, then, is the deep logic of your films?
To make the spectator suffer.

I Do Not Know This Woman

Allow me to go back to what we were talking about a moment ago. Why does Mason begin by drawing the curtains in the first scene of North by Northwest, *in which he meets Grant?*
He thinks it makes it possible for him to resort to violence. Since it isn't his house, he has to be careful.

In this scene, Mason's alleged wife comes in looking for her husband so that he can welcome his guests. She doesn't try to hide anything from them because they don't exist, at least that seems to be the case.
I don't know anything. I don't know the woman in question. I've never had the pleasure of meeting her. I don't know why she came in and why she said that. I don't know her. Behind every mystery there's always an explanation. But that's the subject of my next film. . . . I could have shown the guests having dinner. But to show everything, I would have had to make an eight-hour film.

There is an opposition between shadow and light in your films. Have you been influenced by the expressionists or the work of Fritz Lang?
There are no symbols in *North by Northwest*. Oh yes! One. The last shot, the train entering the tunnel after the love scene between Grant and Eva Marie Saint. It's a phallic symbol. But don't tell anyone.

I Am O

Yet in Vertigo *a shadow becomes a nun.*
That's for a purely dramatic reason. Kim Novak is not in her normal state of mind. She thinks that the dead woman has returned (the shadow of the dead) and right after that she kills herself. It's an apparition of the dead that kills her.

As for expressionism, I say to you that I've been influenced by no one. I never go to the movies. In thirty-five years I've only once been on another set, when I was made to visit Paramount Studios. I'm too nervous to be able to stay on a set.

I never look in a viewfinder. I take a pencil and draw a plan for the cameraman when there's a difficulty. My film is finished before being shot. That's why it took me a year to prepare *North by Northwest*. If I go to the rushes afterward, it's to see if the hair and the face of Eva Marie Saint are as they should be. I know everything.

When you imagine a scene, what is the most important thing for you?

Its significance for the whole picture. It's a piece of the whole. Not only the dialogue and acting, but, just as important, the dramatic objective of the scene; everything should serve a specific purpose: colors, atmosphere, everything. For example, in the scene at the United Nations, I wanted to create an atmosphere out of nothing. As in *Strangers on a Train,* in the scene in which the silhouette of Walker appears against the monument. These are the kind of scenes that have nothing clichéd about them. It's always necessary to have striking settings in the film.

Which lines dominate in a composition?

The horizontal and the vertical. In cinema, there are only two dimensions. Depth of field doesn't count for anything, except the illusion of the moment. Everything is round for me; it's a question of temperament. I'm a round temperament. I am O, others are I.

In your films, the most impressive design seems to be the spiral, the serpentine.

I use it to avoid clichés. In *Vertigo,* Stewart kisses Novak in the stable just before she dies. The cliché would be to have a close-up. . . . One must feel the scene, not see it. That's why I made that turning movement. The feeling that the camera expresses should correspond to the kiss itself. In that way, I let the spectator get into the scene, to form a ménage à trois. I never change the size of the frame in a love scene. There should be no interruption, because, in reality, there's no interruption. All the man needs to do is look into the girl's eyes. Meanwhile, his left hand is otherwise occupied. The single shot preserves good taste.

In the love scene on the train in North by Northwest, the camera shifts from the outside to the inside of the train, giving the impression of movement, of sliding.

This way the spectators don't forget they're in a train. The cliché would be to make two separate shots, with the second one showing the train passing by. It would make one believe the purpose was to watch the train pass. And that's much too static. I should have shot everything inside a real train, at the very hour when the action was taking place. We could have built a platform with a camera in the train.

You don't use the "five-minute take" any more. Weren't you satisfied with the results?

In *Under Capricorn,* that technique didn't suit the subject. In *Rope,* since the subject was out of the ordinary, it required a technique that was equally extraordinary. The film begins at 7:30 P.M. and ends at 9:00 P.M. I wanted the technique to represent the flow of time.

The entire setting of Rope is constructed lengthwise. Why not a right-angle décor?

You don't have perspective. It's necessary to have the kind of perspective that allows for the discovery of other rooms. It's more realistic that way.

It's the most successful technical work I've done, but also the most underrated. The change in lighting was so well done that nobody noticed it. The film begins in broad daylight and ends in the dark of night. There's no transparency, no faking.

At Last Man Created the Zoom

Are variations in lenses used for dramatic purposes in your films?

I sometimes use wide-angle framing because it gives me a very broad perspective. The most sophisticated technique in *Vertigo,* and the most successful, involved the sensation of vertigo itself. I have tried to represent that sensation on the screen for twenty years now. No one has ever succeeded in doing that. I tried it in 1939 with *Rebecca.* Joan Fontaine starts fainting and everything becomes blurred. It wasn't good; it wasn't what I wanted. I wanted to give the impression that she was fainting, to show the room receding away from her. Very far, very far away, like when you're drunk.

What's most interesting to me is the idea of changing perspective within the same shot. To start with a normal vision and end with an unusual one. There have been attempts to do that, but they all failed because the image gives the impression of moving. It wasn't possible. When you look at a wall, the wall stays as it is. It's neither bigger nor smaller. That was the reason the attempts failed.

At last came the zoom, which has been perfected lately. One uses the dolly with the zoom to get the effect one wants. It's very complicated. The variation of lenses during the movement of the camera, thanks to the zoom, gives exceptional dramatic effects. . . .

The United Nations scene in *North by Northwest* has a very dramatic effect. Cary Grant has a knife in his hand. The photographer takes a picture of him and then we see him running through the garden of the building. We have the impression that the whole world is conspiring against his small silhouette.

In *Vertigo* also, the fall during the nightmare scene had a very dramatic effect. It defined Stewart's mental depression. It's truly the desire to return to death. He goes straight down toward his grave. . . .

A Story Full of Charm and Blood

What will your next film be then?

Psycho. P-S-Y-C-H-O.

With Anthony Perkins, Janet Leigh, and Vera Miles. I want to give these last two the roles of average young American women, very normal and very ordinary. It's the story of a young man who manages a motel. You know what a motel is? He lives with his old mother in an old mansion behind the motel, built in the gothic style like the old-fashioned houses in *Vertigo*. And the old woman is a homicidal maniac. But he loves her so much that he hides her in a room and refuses to denounce her to the police. It's a horror movie.

Mr. Hitchcock, your conception of life seems to be very pessimistic. In your films, the villains are always more interesting, more fascinating, than the good guys.

That's true. The villain is always much more interesting. It's like that in life. That's reality, logic.

Psycho won't be a superproduction, but it will be a very strange film. I'll shoot it in Hollywood. I'll build the house and the motel in the big old studios of Universal. It will be easier to shoot there.

It will be a film full of charm and blood. There will be a lot, a lot of blood. Saul Bass will help me with certain lighting compositions.

Of course Robert Burks will be your cameraman.

No. It'll be Jack Russell, who's a specialist in television and black and white. He's very good.[2] When I hired Burks, he was just an honest cameraman at Warners. But I taught him to change his method, to be much more careful. Now that he has a name to defend, he's very careful. Too much so: he's very slow, that's his biggest problem.

I prefer employing television cameramen because they know how to work very quickly. And I want to shoot quickly: I don't want to make an expensive movie because, in all honesty, I don't know if it's going to be successful or not. It's very, very out of the ordinary.

2. So good that we owe him the camera movements of Fuller's *Park Row,* which are among the most beautiful of our time [*Cahiers'* note].

An Interview with Ernest Lehman

John Brady

Brady: *North by Northwest* is such a picaresque script—and you say that you practically lived the Cary Grant role?

Lehman: I'll tell you what I did. I went to New York, went to the United Nations, and spent five days there. I knew there was going to be a sequence in the United Nations, knew I needed a murder to take place there. I spent time in the delegates' lounge, sat around listening to people being paged on the public address system, watched colorful figures come and go. I thought, "Good, it's perfect." It's a great-looking room. It could be a *great* place for a murder. Well, that stuck in my head. In the script I called it the public lounge. Then I went out to Glen Cove, because I knew the Soviet Union's United Nations delegation lived in a mansion there. I met a judge in Glen Cove who happened to have gone to school with somebody I knew in California. He proved most cooperative. I didn't drop in on him unannounced. I told him I was writing a movie and needed a sequence in which a man gets picked up for drunk driving—would he please put me through the whole thing? And he did. I went through the whole damn experience that I wrote for Cary Grant later. They brought in a doctor who gave me an examination as though I were drunk, and I learned the tests he would give me, and whether they would allow me a telephone call, and what words they would use as they bring you into the station house. To me that's good research, and helps in the writing of a screenplay.

Then I went to Grand Central Station, roamed around, got on the Twentieth-Century Limited, went to Chicago, checked in at the Ambassador East, and hung around the lobby and looked the place over and got familiar with it. Then I took a train to Rapid City, South Dakota, and hired a forest ranger on his day off and told him I wanted to climb Mount Rushmore to see what was on top. I got halfway up and realized how dangerous my predicament was. I looked down. One slip and that was it. I said, "Look, I'm not going one step farther. I'm a screenwriter, not a mountain climber." I went down and bought him a Polaroid camera, and *he* went up the next day, photographed the top in all directions, and it turned out there was nothing up there. It was impossible. No way you could do a sequence on top of Mount Rushmore. But I wrote it anyway, and Hitchcock constructed it at the studio.

I also attended a few auctions to get the feel of the Chicago auction scene in the picture. This to me is writer's research. I can't write a sequence in which a man is

From *The Craft of the Screenwriter* (New York: Touchstone Books, 1982), pp. 198–206.

picked up for drunk driving in Glen Cove if I know nothing about it. I've got to find out by going through it. I can't write a murder sequence in the United Nations if I've never *been* in the United Nations and don't know what the sounds are like or who the characters are or what a receptionist would say. I have to go through all that.

Brady: Where did the idea for the Mount Rushmore setting originate?

Lehman: Hitchcock always wanted to do a chase across the faces of Mount Rushmore. You might say in a way it was . . . a goal we had to get to. Who was getting there, and why, who was chasing whom, and why—that was all a total mystery. Mount Rushmore was a shadowy, distant objective that, in a way, gave impetus to the creating of the movie. The sequence became one of the things you remember most about *North by Northwest.*

Brady: So many scenes in that film seem to be a combination of private, intimate, possibly harmful things happening in public places. I wonder if there is some structural theme that you were after.

Lehman: I'd have to read what some French writers on films have to say about it, who interpret these pictures years later. I'm serious. I once saw a French film magazine filled with diagrams of the movements of the characters in *North by Northwest* and how they all have a meaning: going from left to right here . . . and scenes with circular movements there. Hitch and I used to laugh sometimes when we read about the symbolism in his pictures, particularly in *Family Plot.* By mistake a propman had two pieces of wood set up so that they looked vaguely like a cross, and the car goes downhill and crashes through a field, goes through a fence, and knocks over the cross. So some learned New York critic commented: there's Alfred Hitchcock's anti-Catholicism coming out once again. When I was at the Cannes Film Festival with *Family Plot,* Karen Black, Bruce Dern, and I attended a press conference, and some French journalist had the symbolism of the license plate in the picture all worked out: 885 DJU. He had some *elaborate* explanation for those numbers. When he got through explaining it, I said, "I hate to tell you this, but the reason I used that license plate number was that it used to be my own, and I felt it would be legally safe to use." So much for symbolism.

Brady: How did you come by the title *North by Northwest*?

Lehman: The same way we came by the film itself—circuitously. We once had the working title *In a Northwesterly Direction,* which was never used—along with all the ideas we kicked around and never used. I said I wanted to write a definitive Hitchcock film—the Hitchcock film to end all Hitchcock films. Hitch said to me, "I always wanted to do something involving a chase across Mount Rushmore." Then he said, "I had an idea for a scene once where someone is addressing the United Nations General Assembly and the delegate from Peru is asleep. The man who is addressing the General Assembly gets insulted and says he will not continue unless the delegate from Peru pays attention. Someone taps the guy on the shoulder and he falls over dead. The only clue is some doodling he had been doing on a piece of paper looked like antlers on a moose." I said, "That's very interesting." Of course, we never *used* that. But it was like I was saying to myself, "Oh, I see, maybe this picture will have something to do with the United Nations." Then Hitch said, "I've always wanted to do a scene along an automobile assembly line. You start with nothing on the assembly line, then the fender, and various parts come in. It's the longest dolly shot in history. The camera follows a whole car as it is being assembled, from nothing to the completed car, which is then driven off the assembly line, and in the back seat of the car there's a dead body—and it's all in one shot." I said, "That's terrific." Then Hitch said, "I always wanted to see something like a Moral Rearmament Conference in Lake Louise. Some very nice families seem to be gathered there. Suddenly, a twelve-year-old girl pulls out a gun and shoots someone."

I was making notes on all these little Hitchcockian things, which we *never ever* used. I've got a whole slew of them, all kinds of situations. An Eskimo is fishing through a hole in the ice. Suddenly a hand comes up out of the hole. Finally I said, "Well, I see we are starting at the United Nations, and we are moving in a northwesterly direction. We wind up in Alaska, there's a tidal wave, and a plane is trying to take off. . . ." All these touches sound fascinating when you are talking, and, though they came to nothing, that must have been what gave rise to our thinking about this picture—*whatever* it was going to be, moving in a northwesterly direction from New York on to Detroit, then on to Lake Louise and on to Alaska, whatever, whoever, whyever. So that title was around for quite a while.

Finally, when I started really working on the script, the head of the story department at MGM suggested that we call it, as a working title, *North by Northwest*. That's how that title came into being. That was only a working title, too. And I remember after I had finished (I called it *The Man on Lincoln's Nose* for a while), Sammy Cahn came into my office one day and said, "I've got the title song," and he *sang* for me a *love* song called "The Man on Lincoln's Nose." I mean it's like George S. Kaufman and Moss Hart writing a play about Hollywood. Here's this famous songwriter doing "The Man on Lincoln's Nose" in my office. No parody. He was *serious*. That's Sammy Cahn. Give him any title, he'll turn it into a love song, and it'll be a smash. Finally, Hitchcock called me and said, "We've *got* to find a title for this picture." Well, we never did find a title for the picture better than *North by Northwest*. And afterward, we found out that there *was* no such direction. And you should see the hundreds of thousands of words on *that* subject! Ah hah, symbolism . . . they used a direction that doesn't exist. . . .

Brady: How did you develop the crop-dusting scene?

Lehman: My memory isn't *that* good. All I know is that it happened in Hitch's study at his home one afternoon, when we were discussing ways for the heavies to get Cary Grant killed after he arrives in Chicago. I remember Hitch kept talking about a cyclone, and how it menaces Grant from the sky. I said, "Hitch, that's not good." He said, "Oh, that would be wonderful. It's easy to do." I said, "Yeah, but *they're* trying to kill him. How are *they* going to work up a cyclone?" Anyway, now we are up in the sky with a cyclone, right? And I just can't tell you who said what to whom, but somewhere during that afternoon, the cyclone in the sky became the crop-duster plane. Before the day ended, Hitch and I were acting out the entire sequence. The plane making its passes, Grant seeing the cornfield, ducking into the cornfield, the various passes of the plane with a gun; then he sees a car, tries to wave it down, it ignores him, and he races into the cornfield. Crop-dusting poison is going to drive him out. He sees a diesel truck. I remember all that stuff. And that's where it all happened. In the study in Hitch's house. The next day I went to my office and wrote it, naturally with the greatest of ease. I had already seen it all.

Brady: Do you ever use a storyboard when writing?

Lehman: Well, a storyboard is really done by an illustrator who is visualizing or drawing scenes that have been written. That's the director's work with his art director or his illustrator, his sketch artist. As a writer I used to storyboard my script at times, putting index cards up on a board with tacks and standing back and looking at the cards and saying, "Oh yeah, that scene, then that scene, then that scene" . . . all in order. "Gee, that's kind of long. Twenty-eight scenes in the first act. That's kind of a long first act, you know."

Brady: Is it that mathematical?

Lehman: Not really. But sometimes you can see an imbalance. If I've got only five cards there in the second act, it's ridiculous. That first part is going to take an hour and ten minutes to play. And that little second part is going to take fifteen minutes. That's not right.

Brady: Should the three acts be approximately the same time?

Lehman: I don't say anything is that mathematical. No. There's just a kind of feeling about imbalance.

Brady: How visual is your thinking as a screenwriter? Do you try to set scenes as well as establish dialogue?

Lehman: Yes, definitely. I see everything. I occasionally put in an excess amount of direction, like "He turned and walked across the room and looked out of the window for a moment." It's almost like I'm playing the scene in my head. I never, just *never,* put down only dialogue; I'm always acting it out in my head. . . .

Brady: What ingredients do you look for in each act?

Lehman: In the first act, who are the people, what is the situation of this whole story? The second act is the progression of that situation to a point of high conflict and great problems. And the third act is how the conflicts and problems are resolved. That's putting it a little patly, but that's the way it ought to be.

Brady: So you go through the undergrowth and extract the three acts?

Lehman: Well, you try. You do it kind of unconsciously, instinctively. What's the drama here? Where's the conflict? What's the resolution?

Brady: Why don't you write more original screenplays? . . .

Lehman: Well, *North by Northwest* would have been relatively nothing without its being *North by Northwest directed by Alfred Hitchcock.* It wouldn't have been much of anything in someone else's hands. The mere presence of Hitchcock, *plus* his particular skills as a director—and the fact that he could get a Cary Grant with the greatest of ease—was an enormous help. I am not downgrading my screenplay at all, but writing that film doesn't mean that I could have dashed off a dozen *North by Northwests* thereafter and they all would have been successful. Oh, no. I had no illusions about that. I knew that the fact that it was a *Hitchcock* picture made it ultimately memorable. And there *are* no Hitchcocks anymore. God rest his soul. There really aren't. And it wasn't until years later that the picture came into its own. It was successful and highly regarded when it came out, but pretty soon thereafter the whole genre kind of fell into disrepute because along came the James Bond pictures, which were not Hitchcockian in any way, which depended entirely on other things, but they were hugely successful. The *North by Northwest* kind of picture was mild, during that era, compared to what you got in a James Bond picture. Audiences loved the Bond gadgets and the sex and the spoof, the whole number. And so I moved on to other fields, only to team up with Hitch again years later for *Family Plot.* It saddens me to talk about it. I never wanted that to be his last film. I'm grateful that I was part of it. But I returned to him again to write what was to be his next picture, *The Short Night,* because I suspected it might be his last, and I wanted it to be much better than the previous one. Sometimes I think we both knew, on this one, that we were going through the motions. Were we or weren't we? I'll never know. He *wanted* to make it, didn't he? I *wanted* him to make it—isn't that why I wrote it? But did either of us believe that he could? Did either of us ever admit that he couldn't, even to ourselves? Now that Hitch is gone, I think the script will vanish as he did. I don't think it should be made. Not without Hitch.

Reviews

North by Northwest received generally good reviews in the American press, which treated the film as an amusing diversion; consider, for example, the review from *Time* reprinted here. One exception to the rule in America was Stanley Kauffmann of *The New Republic,* who, like James Agee before him, regarded Hitchcock's work in Hollywood as a betrayal of the realistic values in his best British films. In the letters column of a subsequent issue of *The New Republic* (September 14, 1959, p. 3), one of Kauffmann's readers argued that Hitchcock "is not making the same kind of film now that he did in 1935," and that pictures like *Vertigo* and *North by Northwest* ought to be judged on their "own terms." Kauffmann replied: "*Vertigo* was indeed an attempt to do something different, which does not necessarily make it a successful attempt. *Northwest* is surely, element by element, an attempt at a 'real' suspense picture like his early ones; but, to leave tech-nical matters out of it, would the 1935 Hitchcock have tolerated the high sea-side cliffs on Long Island? Or a hero-ine in cahoots with the villain who turns out, not quite surprisingly, to be working for the FBI?"

The auteurists in France, especially the "Hitchcockians" at *Cahiers du Cinéma,* saw *North by Northwest* as further evidence of the director's deep-est ethical, psychological, and aes-thetic concerns. This group used the release of the film as an occasion for debate with Eric Rohmer and Claude Chabrol, who had recently written a provocative book describing Hitch-cock as a Catholic artist (see the bibli-ography). The review reprinted here, translated by Lahcen Hassad and the editor, was written by Luc Moullet, one of the most willfully delirious of the *Cahiers* critics. Moullet argued that Hitchcock was anything but a Catholic type; on the contrary, he claimed, Hitchcock's style implied an anti-Catholic formalism and a "sub-lime" pop sensibility.

Time

North by Northwest (MGM). While in Manhattan shooting the early scenes of this film, director Alfred Hitchcock grumbled that newspapers tell too many "outlandish stories from real life that drive the spinner of suspense fiction to further extremes." "Further extremes" turns out to be a point on Hitchcock's compass. Direction: *North by Northwest.*

Smoothly troweled and thoroughly entertaining, *North by Northwest* wears its implausibilities lightly, bobs swiftly past colored picture postcard backgrounds from Madison Avenue to South Dakota's Mount Rushmore, the United Nations Secretariat to George Washington's wattles. As the story begins, adman Cary Grant has little on his mind but Trendex and his waistline (he reminds himself to "think thin") until enemy agents mistake him for a U.S. counterspy and kidnap him from a cocktail lounge in the Plaza Hotel. Spy ringleader James Mason (as polished and heavy as a Kremlin banister) invites Grant to spill all he knows. But all the adman knows has long since been run up flagpoles.

The bad guys force a fifth of bourbon down Cary and turn him loose in a sports car to destroy himself—but he merely gets arrested and comes back after them to clear his name. They frame him with a knife murder committed in a reception lounge of the United Nations and, when he flees the city, arrange for a purring hood-nymph (Eva Marie Saint) to pick him up on the Twentieth-Century Limited. But Cary has made his way to her berth before the train makes Albany. The villains lure him out onto an Indiana cornfield, where a crop-duster in a biplane strafes him. He comes through it all looking like an ad for Brooks Brothers. And by now the villains are beginning to catch on to what U.S. moviegoers could have told them all along: it will take a lot more than an army of Communist spies to do away with Cary Grant.

But even Cary eventually shows a touch of strain as the film's glibly rococo plot closes in on Mount Rushmore ("I don't like the way Teddy Roosevelt is looking at me") and he is up to his immaculate collar in spies and counterspies, including a tweedy troubleshooter from Washington (Leo G. Carroll), the only man alive who seems to understand what is going on. The final scenes leading to the inevitable chase fairly tingle with Hitchcock-signature direction (such as a closeup of an oncoming fist). The suspense is beautiful as the bad guys nearly wipe out all the good guys and almost get away with the microfilm. Then Hitchcock reaches *North by Northwest's* ultimate "further extreme": a fugitive Eva Marie Saint scrambling down Thomas Jefferson's forehead in high heels.

From *Time,* August 17, 1959, pp. 78, 80.

The New Republic

Stanley Kauffmann

The decline of Alfred Hitchcock is no longer news. It is quite clear that the director of *The Lady Vanishes* and *The 39 Steps* is dead and that an obscene ghost is mocking him by superficially imitating him. His last film, *Vertigo,* was an asinine, unredeemed bore. His latest, *North by Northwest,* starts more promisingly but soon loses us in cliché and preposterousness. (Why didn't the Long Island police know the woman in the mansion was an impostor? Why was the United Nations delegate murdered? Etc., etc.) Like an old whore struggling desperately for remembered rapture, Hitchcock fumbles for his early ability to render familiar scenes and objects scary. But the urgent, encompassing reality of his first films is missing, and without it his antics simply look foolish.

The scene in the cornfield in which a crop-dusting plane strafes Cary Grant is probably the low point in Hitchcock's career—pure comic book stuff. And in the climax (this time it's the Mount Rushmore Memorial instead of the Statue of Liberty), all I could think of, as Grant and Eva Marie Saint scrambled down the huge face of Washington, was whether the Actors Studio, of which Miss Saint is an alumna, would have approved her performance. But then The Method provides little guidance for hiding under Washington's right nostril.

A much-publicized trademark of a Hitchcock film is a brief appearance by [the director] himself. Equally standard by now is a huge two-shot scene, long protracted, in which the hero and heroine nibble each other's ears and neck, and converse in suggestive dialogue. It has the same relation to sex that Hitchcock's recent pictures have to suspense.

From *The New Republic,* August 10, 1959, p. 23.

Cahiers du Cinéma

Luc Moullet

R oger Thornhill (Cary Grant), a very busy New York publicist, is mistaken for American counterespionage agent George Kaplan by the minions of foreign spy Phillip Vandamm (James Mason), who kidnap him, try in vain to kill him, and end up accusing him of a crime of their own doing—thereby forcing Thornhill to flee the police and go to Chicago to look for Kaplan, the only person capable of saving him; this Thornhill, en route to Chicago on a train, is seduced by Eve Kendall (Eva Marie Saint), who helps him arrange an appointment with Kaplan, which turns out to be an ambush from which he escapes, only to discover that Eve is Vandamm's mistress; after managing to avoid the clutches of Vandamm by getting arrested by the police, he is turned over to an American spymaster (Leo G. Carroll), who informs him that Kaplan has never existed and is nothing more than bait for Vandamm, designed to protect the real agent. . . . Eve, who, now that Vandamm senses her love for Thornhill, is in mortal danger in South Dakota, where Cary saves her by pretending to be shot; then, after jumping from the window of a hospital where Carroll locks him up, Cary learns that Vandamm is aware of the shooting hoax and is making preparations to throw Eve into the Pacific from a plane taking him and a set of microfilms to Russia (Oh my God! I am extrapolating here); but Cary manages to save Eve and get the microfilms from Vandamm, at the price of almost falling down the vertical slopes of Mount Rushmore, where the figures of the greatest American statesmen are engraved.

What one will not do to please the readers of *Cahiers* who may not have seen this extraordinary film, and my chief editors, who did not understand the story and asked me to relate the plot of a two-hour-and-sixteen-minute-long masterpiece (a good deal clearer than my précis)—a picture that was shot for a million and a half in the weeks between August 27 and December 24, 1958; that moves quicker than any other Hitchcock; and that, in adopting the title *North by Northwest,* pays discreet homage to Shakespeare's *Hamlet:* oh well, the picture ends with Cary marrying Eva.

Unlike *Vertigo,* which is a highly serious film, *North by Northwest* is an entertainment. What do I mean? That the characters in *Vertigo* have a consistency, whereas in *North by Northwest* they have none—or, more precisely, they parody the parody of consistency they have in *Vertigo.* The film makes one laugh and it has no very precise message. There are numerous flaws—banal expository scenes;

Translated by the editor and Lahcen Hassad from "La Concierge et le bûcheron," *Cahiers du Cinéma* 102 (December 1959): 52–55.

failures in the Technicolor as printed by Metro; ideas from Hitchcock's earlier work that are executed with less panache. Everybody knows these problems and it's useless to talk about them: besides, a critique is no place for carping complaints. Let's talk about the best parts: this film has some twenty scenes that are sublime, and among them are three or four that easily surpass the most beautiful shots of *Rope, Under Capricorn, Strangers on a Train, I Confess, The Wrong Man,* and *Vertigo.* I am referring specifically to the ambush in the fields of Illinois, and to the scene at the United Nations. Consider the best of these, the ambush: it serves as a definition of Hitchcock's art. We should quickly note that this scene is inscribed in the margins of the film: here is a movie made up entirely of very short subordinations—I love short phrases with no main clause. Its beauty, like any other beauty, provides access to a metaphysics, in the broad sense of that word, which does not at all conform to the Christian idea of narrative. In his small book, Rohmer calls Hitchcock "a practicing Catholic."[1] I don't think so. Catholicism is another pair of shoes; it is Rossellini. Some may argue that the meaning, the external moral structure, of Hitchcock's work is Catholic. But that does not mean that he is a true Catholic. Hitchcock is one of those directors who seeks perfection. And such a quest runs counter to a moral injunction of the Church: we humans, who are imperfect, should never crave perfection—such desires are folly. We should not be surprised, however, if the anxious desire for perfection gives rise to contradictions that are nonetheless quite productive. It is obvious that Catholic thought, among all other forms of thought, is the kind that strikes the deepest chord in humanity, the kind that has the strongest dramatic power—and we could elaborate for pages on the theme of the communion of saints in *North by Northwest* or anywhere else. But if Hitchcock's mind is subject to the moral and commercial preeminence of Catholicism, his soul is not or is only rarely so. He is a Catholic in the sense that he looks for the perfect subject matter, since only a Catholic subject can be perfect. But it's quite rare when the actual form of his films corresponds to Catholic ideas. This happens in certain of his films that are less commercial, less acclaimed, like *The Wrong Man.* Hitchcockian Catholicism is essentially symbolic, and thus inconsistent.

The consistent and sole defining element of Hitchcockian metaphysics is the drive toward formal perfection: every shot in Hitchcock is determined by an implacable logic, and not by personal taste. This preoccupation with the mechanisms of art, which is the only common element of the series of interviews we published with him in this journal, is generally closer to the spirit of the Reformation than to the attitudes of the Roman Church. One name seems to me irresistably connected with such a spirit—the name of Cecil B. De Mille. Hitchcock and De Mille, the two masters of Paramount, are also the most famous directors on earth.

---

1. Eric Rohmer and Claude Chabrol, *Hitchcock: The First Forty-four Films,* trans. Stanley Hochmann (New York: Frederick Ungar, 1979), p. 116. [Editor's note.]

They are both obsessed with perfection and recipes. Another of their common traits is that, unlike Catholics, they do not regard love as a natural phenomenon. De Mille plays on the affinity of sex and religion with a perversity that borders on sadism. Hitchcock, more clearly in his interviews and television films than in his feature pictures, reveals a taste for a provocative obscenity that has nothing beautiful about it. And what is *North by Northwest,* if not a more intelligent and edifying De Mille? It is made up of a continuous series of effects of the most brilliant artificiality. But where will we end up if we abolish artificiality from art? Hitchcock's aesthetics is an aesthetics of punching, based solely on dramatic power: here we are as far as can be from the pulpit and the teeming life of Roman Catholic directors. With its fascinating forward and backward traveling shots, its stupefying tricks, Hitchcock's film is entirely based on a monism of technical effects, on a schematization so unprecedented and so abstract as to border on the sublime. Yes, the film is beautiful because we see that it is fake, that it hides nothing, that it gives nothing. It is beautiful because it is false; yet we will be the first to pounce upon anyone who casts doubts on its truthfulness. In the same way that De Mille represents the Red Sea and the burning bush as if they were animated drawings, Hitchcock adheres strongly to the cartoon tradition. The fact that he works with Saul Bass is proof enough. And yet *North by Northwest* is better than an animated cartoon. . . .

The ambush scene, which approximates some kind of Puritan schematism, shows very well how Hitchcock's work has nothing to do with Catholic metaphysics. Yet it is one of his best achievements. We show good breeding when we consider *North by Northwest* a minor work. But it is wrong to base such a judgment on the lightness of the subject and not on the various internal weaknesses of the film. The lack of serious intention makes us see Hitchcock as he really is, and disencumbers us of various prejudices that normally hinder our view. We must cling to the physical sensations we experience when we watch his films—physical sensations quite alien to the simplified Catholic metaphysics of the scripts. We must watch *North by Northwest* through the eyes of the concierge and the woodcutter, which are my eyes; because it is for their gaze that Hitchcock makes his films—films ingenious enough to bring about in their own way the reunification of the social classes.

Commentaries

The literature on Hitchcock is considerable, and the items reprinted here are not to be taken as superior to numerous others that I have, for a variety of reasons, been forced to omit. I regret that space does not permit me to reprint some of the longer writings on *North by Northwest*—especially the work of Raymond Bellour, Lesley Brill, Stanley Cavell, and Geoffrey Hartman, some of whose writings are listed in the bibliography. I also wanted to include an extract from Tania Modleski's fine book on Hitchcock; unfortunately, she mentions *North by Northwest* only once or twice in passing. The commentaries I have chosen are nevertheless indicative of the range and quality of the critical attention the film has received.

Every study of Hitchcock since 1965 has been indebted to Robin Wood's analysis of the director's major American films. A gifted writer who has often acknowledged his indebtedness to F. R. Leavis, Wood was the first critic in English to view Hitchcock in moral and ethical terms, as an exemplar of what Leavis called "the great tradition." Wood's attitudes toward Hitchcock have changed over the years (as can be seen from the footnotes he added to later editions of his work), but he continues to insist that the best art—such as Hitchcock's—functions as a criticism of life.

The other two writers examine the film in terms of Hitchcock's entire oeuvre. Marian Keane sees *North by Northwest* as Hitchcock's complex, self-reflexive meditation on his own authorship and place in cinema history. Slavoj iek uses Hitchcock to explain the psychoanalytic theory of Jacques Lacan, and vice versa; in a witty, erudite discussion of the "family secret" of late capitalism, he speculates on various ways in which *North by Northwest* expresses buried anxieties of the culture at large.

North by Northwest

Robin Wood

There are no symbols in North by Northwest. Oh yes! One. The last shot, the train entering the tunnel after the love scene between Grant and Eva Marie Saint. It's a phallic symbol. But don't tell anyone.

Alfred Hitchcock, Cahiers du Cinéma 102

O f Hitchcock's six most recent films, *North by Northwest* is that which corresponds most nearly to the conventional estimate of him as a polished light entertainer. That, beside its immediate neighbors, it is a lightweight work, a relaxation, in which we see Hitchcock working at something less than full pressure, I do not deny. That it is trivial or frivolous, not worth serious attention, I reject absolutely. When I spoke of the unbroken series of masterpieces from *Vertigo* to *Marnie,* I had not forgotten *North by Northwest.*

A light entertainment can have depth, subtlety, finesse. It can embody mature moral values; indeed, it seems to me that it *must.* If I fail to be entertained by *Goldfinger,* it is because there is nothing there to engage or retain the attention; the result is a nonentity, consequently tedious. The essential triviality of the James Bond films, in fact, sets off perfectly, by contrast, the depth, the charm, the integrity of Hitchcock's film.

A film, whether light entertainment or not, is either a work of art or it is nothing. And the basic essential of a work of art is that it be thematically organic. *Goldfinger* is a collection of bits, carefully calculated with both eyes on the box office, put end to end with no deeper necessity for what happens next than mere plot; nothing except plot develops in the course of it, and, obviously, the essence of an organic construction is development. But *Goldfinger,* I shall be reminded, doesn't take itself seriously: so much the worse for it. And if it doesn't why should anyone else—for I find it difficult to see how the adult mind can occupy itself with something that cannot, in some sense, be taken seriously. *North by Northwest,* on the level of plot (if one can imagine its plot divorced from its subject, which is more difficult than may at first appear), also doesn't take itself seriously: we are not, in other words, expected to believe, literally, *this could happen.* But it is a very superficial glance that sees no more there than the plot. The tongue-in-cheek element on plot level has the function of directing our attention to other levels. On the other hand the self-mocking aspect of the Bond films is merely a very shrewd means of permitting the spectator to indulge any penchant for sadism and sexual "kicks" he may have without any accompanying discomfort.

From *Hitchcock's Films Revisited* (New York: Columbia University Press, 1989), pp. 131–141.

The sociologist and the critic have territory in common, certainly; but *Goldfinger* and its success, the wide popular and critical success of a film that has scarcely more to offer than a boys' comic paper, seems to me to belong strictly to the sociologist. Even to compare it with *North by Northwest* will seem slightly ridiculous to Hitchcock's admirers, but a moment's reflection will be enough to remind them that the obvious distinction between the two films has not been made everywhere.

I have allowed that *North by Northwest* is a comparatively relaxed film, a divertissement; that is to say, one must not demand of it the concentrated significance, the extraordinarily close-knit organization of *Vertigo* and *Psycho*. Nevertheless, it has a coherent and satisfying development, a construction sufficiently strong and clear to assimilate the occasional charming but irrelevant little *jeux d'esprit* (the strange lady's reaction to Cary Grant's nocturnal passage through her room as he escapes from the hospital in which the head of the CIA has imprisoned him[1]) permissible in a work of this nature. Like *Vertigo* (to which it is also linked through its equivocal heroine), it can be regarded as falling into three movements corresponding to the main stages in the evolution of the hero's attitude. The first lightly sketches all that is relevant (for the purposes of the film) of his general situation and outlook, and has him mistaken for George Kaplan and wanted by both spies and police; it closes with the revelation that George Kaplan doesn't exist. The second sees him involved with Eve Kendall and traces the abrupt shifts in his relationship with her as he (as well as the spectator) becomes increasingly frustrated, baffled, disillusioned, by the ambiguity of her position and behavior. The last movement begins when he learns the truth about her and—the real turning point of the film—voluntarily accepts his role as Kaplan, and culminates in the cementing of their relationship.

North by Northwest bears an obvious resemblance to both *The 39 Steps* and *Saboteur;* its immense superiority to both films scarcely needs to be argued, but it is worth noting that Hitchcock himself, when asked why he had remade *Saboteur,* replied that in the earlier film the characters were not interesting, and that he made an elementary mistake in having the villain, not the hero, dangle from the top of the Statue of Liberty. The second point is by no means a trivial one, and is intimately connected with the first. It is not so much a greater complexity of the characters in *North by Northwest* that makes them more interesting, but their relationship to the action. Both *The 39 Steps* and *Saboteur* have heroes quite unpredictably and abruptly plunged into hair-raising adventures, but the adven-

---

1. All three of the commentators reprinted in this volume describe the fictional spy agency in the film as the CIA. The error is understandable, since Hitchcock and Lehman clearly intended to satirize that organization (see the Introduction). It should be noted, however, that the film gives the agency the name United States Intelligence Agency (shot 302). The target of the film's satire is best described as what the Professor calls the "alphabet soup" of modern surveillance organizations. [Editor's note.]

tures bear no really organic relationship to the men; there is not the same point in these things happening to Richard Hannay and the hero of *Saboteur* as there is in their happening to Roger Thornhill. Similarly, there is no point at all in having Fry (the "saboteur" of the title) hang by his coat sleeves from the Statue of Liberty, beyond the prolonging of a simple suspense as an end in itself; there is every point in Roger Thornhill, the previously irresponsible, unattached advertising man, having to hang onto a ledge on Mount Rushmore by one hand, holding the woman he loves by the other, while the homosexual spy Leonard, the film's ultimate representative of the sterile and destructive, grinds the hand with his foot.[2] The difference can be summed up (with some unfairness in simplification to the earlier films) by saying that *North by Northwest* has a subject as well as a plot.

In fact, at a deeper level the film has more in common with *Rear Window* than with *Saboteur* or *The 39 Steps.* The film begins with shots of New York traffic and New York crowds: a sense of apparently aimless and chaotic bustle and movement. From this emerges Roger Thornhill, dictating to his secretary on his way home by lift, crowded pavement, taxi: emerges from it as its typical representative and product. In an exposition of masterly compression we learn all the essential things about him: he is brash, fast-talking, overconfident on the surface; entirely irresponsible and inconsiderate of others (he cheats a man out of his taxi by pretending his secretary is ill, then cheerfully justifies this to her by telling her he has made the other man "feel like a Good Samaritan"); a heavy drinker; a divorcé (twice, it transpires); surprisingly dominated by his mother, who, he says, is "like a bloodhound" in still sniffing his breath to find out if he has been drinking. Indeed, he is a man who lives purely on the surface, refusing all commitment or responsibility (appropriately, he is in advertising), immature for all his cocksureness, his life all the more a chaos for the fact that he doesn't recognize it as such; a man who relies above all on the exterior trappings of modern civilization—business offices, cocktail bars, machines—for protection, who substitutes bustle and speed for a sense of direction or purpose: a modern city Everyman, whose charm and self-confidence and smartness make him especially easy for the spectator to identity with, so that at the start we are scarcely conscious of his limitations as a human being. We can quite happily and thoughtlessly attach ourselves to his smug confidence in being in control of his environment.

And then, abruptly, within ten minutes of the start of the film, the ground is cut away from under his/our feet. Hitchcock's sense of the precariousness of all human order has never been more beautifully expressed (though conveyed elsewhere—in *The Wrong Man* and *The Birds,* for instance—with greater intensity and overt seriousness) than in the mistake, due to sheer chance, by which

2. This sentence was written by a gay male who at that time was desperately trying to reject and disown his own homosexuality. It is not, I think, an inaccurate description of the effect of the film at this point, but I am deeply ashamed of its tone and implicit attitude. [Wood's note.]

Thornhill, going to send a telegram to his mother, finds himself kidnapped by gunmen. In the lobby of a crowded hotel, in whose lounge bar he has just been drinking with associates, chaos abruptly takes over.

The remainder of the film's first movement is devoted to a systematic stripping away of all the protective armor of modern city man on which Thornhill relies for his safety. In the midst of crowds, he becomes completely isolated. The opportunist has been defeated by chance. The man who deprived others of their taxi is imprisoned in a car he can't get out of, unable even to attract attention. He is taken to the house of a Mr. Townsend where all his "proofs" of identity are disdainfully refused. The heavy drinker is forced to gulp down immense quantities of bourbon as a preliminary to a "drunk driving accident." The fact that he is a heavy drinker, of course, makes it feasible that he should be able to frustrate his potential murderers by escaping his "accident"; but we are also left to reflect on the appropriateness of such a death—it is precisely the way in which Thornhill might eventually have died. The hair-raising drive in a car almost out of his control is a logical extension of his basic situation. And Hitchcock is so little interested in his spies *as* spies, the spectator is so little encouraged to inquire into the precise nature of their activities, that it becomes very easy to accept them as simply the embodiment of the forces of disorder and subversion: we are no more interested in their rational motivation than we are in that of the birds two films later. Like the birds, they are not so much a projection of the chaos underlying modern order as the agents whereby that order is destroyed, the chaos forced upon the characters' consciousness.

Thornhill's sense of personal identity is clearly weak, and undermined by the spies' unshakable conviction that he is George Kaplan; and indeed as an integrated human being he has about as real an existence. At the police station, he tells his mother on the phone, very emphatically, "This is your son, Roger Thornhill"—as if he had been brought to the point of doubting it. The only relationship of any apparent strength, with his mother, proves worse than useless, her skepticism undermining him at every step; it is parodied when he returns with the police to the Townsend mansion by the false Mrs. Townsend's effusive, motherly, yet equally cynical, treatment of him. The parallel is emphasized by Hitchcock's having the two women (who look very much alike) stand in similar postures, hands folded before them. One of the film's funniest and most uncomfortable moments comes when, descending from their exploration of Kaplan's rooms in the hotel lift, Thornhill's mother remarks gaily to the two men who almost sent her son over a cliff the night before, "You gentlemen aren't *really* trying to kill my son, are you?", and the whole lift load—mother, killers, other passengers—laugh uproariously at the joke while Thornhill stands helplessly in their midst.

With characteristic Hitchcockian outrageousness, Thornhill's final plunge into chaos is set in the supreme symbol of potential world order, the United Nations building. After the knifing of the real Townsend, we see Thornhill running frantically, a microscopic figure, in a shot taken from the top of the building, looking directly down on him; the smug, self-confident advertising man, so sure of the effectiveness of his personality, reduced to an almost indistinguishable speck, and a completely isolated speck, for he is now (as Thornhill) pursued by the forces of order as well as disorder (as Kaplan). It is at this point that we leave him for a moment to learn the truth: the meeting in the intelligence bureau reveals that Kaplan (on whose whereabouts Thornhill's fate depends) doesn't exist—is a convenient invention, a "nonexistent decoy" designed to divert the spies' attention from the *real* agent. What is to be done to protect Thornhill? Nothing. He is to be left to fend for himself, thrown back on his own resources, all civilized protections removed. The first movement of the film ends with the agent's epitaph on an unknown nonentity: "Good-bye, Mr. Thornhill, wherever you are."

The second movement begins with Thornhill, in the station, again among crowds, into which we see him, in long shot, disappear. The ensuing sequence gives us the train journey, Thornhill's meeting with Eve Kendall, and the first stage in their relationship. The superficial Eve—it is all we see for some time— suggests that she is the perfect counterpart for Thornhill: worldly, amoral, quite without depth of feeling, quite uncommitted to anything or anyone, taking sex as she would a cocktail (she says to him, with a sly suggestiveness, "It's going to be a long night. . . . And I don't particularly like the book I've started. . . . Do you know what I mean?"). There is a slight hint of nymphomania. She seems to be offering exactly the kind of relationship he would want: love-making without involvement, sex without responsibilities. But already, as they begin to make love after she has hidden him in her wall-bed from the searching police, one begins to be aware of undercurrents. He wonders why she isn't afraid of him, a supposed murderer; she asks him if he is planning to murder her. He asks, "Shall I?"; she murmurs, "Please do," and they kiss. It is all playful on the surface; but as they kiss his hands encircle her head as if either to strangle or to crush her, and hers move to his to draw him down, in an attitude of surrender. We realize his sudden sense of the danger of involvement and also her barely concealed weariness and yearning. It is all done with a marvelous delicacy that is in fact profoundly characteristic of Hitchcock, although this is not often recognized. The scene ends with a shot of her looking over his shoulder, her eyes deeply troubled; then she sends the message along to Vandamm: "What do I do with him in the morning?"

What she does is to arrange for him to be machine-gunned from a plane. The attempt on his life is prefaced by their parting, which ends with the beautiful shot of his hand tentatively covering hers on the handle of her case, as she draws back: their mutual involvement is suggested with remarkable economy. What we seem to have here (for we still take Eve very largely at her face value) is the old cliché of the wicked woman drawn into true love against her will. A cursory comparison with what Guy Hamilton makes of the Pussy Galore/James Bond relationship will reveal the extent to which a "light entertainment" can have grace, sensibility, and moral depth if it is directed by Hitchcock.

The crop-dusting sequence is justly famous and seems widely accepted as one of Hitchcock's most brilliant set pieces. What is not so often noticed, however, is its dependence for much of its effect on its context. Certainly, it is brilliant in itself, an object lesson in the building up of a suspense through the repeated cheating of the audience's expectations, ending in the *frisson*-producing line, "That plane's dustin' crops where there ain't no crops," and the subsequent explosion into violent action. Yet the sequence retains its magic however many times one sees the film—even after one knows, shot by shot, what comes next, and it is worth asking why this should be. The sequence occurs at almost exactly midpoint in the film. Immediately behind it is our knowledge of Eve Kendall's treachery (*we* know Thornhill is going to be attacked, though *he* doesn't) and all the emotional tension generated by their relationship. But there is much more behind it than that. Hitherto in the film, Thornhill has always been *inside:* inside cities, buildings, vehicles: and we know him as a man at home in the complacency-encouraging security of office and cocktail bar. Now, suddenly, he is in open country. And not merely open country: a flat landscape, treeless, houseless, shelterless, parched, stretching away apparently to infinity on all sides. In the midst of this he stands, an isolated speck with the whole world against him, absolutely exposed and vulnerable: modern man deprived of all his amenities and artificial resources. The bus— his last contact with other people, with civilization—moves away, the crop-dusting plane turns and flies toward him. . . . It is a marvelous conception, central to the film in more ways than position.

Thornhill's first image of Eve is now shattered; the second is equally misleading—though both bear some relationship to the real Eve. When they meet again in the hotel, she runs up to him, and we see her relief: relief not only that he isn't dead but that she hasn't been responsible for his death. His hands go around her head again to embrace her, in the gesture he used on the train; only this time they don't quite touch. He hesitates, moves away, makes a sarcastic remark about "togetherness." Another familiar Hitchcock theme is touched on: the necessity for a trust based on instinct, even when it is quite unreasonable. Their separation is expressed by restless crosscutting, their partial reconciliation (on his side clearly provisional and suspicious) by a beautiful camera movement that unites them in one image as she moves toward him. She helps him remove his jacket to have it cleaned, and he says, "When I was a little boy, I wouldn't even let my mother undress me"; she tells him he is a big boy now. It is one of those unobtrusive, almost offhand exchanges that reveals a great deal. Before she leaves, he asks her, "Ever *kill* anyone?"—we are made to remember that (whatever her motives) she did in fact connive in the attempt on his life.

This middle movement of the film closes with the auction scene, which gives us Thornhill's view of Eve at its most bitterly disillusioned ebb. Vandamm is standing behind her, his hand closing around the back of her neck in what constitutes at once a caress and a threat. A close-up emphasizes this, and we connect it with Thornhill's embraces, but this is far more sinister, and expresses the precariousness of Eve's position (before we know the truth about her). Thornhill calls her a "statue" and tells her: "Who are you kidding? You have no feelings to hurt." We see, but he doesn't, that she is in tears: the sequence is a condensed recapitulation of *Notorious*. This is not so banal as it sounds. We are aware by this time of the potentially healing power of the relationship on both sides (though we still don't know the real nature of Eve's need); but it appears—as Thornhill escapes, thanks to the police—irremediably broken.

The final movement opens with the reversal of this situation. At the airport, the head of the CIA tells Thornhill the truth about Eve, and he accepts his role as Kaplan for her sake. Immediately before, he uses a phrase that unites his two images of her: "That treacherous little tramp." Suddenly he learns that her life may depend on him, and, in agreeing to be Kaplan, he is accepting his responsibility and his involvement in a deep relationship. The sexual basis of his previous refusal of commitment, rejection of responsibility, is clear: he has survived two marriages that have left him, apparently, completely unaffected. As he accepts, his face is suddenly illuminated by the light of the plane; and we cut to the first shot of Mount Rushmore. The cut has great emotional effect, because it abruptly defines for us, with marvelous economy, the evolution of the hero. For if the significance of Mount Rushmore is dramatic rather than symbolic, it is because "symbolic" suggests something too precise and too simple. It is not a symbol of democracy standing against the wicked agents; but certainly, in its emotional effect it suggests the order and stability toward which Thornhill is progressing, and to which the acceptance of a strong relationship with its accompanying responsibilities is the essential step.[3]

The scene of his reconciliation with Eve (after the false shooting) is perhaps the most beautiful in the film. First, the location: for the first time in the film we are among trees, cool calm sunlight, and shade—the effect is more a matter of context than of the intrinsic beauty of the scenery, and (as usual in this film, indeed in all Hitchcock's work) more of overtones and associations than of overt, clear-cut symbolism; it is an apt setting for the beginning of new life. Second, the mise-en-scène. As the "dead" Thornhill gets out of the back of the car, the camera tracks back to reveal Eve standing by *her* car to the right. We see them in long shot gazing at each other from the extremities of the screen, across the space of trees and filtered sunlight, everything still, the two hesitant, as if shy of each other. Then a shot of Thornhill as he begins to move: the camera tracks with him, left to right. Cut to a shot of Eve as *she* starts forward: the camera tracks with her from right to left. And so they are united: Hitchcock beautifully involves the spectator in their

3. The effect now seems to me more equivocal and ironic. Mount Rushmore becomes (as Andrew Britton points out in his monograph on Cary Grant [page 12]) the final obstacle to Thornhill's rescue of Eve, connected to the film's two monstrous though opposed authority figures, Vandamm and the Professor. [Wood's note.]

movement toward each other, their movement toward the "togetherness" that was earlier (for Thornhill) a contemptuous sneer.

We, and Thornhill, see at last the real Eve; or perhaps it is truer to say that the real Eve now *emerges:* her true identity is created—or at least crystallized—by the relationship, superseding (or perhaps assimilating) her two earlier personae. But it is made clear that those earlier Eves, partly artificial, are what she could have become, just as the real Judy Barton contains elements of her two adopted "personalities" (in *Vertigo* the distinction between them is of course much greater). It is the real Eve who tells Thornhill, with a touching gentleness, how deeply his words hurt; but almost at once, we get a glimpse of the first Eve, the Eve of the train journey, in her description of her relationship with Vandamm: "I had nothing better to do that weekend, so I decided to fall in love." Then her comment on her decision to help Intelligence ("Maybe it was the first time anyone ever asked me to do anything worthwhile.") gives us the potentially ruthless Eve—ruthless in a good cause—who could send Thornhill (with whatever qualms) to his death, and who is still ready to sacrifice their relationship for the "cause." The strands are drawn together in the ensuing dialogue exchange: "Has life been like that?" he asks her, and she assents. "How come?"—"Men like you."—"What's wrong with men like me?"—"They don't believe in marriage." He tells her he's been married twice; her comment: "See what I mean?" Circumstances have steered her toward being one or the other of the earlier Eves; now, in the relationship with Thornhill, her true self can be realized.

She makes it clear that this marriage is one, at last, that he will not easily escape. His reaction is jocular, cynical—"I may go back to hating you. It was more fun." His expression and tone belie the words, but they serve to bring before us the man's previous fear of real involvement, of responsibility. Hitchcock—here and in *Rear Window*—gives us no simple "redemption through love," no abrupt transformation; just a delicate intimation of the potential healing power of a balanced, permanent relationship. Eve reminds him that he is meant to be critically wounded; he replies, "I never felt more alive."

That charming father figure, the head of the CIA, whom Jean Douchet appears to suggest is some kind of Divine Instrument, seems to me to come out of things pretty badly. The film is surely solidly behind Thornhill in rejecting the use of a woman to get people like Vandamm: prostitution, in however admirable a cause, remains prostitution. Mixed morality—the pursuing of a good end by conventionally immoral means like Mark Rutland's in *Marnie*—is justified by Hitchcock only as the outcome of powerful instinctive drives, of basically right feelings, not when it comes to cold calculation: justifiable, therefore, only on the personal level, not on the political. We are entirely behind Thornhill, then, in his attempts to extricate Eve—in the determined positive action that results from his acceptance of personal responsibility.

Before the Mount Rushmore climax, we have Thornhill's attempts to rescue Eve from Vandamm's house, Vandamm's discovery of her true nature, and his plans to dispose of her over the sea. Leonard is built up here as the incarnation of destruction and negation. His motive is sexual jealousy—jealousy of Eve, his rival for Vandamm. He discloses the truth about Eve in a melodramatic, vindictive way, by "shooting" Vandamm with her blank-loaded revolver.

The climax is played out on and around the imperturbable stone faces of the presidents, with their suggestion of stability and order forming a background to Thornhill's desperate struggle to save himself and Eve for life. As they dangle from a ledge by their hands, they discuss—with total absurdity on a naturalistic level—Thornhill's first two marriages: "My wives divorced me. . . . I think they said I led too dull a life." The struggle for life against the destructive elements (the spies) is thus combined with the cementing of the relationship, the sealing off of the past. The joining of the lovers' hands derives some of its emotional and moral force from our view of it as the climax of a sequence of shots of their hands touching (to mark phases in the relationship) earlier: her sensuous caressing of his hand over the lunch table on the train, when she looked at his "R.O.T." matchbook; his pressure on her hand at the Chicago station as they said good-bye, after she had arranged the "meeting" with Kaplan. Eventually, Thornhill is hanging by one hand, holding the dangling Eve by the other, a great abyss beneath them: final test of stamina, with everything staked on his powers of endurance and determination. Leonard stands above them; Thornhill's "Help! Help me!" is given great force. Then Leonard treads on Thornhill's hand. Thornhill survives the trial for long enough: Leonard is shot down. We see Thornhill pulling Eve to safety. An abrupt cut, but with overlapping dialogue, makes the action culminate in his pulling her up into bed on a train, as "Mrs. Thornhill"—a beautiful way of expressing the link between his survival of the ordeal and their relationship. The last shot is of a train entering a tunnel: the "phallic symbol" toward which the whole film has moved.

It will be objected that this account of *North by Northwest* makes it far too serious. But its charms, its deftness, the constant flow of invention, its humor and exhilaration, are there for all to see. All I have tried to do is adjust the balance: not to turn a light comedy into an unsmiling morality play, but to suggest why *North by Northwest* is such a very, very good light comedy.

The Designs of Authorship: An Essay on *North by Northwest*

Marian Keane

North by Northwest occupies a central, though not easily grasped, place in Hitchcock's work. It immediately precedes *Psycho,* one of Hitchcock's darkest films, and brings together threads and themes of his earlier work, especially *The 39 Steps,* which it explicitly echoes. In the character of Eve Kendall, much of the Ingrid Bergman character in *Notorious* is duplicated; and in the Grant character's plea for help at the end of the film, a harbinger of *Marnie* can be heard. Yet *North by Northwest* marks the occasion of many endpoints in Hitchcock's work. In a way, it is his homage to Hollywood films and his farewell to them, and it is also his declaration of his own place within Hollywood's history. It is the last time he employs a star cast that survives in the film; the last time his wit and comedy fill a film to his audience's deep satisfaction; the last time he grants his audience what feels like a completely happy ending.

North by Northwest is and is not a comedy. As a comedy it stands as Hitchcock's working of a Hollywood genre of comedies, identifiable in part by their witty, fast-paced dialogue. The Cary Grant persona from these comedies emerges fully through his role and the film's explicit allusion to his earlier film roles. Like the 1930s comedies,[1] *North by Northwest* ends with (something like) a remarriage. At least, it is the Grant character's third marriage, and the Saint character's second intimate liaison that we know of. They take the train back to Chicago, in repetition of their first erotic encounter because, Grant tells her, "I'm sentimental." And their collapse onto the train berth closes with not quite an embrace,[2] though their union is something we do not doubt. Won in the face of its alternative fall, which would have been to their deaths, their marriage conjoins and closes the dual strains of the film's plot, one of which called for their deaths, one of which allowed and affirmed their love, and specifically, their marriage.

1. I refer here to the body of critical and theoretical works by Stanley Cavell that set out the nature of, and read in the particular, a genre he has isolated and named "Comedies of Remarriage." I refer specifically to his brilliant essay, "Leopards in Connecticut," *Georgia Review* 30, no. 2 (Summer 1976): 233–262, and to "The Pursuits of Happiness: A Reading of *The Lady Eve,*" *New Literary History* 10 (1979): 581–601. This essay owes a great debt to Cavell, not only to his writings, but to the numerous lectures by and conversations with him, to which this essay only represents a part of my debt.
2. This feature of the Comedies of Remarriage of closing on an "awkward" embrace or kiss is discussed by Cavell in "Leopards in Connecticut," 247–248, as a crucial feature of the genre.

From *Wide Angle* 4, no. 1 (1980): 44–52.

Though on the one hand *North by Northwest* is a romantic comedy and true to characteristics of a Hollywood genre, it is also a Hitchcock film. Thus, there are ways in which Hitchcock inserts himself, the history of his own filmmaking, into the generic aspects of the film. (This is one way of announcing that the history of Hollywood film genres is both encompassed by, and cannot be considered without the inclusion of, Hitchcock's work.) This film incorporates the romantic comedy features with classic Hitchcockian strategies: Thornhill/Grant's mistaken identity (as in *The Wrong Man*), a deep concern with theater, the threats of murder and violence. Most importantly, alternative plots, or scripts, share the world of the film's romance. Thus the possibilities of *North by Northwest* are both comic and tragic, where tragedy not only stands in the possibility of Thornhill's and Kendall's deaths, but in their metaphoric deaths by continued service to the Professor or Vandamm.

In the characters of the Professor and Vandamm, Hitchcock continues a lineage of figures whose intentions resemble and also challenge his own act of authoring the world of the film.[3] Both characters have scripts that are subversive to Hitchcock's own, and both devise little acts of theater, of playacting and violence, in order to achieve their ends. The Professor's plot is inseparable from Vandamm's, and both strategies are inseparable from Hitchcock's. Through these characters, and by distinguishing himself from them, Hitchcock announces who he is as a filmmaker, asserts his own presence, and contemplates the conditions of his authoring presence behind the camera. Within his work, these surrogate, subversive author-figures function centrally as one means of meditating on his own art and act of filmmaking.

That Hitchcock's relationship with the characters of Vandamm and the Professor involves the act of authorship is apparent in the shots that introduce either character. Vandamm is the second[4] author-figure to enter the camera's gaze, during the intricate, and to his mind unsuccessful, encounter with Thornhill/Grant in the elegant Townsend library. Vandamm (James Mason) enters the room through a set of double wooden doors, which, framed in long shot, heighten the

---

3. William Rothman's study of Hitchcock's authorship, *Hitchcock: The Murderous Gaze* (Cambridge, Mass.: Harvard University Press, 1982), deals centrally with the author-figures and their significance in Hitchcock's work as they appear in five Hitchcock films. The debt this essay owes to Rothman's work is but a small fraction of its real debt to him for his patience in seeing it to its completion. Throughout, my reading of *North by Northwest* is modeled on Rothman's manner of reading Hitchcock films.

4. The first author-figure to appear is Hitchcock himself, in a telling and humorous shot. During the title sequence, as his name cuts across the screen, Hitchcock runs to catch a bus, which shuts its doors in his face. The shot comments ironically on New York City's rush hour rudeness, and also suggests that Hitchcock is necessarily closed out of the world of his film. As with Octave/Renoir's realization at the end of *Rules of the Game*, Hitchcock here acknowledges that his position behind the camera mandates his physical omission from the world viewed.

theatricality of his arrival. It is important to remember that in this scene Vandamm presents himself as Lester Townsend, masking his real identity with an act. He will accuse Thornhill/Grant of assuming roles, of the very kind of playacting in which he indulges, throughout the film. Compositionally, the placement of this doorway represents a kind of frame-within-the-frame, similar to the way in which windows function throughout the film. The doorway also resembles a stage curtain, like the curtains on the opposite side of the room that Vandamm will make an event of drawing. These compositional elements bear out something also clear in Mason's formal and restrained acting (which can be compared, in opposition, to Grant's outrageous performances at the art auction or when driving while drunk in "Laura's Mercedes"). His presence in the world of the film is a self-conscious performance, an act that takes place as if on a stage. In each of his scenes, his every gesture is charged with the knowledge that he is performing.

In this introductory shot of Vandamm, the camera is located behind the desk opposite the doorway, on the far side of the room. Though Thornhill/Grant stands behind the desk to its left, this shot does not represent his point of view. He is looking out of the window to the lawn, where he sees Vandamm's agent Leonard for the first time. It is worth noting that this initial view of Leonard (Martin Landau), croquet mallet upraised in one hand, implies his potential for violence, and, in the composition of windowpane frames dividing his body in two, also foretells his death at the film's end.

In its framing and dramatic timing, including as it does the closed doorway just prior to Vandamm's entrance, this shot is underscored as Hitchcock's own private view. Specific compositional characteristics of the shot are echoed in the first full view of the Professor during the CIA conference room scene. In both, Hitchcock places the camera directly opposite its subject character, and on the opposite end of a writing surface. In the library, the camera views Vandamm from across the desk; in the CIA office, it takes up the only unoccupied chair (we can read: Hitchcock's chair[5]) at the end of a long table covered with writing tablets and pens.

In fact, the entire CIA sequence resembles a scriptwriting meeting.[6] Its five characters ponder the problem of what to do now that their scripted character has become real. Thornhill ("the poor sucker"), mistaken for the nonexistent Kaplan, has been trapped in a world where this hidden, sheltered group of authors plot his fate. "If it's so horribly sad," one of the advisors says, "how is it I feel like laughing?", a remark we can understand to be addressed to the whole of *North by Northwest*.

Though this scene is the Professor's, Hitchcock's presence is strongly manifest. As in the Townsend library scene, and that which takes place at Vandamm's Rapid

5. A critical point made by William Rothman in a lecture at Harvard University, spring 1978.
6. Ibid.

City home, the camera ascends to a high-angle position at a particular moment. The Professor declares that the CIA will "do nothing" to save Thornhill now that he faces the real consequences of their invented decoy agent. His survival is, the Professor states, "his problem." The camera assumes a high-angle, vertiginous position at this moment when Thornhill's fate seems sealed. "Good-bye, Mr. Thornhill, wherever you are," intones the female advisor; framed within the shot, on an angle, is the desk surrounded by the scriptwriters, inclusive of the empty chair that invokes Hitchcock's presence. The camera moves to the same high position when Vandamm tells Thornhill/Grant that his confession will at least afford him "the opportunity of surviving the evening" in the Townsend library. And again, Hitchcock marks the moment of an incipient death, or its threat, when he raises the camera above Vandamm and Leonard at Vandamm's home. Eve will be disposed of, Vandamm states, "from a great height. Over water."

Significantly, the place occupied by the camera in the initial views of the Professor and Vandamm is assumed at later moments in either scene by the would-be author-figure. When Vandamm reads Thornhill/Grant the sparse itinerary of George Kaplan's past, present, and future travels—a document that stands as his only information about the Professor's script—he stands behind the desk. In the CIA sequence, the Professor recounts the story of Kaplan's invention as a fictive character and, to the dismay of his advisors, asks, "What can we do to save him, without endangering our own agent?" Raising the safety of the agent and the secrecy of her real role in relation to Vandamm as his priority concerns, the Professor relinquishes responsibility for Thornhill's future. At these moments, he stands behind (Hitchcock's) empty chair, with the room's large windows squarely behind him.

The introductory shots of these characters and the subsequent occupation of the camera's positions in them by the Professor and Vandamm reveal aspects of Hitchcock's presence in *North by Northwest,* two of which we will set out here: first, that he is in opposition to the plans of these characters, and second, that the specific challenges each raises for Hitchcock, threats of which he is aware, are those of authorship. Clearly, the Professor's invention of George Kaplan, a name or character without a player, poses the same problems as a film script's characters prior to the selection of performers. This status of the figure of Kaplan is borne out in the Professor's request that Thornhill/Grant "go on being [Kaplan]" through the Mount Rushmore scene.

Though Vandamm is ignorant of important elements of the Professor's script, such as that Eve is a spy, he nonetheless has a plotted strategy all his own. Like the Professor's plot, Vandamm's play requires (play)acting with the intent of decep-tion for realization. His performance as Townsend, his sister's part as his wife (Mrs. Townsend), and Eve's act of seductress are all pieces of theater directed by Vandamm. The Professor's play, on the other hand, rather than attacking and exposing Vandamm's operations, takes up a role within them, penetrating them by performances designed for Vandamm as audience and for his deception. Though the Professor's play is more completely worked, Vandamm's harbors a special secret; what that secret really is, we never learn. What we do know is that his secret is embodied in a little film, itself embodied, engorged, or swallowed, into the belly of a miniature demigod statue.

The character of Vandamm dwells in what Norman Bates will aptly name "a private trap" in *Psycho;* in certain ways, he and Norman resemble each other. Whereas Norman will continue to "light the lights and change the beds" even in the absence of clients for his motel, Vandamm maintains a similar routine of formalities. Vandamm's "private trap" is the world of theater, of mere performances rather than actions truly meant, feelings really felt. His initial interview with Thornhill/Grant proves him to be both an admiring audience and a disbeliever of reality. "So you see," he says wearily, "there's very little sense in maintaining this fiction [we can read: Hitchcock's script] that you're deceiving us, any more than *we* are deceiving *you*."

The library scene is a little piece of theater Vandamm expertly designs to achieve an unmasking. His first gestures of closing the drapes and lighting two lamps, which throw light directly and brilliantly on Thornhill/Grant's face, transform the room into a theatrical space, a stage. In one of his customary strategies, Vandamm accuses Thornhill of creating this stage likeness, thereby diverting responsibility from himself. As Thornhill announces that he has tickets for a play at a theater in New York, Vandamm tells him, "With such expert playacting, you make this very room a theater."

The particular means by which Vandamm attempts to effect Kaplan's emergence, to cut through the guise of Thornhill and reveal the real person, is confronting Thornhill with the facts of his "real" identity. By staging a play within which Vandamm assumes he knows the truth about Thornhill, this scene presents the first elucidation of the film's title reference to *Hamlet*. (Hitchcock explicitly alludes to the same play-within-a-play scene in *Hamlet* in *Murder!*) The title of *North by Northwest* is taken from act II, Scene ii, in *Hamlet,* in which Hamlet greets the players who come to Elsinore:

> HAMLET: Gentlemen, you are welcome to Elsinore.
> Your hands. Come then.
> T'appurtenance of welcome, is fashion
> and ceremony. Let me comply with you in garbe,
> lest me extent with the players,
> which I tell you must show fairly outwards,
> should appear more like entertainment than yours.
> You are welcome.
> But my uncle-father and aunt-mother are deceived.
> GUILDENSTERN: In what, my dear lord?
> HAMLET: I am but mad north, northwest;
> when the wind is southerly,
> I know a hawk from a handsaw. (379–388)

In Vandamm's play, every line turns on the subjects of acting and deception. Vandamm acknowledges that Thornhill/Grant is a "man of many names" and agrees "to accept [his] current choice." "Roger Thornhill" is understood by Vandamm to be an act, a falsity. On one level, Vandamm is erroneous in his refusal to accept that this man is Roger Thornhill, Madison Avenue advertising executive, master of "the Expedient Exaggeration." At another level, a level of which Vandamm is unaware, the issue uncovered is that of who the actor Cary Grant is, since Roger Thornhill and George Kaplan become two of his many names, two of the roles he plays in front of the camera.

North by Northwest makes a point of being a film tailor-made for Cary Grant, and not merely in the resuscitation of his 1930s comedy persona. Every aspect of his charm, wit, and physical ease becomes a part of the character Roger Thornhill. By contrast, George Kaplan is not, at the start, a role for Grant. Clearly the Professor did not have him in mind when he ordered a suit and a comb full of dandruff, outlining features of Kaplan. Kaplan, however, is a role Thornhill/Grant comes to accept, to play in *North by Northwest:* it is as Kaplan that he dies in the cafeteria at Mount Rushmore.

The part of Roger Thornhill is not altogether different than that of Kaplan; the task of playing Thornhill, though, involves Grant's understanding and acknowledgment that he is acting in a film directed by Alfred Hitchcock. Revealing this process of Thornhill/Grant's dawning realization of the camera, the camera, time and time again, functions independently of his gaze. In these special views, the camera points out particularly menacing, threatening elements of the world of the film of which Thornhill/Grant is unaware. This knowledgeability of the camera is shown, for example, in its sweeping tracking movement, during the Oak Room bar scene, when it focuses on the two ominously waiting thugs in the corridor. Similarly, when Thornhill/Grant and his entourage of disbelievers, his mother and the detectives, leave the Townsend mansion, the shot that views their disappearing car turns to frame the figure of a gardener trimming the hedges. In the next, closer, shot, the gardener raises his head into the frame and turns to watch Thornhill's departure. This figure who frighteningly penetrates the limits of the frame is Vandamm's knife-wielding thug.

Yet another instance of the camera's independent gazing occurs in the United Nations lobby. Here, the camera's movement is almost exactly like the movement in the Oak Room bar scene. Thornhill gives his name ("George Kaplan") to the information desk and asks that Lester Townsend be paged. Thornhill then turns his back to the camera, surveying the room for Townsend's arrival. At the exact moment that his back is turned, the camera pans right quickly, to the doorway, where the knife thrower waits, framed next to a highly polished statue.

These shots emphasize Thornhill/Grant's unawareness of the camera, his denial of its presence. The camera movements undertaken at the times Thornhill turns away reveal its perspicuity in the world of the film and also, with each shot beginning its motion from a frame Thornhill/Grant occupies, imply his absented view. In other words, these are views that are available to Thornhill/Grant, but that require his acknowledgement of the camera.

As in other of his films,[7] Cary Grant's dilemma in *North by Northwest* is that he does not know about the world he inhabits, how it works or what lies in store for him; he also does not know, on a deeper level, what he is to do. His manner of surviving his thrownness[8] in the world he discovers himself to inhabit relies upon his intelligence and physical agility and most importantly on his comic wit.

Grant appropriates the gaze and frame of the camera at a crucial moment in *North by Northwest*. On the runway of the airport in Chicago, the Professor tells Grant that Eve Kendall (Eva Marie Saint) is a double agent. In a close-up shot, Grant's look of sudden realization is underscored by the increase of light illuminating him. This shot fades into a long shot of Mount Rushmore, within which a binocular iris movement enlarges and isolates the faces carved in its surface. In the third shot of this point-of-view sequence, the camera frames Grant peering through a large, cameralike, tourist's binocular. His possession of this frame is complete, however, only after his discovery that the Professor's plan does not allow him to leave with Eve. His escape from the hospital window, echoing by opposition his inability to escape from the car taking him to Townsend's mansion, (where he is framed completely, and enclosed by the car window) leads to his act of contacting Eve through the ladderlike (and framelike) windows of her room at Vandamm's house.

However, fully apparent from the beginning of *North by Northwest* is the fact that the Thornhill figure framed by the camera is Cary Grant. He himself disparages the name (as Vandamm disparages Kaplan and Thornhill) to Eve, telling her that the "O" middle initial stands for "nothing." The film's finest sight gags occur when Grant tries, unsuccessfully, to disguise his face or when the camera frames his face making faces, such as in his drunk driving sequence. . . . "I know. I look vaguely familiar," Grant admits, "You feel you've seen me somewhere before." "Mmmm," she responds. If *North by Northwest* is, as Hitchcock tells Truffaut, "one long joke" in any way, it is as an extended comedy revolving around Grant's face. The joke is its unmistakable singularity, familiarity, sculptural fitness in the frame.

Grant's entrance into the world of *North by Northwest* repeats, as many of the film's images do, features of the film's opening credit sequence. The initial single-color blank screen hinges itself, graphically, to the wall of (what we take to be) a building previously invisible as window frames take their shape. These rectangular outlines, resembling film frames, transform into a reflective, mirror-

7. Specifically, I refer to Grant's work in the 1930s comedies, most importantly in *Bringing Up Baby*, but also in *The Awful Truth* and *His Girl Friday*. Henry Fonda suffers the same dilemma in *The Lady Eve*.

8. Stanley Cavell discusses the problem of thrownness in its philosophical context in "What Becomes of Things on Film," *Philosophy and Literature* 2, no. 2 (Fall 1978): 249–257. I refer to pages 249–251 specifically.

like surface containing the image of traffic moving on the street below. The screen, in this sequence, conjures itself a screen on which frames take shape and which open onto reflected depth. Cary Grant enters the world of *North by Northwest* from an elevator, the doors of which are initially shut. Thus his appearance occurs in an image that begins in flatness and opens onto depth, a depth from which he steps. This opening movement of the elevator doors duplicates features of the opening sequence's flatness. Like the image conjured in depth, Grant's appearance marks his "birth" or magical emergence into the film. And he is born into the frame of *North by Northwest* already in possession of his screen identity.

Without doubt, Grant's entrance is also theatrical. Like Vandamm's entrance into the Townsend library, or Eve Kendall's sudden appearance from an unviewed doorway into the long, thin train corridor, or even the Professor's withheld presence in the CIA office scene, *North by Northwest* makes theater as much its subject as it does film. The importance of the opening credit sequence lies in its deeply meditative relation to the subjects addressed by the film. At the outset, it declares the film's relationship to the worlds of Hollywood films wherein magical powers oversee lovers to their proper conclusions.[9]

Further, this opening sequence speaks to the dilemmas Grant faces within the world of the film, specifically that he must learn what that world is and whose magic obtains. The deep issue raised in the magical appearance of the film's image regards what the world so conjured actually is. Partially, this is a question about the presence of the director, whose hand, itself a secret, creates the image of the world we view. But also, this is partially a question about the nature of the film image conjured out of the screen itself. This magic remains that of one unseen; the world conjured announces itself as a miniature, the reflection of a world projected on the flat and receptive screen.

In turn, Grant's magical appearance into the world of the film raises issues that are repeated in the question addressed to him—who is he?—throughout the film; the most anyone knows is his familiar face and his ability to act. His entrance and presence, seemingly an immortal presence affirmed by the failures of repeated attempts to kill him, revolve around the issue of who it is that Cary Grant becomes (who anyone becomes) on film.[10]

9. Magic is an especially important feature of the genre of comedies set forth by Cavell. Usually, as in *The Lady Eve,* the father (or Senex figure) holds the magical power in the world of the film. Ibid. See also Cavell's critical and theoretical work on this subject, particularly "The Pursuits of Happiness," pp. 584–589.

10. This is the problem Cavell sets out at the close of "What Becomes of Things on Film" as "an undertaking of what we might call film theory," that is, "to explain how these appearances . . . are made possible by the general photogenesis of film altogether, by the fact, as I more or less put it in *The World Viewed,* that objects on film are always already displaced, *trouvé* (i.e., that we as viewers are always already displaced before them)" would be this undertaking (p. 256). It was this statement of Cavell's that led to my understanding of this problem in *North by Northwest.*

North by Northwest confronts this problem through the designs invented by the Professor and Vandamm, in part. It is in juxtaposition to the playacting that both demand that another acting, one that Hitchcock stands behind, presents itself. And this alternation of acting and its opposite, or playacting and its real counterpart, is also at the core of *Hamlet*. In a scene earlier than the one of the title's reference, Hamlet sets out the problems of acting revived and explicit in *North by Northwest*. Hamlet is responding to his mother's accusation that his grief at his father's death "seems so particular" on him. He replies:

> *Seems*, madam! Nay, it *is;* I know not *seems.*
> 'Tis not alone my inky cloak, good mother,
> Nor customary suits of solemn black,
> Nor windy suspiration of forc'd breath,
> No, nor the fruitful river in the eye,
> Nor the dejected 'havior of the visage,
> Together with all forms, modes, shows of grief,
> That can denote me truly; these indeed *seem,*
> For they are actions that a man might play;
> But I have that within me which passeth show;
> These, but the trappings and the suits of woe. (I.ii.78–86)

It is Vandamm in *North by Northwest* who makes the claims that Grant's performances are playacting, that they, in fact, "seem." He charges Grant with playing the outraged Madison Avenue advertising man, the peevish lover, and the wrongly accused fugitive from justice at the art auction scene in the same way he accuses Grant of "playacting" the role of Thornhill in the Townsend library. Vandamm's plight in *North by Northwest* is of a man who cannot see; it is to him that we might direct Gloucester's statements to his son in *King Lear,* when he claims that Edgar is a man "that will not see because he doth not feel" (IV.i). At the close of *North by Northwest,* we witness not the single, simple demise of Vandamm's import-export trading of national secrets, but the cataclysmic plunge of his world, its ways, its old routines. Believing everybody capable of (play)acting, of falsifying who they are, what they feel, and where their loyalties fall and reside, Vandamm knows he can be deceived at every turn, each encounter. In the face of this possibility, to ward it off, he himself playacts, masks who he is to preserve his feelings.

Yet believing the world capable of lying, Vandamm tragically misplaces his trust. He cannot see that Thornhill/Grant is not Kaplan, but neither can he see that Eve no longer loves him or that Leonard does love him. Vandamm's inhumanity is registered in his timely exits from the scenes of violence happily executed by Leonard. Grant's coerced drinking at the Townsend library . . . , and Eve's seduction of Grant on the train, are performances that occur at Vandamm's demand. In a similar way the Professor runs inside the Mount Rushmore cafeteria the moment Vandamm, Leonard, and Eve arrive to meet Thornhill/Grant. Both author-figures, maintaining the privilege of keeping themselves on the periphery of the acts they command, or hidden but aware of them, take their physical removal to mean they are not responsible for the things that take place.

The deeply sympathetic strain of Vandamm's character is his aestheticism. There are formalities to Vandamm's world and authorship, routines that Hitchcock proves do not hold in the world of the film. Vandamm asks that Eve seduce Grant, but expects her to have no feelings about it; even Leonard's declaration of his feelings shocks Vandamm at the close of the film. One formality that obtains for Vandamm is that the world carry with it no real consequences for actions, and it is for him that the ending of *North by Northwest* stands as a tragic revelation. In a film full of fake bullets, fake deaths, and fake identities, Leonard's fall to death forces Vandamm to say, "That wasn't very sporting, using real bullets!" His sense of theatrical formality throughout the film caused him to deny the reality of his own situation and those into which he placed others. And, without acknowledging the actions, feelings, and human beings in *North by Northwest* to be real, Vandamm artfully placed himself above its world. It is Vandamm at the film's close who suffers most for the turn Hitchcock's film took toward the dimensions of its own reality, warranting deaths, affirming love.

The Professor, too, holds himself outside the world of *North by Northwest*. "Getting too old for this kind of work," he grumbles to Thornhill/Grant as they run to catch the plane to Rapid City. His intervention became warranted only when Grant "severely overplayed" his part at the art auction, endangering Eve's life. The Professor's reemergence into the world of the film, after his declaration that he would do nothing to save Thornhill, is necessitated by the fact that the play has swung out of control. Thus he designs one last act, one that "will satisfy" Vandamm: the act of Kaplan's death. Whereas Vandamm's goal is the preservation of a little statue, the Professor's is national security. And like Vandamm, the Professor's aim and methods are not vindicated by Hitchcock in the end. The Professor's tragic flaw, although not laced with the homosexual undercurrent revealed in Vandamm, is that his desire for national security outweighs his humanity. He lies to Thornhill/Grant, telling him that after meeting Vandamm in the cafeteria, he and Eve will be together. And like Vandamm, the Professor undertakes no actions on his own; the state trooper fires the fatal bullet that fells Leonard from the top of Mount Rushmore.

Both surrogate author-figures are present by proxy in the difficult scene between Eve and Thornhill in her Chicago hotel room. There, they appear in the form of statues, two Chinese sculptures placed on the bureau, next to a television set.[11] The restraint with which she asks that Grant leave, "no questions asked,"

---

11. Television sets appear in *North by Northwest* in three scenes, each time representing one of the author-figures' access to the other characters in the film, particularly Eve and Thornhill, by viewing them from a hidden location. In brief, these television sets duplicate features of the film frame and

reveals the controlling power these two figures wield over her, the force with which they demand that she deny her real feelings and relinquish them in the acts they demand of her. The (re)marriage desired by Kendall/Saint and Thornhill/ Grant requires their acknowledgment, not only that they act out of love, but that they act under Hitchcock's gaze. Their escape occurs at Grant's discovery that both the Professor and Vandamm are birds of prey, called by Hamlet a hawk and a handsaw, or his uncle-father and aunt-mother. The kernel of Grant's ability to deceive these watchful, plotting authors derives from, Hitchcock reveals to us, his immortality on the screen once he acknowledges Hitchcock's camera.

Yet this is not to say that Hitchcock shares nothing with these birds of prey. Surely the designs of the Professor and Vandamm, their efforts and desires to kill and demand performances, are also those of Hitchcock's camera. His camera's own immortality as a mythical bird with an appetite for murder becomes the subject of *Psycho*. Even in *North by Northwest,* Grant and Saint are pressed to the extreme, to begging for assistance to survive their perches on Mount Rushmore. It is Grant who must look directly into the camera, which represents at that moment Leonard's point of view, and beseech it for help. Hitchcock's allegiance with Leonard here is not accidental; the faces of the camera are revealed in both of their possibilities, human and inhuman. Hitchcock also speaks to the desires of his audience in this shot, desires that contain both the wish to see Grant and Saint fall and the wish to see them survive.

In accepting the conditions of a romantic comedy of remarriage, Hitchcock declares that its world, like the world of any film (a world that happens before and includes the camera), is not without its dark desires. The myth of the Hollywood screen romance, which emerges from and creates "such stuff as dreams are made on," is revealed to include the preying possibilities of the camera's (and audience's) gaze under Hitchcock's magical hand.[12] *North by Northwest* affirms the comedy of remarriage, but reveals tragic possibilities that reside in its (film) myth as a result of its very nature as a film.

---

screen and reveal the author-figure's private viewing access to the world of the film. One television set is in the Professor's CIA office, where it symbolizes a global control in much the same way as the Professor's globe in *The 39 Steps* (cf. Rothman, *The Murderous Gaze,* Chapter 3) symbolizes this. Most clearly, the television set on which Vandamm's housekeeper spies Grant, in reflection, sneaking down the stairs and arrests him (with Eve's fake gun) reveals the privileges of viewing they permit.

12. This awareness of the camera, or of a film genre, is not to be found in *North by Northwest* alone. Though Hitchcock's camera, and the film's acknowledgments of it, are different from those in the other comedies of remarriage as set out by Cavell, the comedies he reads share this self-consciousness, and address the issues of the screen and camera, and that of the viewer. Thus the specific working of the genre is Hitchcock's in *North by Northwest,* but this central characteristic of the film as a comedy of remarriage is shared by the other films Cavell isolates, each in a different way.

The Hitchcockian Blot

Slavoj Žižek

n writing Poe's "The Purloined Letter," Lacan makes reference to a game of logic: we take a random series of 0s and 1s—100101100, for example—and as soon the series is articulated into linked triads (100,001,010,etc.), rules of succession will emerge (a triad with 0 at the end cannot be followed by a triad that has 1 as its middle term, and so on).[1] The same is true of Hitchcock's films: if we consider them as a whole we have an accidental, random series, but as soon as we separate them into linked triads (and exclude those films that are not part of the "Hitchcockian universe," the "exceptions," the results of various compromises), each triad can then be seen to be linked by some theme, some common structuring principle. For example, take the following five films: *The Wrong Man, Vertigo, North by Northwest, Psycho,* and *The Birds:* no single theme can be found to link all the films in such a series, yet such themes can be found if we consider them in groups of three. The first triad concerns "false identity": in *The Wrong Man,* the hero is wrongly identified as the burglar; in *Vertigo* the hero is mistaken about the identity of the false Madeleine; in *North by Northwest* Soviet spies mistakenly identify the film's hero as the mysterious agent "George Kaplan." As for the great trilogy *Vertigo, North by Northwest,* and *Psycho,* it is very tempting to regard these three key Hitchcock films as the articulation of three different versions of filling the gap in the Other. Their formal problem is the same: the relationship between a lack and a factor (a person) that tries to compensate for it. In *Vertigo,* the hero attempts to compensate for the absence of the woman he loves, an apparent suicide, on a level that is literally *imaginary:* he tries, by means of dress, hairstyle, and so forth, to recreate the image of the lost woman. In *North by Northwest,* we are on the *symbolic* level: we are dealing with an empty name, the name of a nonexistent person ("Kaplan"), a signifier without a bearer, which becomes attached to the hero out of sheer chance. In *Psycho,* finally, we reach the level of the *real:* Norman Bates, who dresses in his mother's clothes, speaks with her voice, etc., wants neither to resuscitate her image nor act in her name; he wants to take her place in the real—evidence of a psychotic state.

If the middle triad, therefore, is that of the "empty place," the final one is in its turn united around the motif of the *maternal superego:* the heroes of these three films are fatherless, they have a mother who is "strong," who is "possessive," who disturbs the

---

1. *Ecrits* (Paris: Sevil, 1966), pp. 54–59.

From *Looking Awry: An Introduction to Jacques Lacan Through Popular Culture* (Cambridge, Mass.: MIT Press, 1991), pp. 98–104.

"normal" sexual relationship. At the very beginning of *North by Northwest* the film's hero, Roger Thornhill (Cary Grant), is shown with his scornful, mocking mother, and it is not difficult to guess why he has been four times divorced;[2] in *Psycho* Norman Bates (Anthony Perkins) is directly controlled by the voice of his dead mother, which instructs him to kill any woman to whom he is sexually attracted; in the case of the mother of Mitch Brenner (Rod Taylor), hero of *The Birds,* mocking disdain is replaced by a zealous concern for her son's fate, a concern that is perhaps even more effective in blocking any lasting relationship he might have with a woman.

There is another trait common to these three films: from one film to the next, the figure of a threat in the shape of birds assumes greater prominence. In *North by Northwest* we have what is perhaps the most famous Hitchcockian scene, the attack by the plane—a steel bird—that pursues the hero across a flat, sun-baked landscape; in *Psycho,* Norman's room is filled with stuffed mounted birds, and even the body of his mummified mother reminds us of a stuffed bird; in *The Birds,* after the (metaphorical) steel bird and the (metonymic) stuffed birds, we finally have actual live birds attacking the town.

The decisive thing is to perceive the link between the two traits: the terrifying figure of the birds is actually the embodiment in the real of a discord, an unresolved tension in intersubjective relations. In the film, the birds are like the plague in Oedipus's Thebes: they are the incarnation of a fundamental disorder in family relationships—the father is absent, the paternal function (the function of pacifying law, the Name-of the-Father) is suspended and that vacuum is filled by the "irrational" maternal superego, arbitrary, wicked, blocking "normal" sexual relationship (only possible under the sign of the paternal metaphor). The dead end *The Birds* is really about is, of course, that of the modern American family: the deficient paternal ego-ideal makes the law "regress" toward a ferocious maternal superego, affecting sexual enjoyment—the decisive trait of the libidinal structure of "pathological narcissism": "Their unconscious impressions of the mother are so overblown and so heavily influenced by aggressive impulses, and the quality of her care is so little attuned to the child's needs, that in the child's fantasies the mother appears as a devouring bird."[3]

From the Oedipal Journey to the "Pathological Narcissist"

How should we locate this figuration of the maternal superego in the totality of Hitchcock's work? The three main stages of Hitchcock's career can be conceived

---

2. Žižek is in error here: Thornhill's mother does not actually appear in the film's opening scenes; she is, however, concisely and vividly described. In addition, Thornhill has been divorced twice, not four times. [Editor's note.]

3. Christopher Lasch, *The Culture of Narcissism* (London: Abacus, 1980), p. 176.

precisely as three variations on the theme of the impossibility of the sexual relationship. Let us begin with the first Hitchcockian classic, *The 39 Steps:* all the animated action of the film should not deceive us for a minute—its function is ultimately just to put the love couple to the test and thus render possible their final reunion. It is on account of this feature that *The 39 Steps* starts the series of Hitchcock's English films of the second half of the 1930s, all of which, with the exception of the last (*Jamaica Inn*), relate the same story of the *initiation of an amorous couple.* They are all stories of a couple tied (sometimes literally: note the role of handcuffs in *The 39 Steps*) by accident and then maturing through a series of ordeals. All these films are thus actually variations on the fundamental motif of the bourgeois ideology of marriage, gaining its first and perhaps noblest expression in Mozart's *The Magic Flute.* The parallel could be here expanded to details: the mysterious woman who charges the hero with his mission (the stranger killed in Hannay's apartment in *The 39 Steps;* the nice old lady who vanishes in the film of the same title), is she not a kind of reincarnation of the "Queen of the Night"? The black Monostatos, is he not reincarnated in the murderous drummer with blackened face in *Young and Innocent?* In *The Lady Vanishes,* the hero attracts the attention of his future love by playing what? A flute, of course!

The innocence lost on this voyage of initiation is best presented in the remarkable figure of Mr. Memory, whose number in the music hall opens and closes the film. He is a man who "remembers everything," a personification of pure automatism and, at the same time, the absolute ethic of the signifier (in the film's final scene, he answers Hannay's question "What are 'the thirty-nine steps'?", although he knows the answer could cost him his life—he is simply obliged to honor his public engagement, to answer any question whatsoever). There is something of the fairy tale in this figure of a Good Dwarf who must die in order that the liaison of the amorous couple finally be established. Mr. Memory embodies a pure, asexual, gapless knowledge, a signifying chain that works absolutely automatically, without any traumatic stumbling block hindering its course. What we must be careful about is the precise moment of his death: he dies after answering the question "What are 'the thirty-nine steps'?", i.e., after revealing the MacGuffin, the secret propelling the story. By disclosing it to the public in the music hall (which stands here for the big Other of common opinion), he delivers Hannay from the awkward position of "persecuted persecutor." The two circles (that of the police chasing Hannay and that of Hannay himself in pursuit of the real culprit) rejoin, Hannay is exonerated in the eyes of the big Other, and the real culprits are unmasked. At this point, the story could end since it was sustained solely by this intermediary state, by Hannay's ambiguous position vis-à-vis the big Other: guilty in the eyes of the big Other, he is at the same time on the track of the real culprits.

It is this position of the "persecuted persecutor" that already displays the motif of the "transference of guilt": Hannay is falsely accused, the guilt is transferred onto him—but whose guilt is it? The guilt of the *obscene, "anal" father* personified by the mysterious leader of the spy network. At the film's end, we witness *two* consecutive deaths: first the leader of the spy ring kills Mr. Memory, then the police, this instrument of the big Other, shoot down the leader, who falls from his theater box onto the podium (this is an exemplary place of denouement in Hitchcock's films: *Murder!*, *Stage Fright*, *I Confess*). Mr. Memory and the leader of the spy ring represent the two sides of the same pre-Oedipal conjunction: the Good Dwarf with his gapless undivided knowledge, and the mean "anal father," the master who pulls the strings of this knowledge-automaton, a father who exhibits in an obscene way his shortened little finger—an ironic allusion to his castration. (We encounter a homologous split in Robert Rossen's *The Hustler*, in the relationship between the professional billiard player, an incarnation of the pure ethic of the game [Jackie Gleason], and his corrupt boss [George C. Scott].) The story begins with an act of "interpellation" that subjectivizes the hero, i.e., it constitutes him as desiring by evoking the MacGuffin, the object-cause of his desire (the message of the "Queen of the Night," the mysterious stranger who is slaughtered in Hannay's apartment). The Oedipal voyage in pursuit of the father, which constitutes the bulk of the film, ends with the "anal" father's death. By means of his death, he can assume his place as metaphor, as the Name-of-the-Father, thus rendering possible the amorous couple's final reunion, their "normal" sexual relation, which, according to Lacan, can take place only under the sign of the paternal metaphor.

In addition to Hannay and Pamela in *The 39 Steps*, couples tied by chance and reunited through ordeal are Ashenden and Elsa in *The Secret Agent*, Robert and Erica in *Young and Innocent*, Gilbert and Iris in *The Lady Vanishes*—with the notable exception of *Sabotage*, in which the triangle of Sylvia, her criminal husband Verloc, and the detective Ted foreshadows the conjuncture characteristic of Hitchcock's next stage (the Selznick period). Here, the story is, as a rule, narrated from the point of view of a woman divided between two men, the elderly figure of a villain (her father or her aged husband, embodying one of the typical Hitchcockian figures, that of a villain who is aware of the evil in himself and who strives after his own destruction) and the younger, somewhat insipid "good guy" whom she chooses at the end.[4] In addition to Sylvia, Verloc, and Ted in *Sabotage*, the main cases of such triangles are Carol Fisher, divided between loyalty to her pro-Nazi father and love for the young American journalist, in *Foreign Correspondent;* Charlie, divided between her murderous uncle of the same name and the detective Jack, in *Shadow of a Doubt;* and, of course, Alicia, divided between her

---

4. Here it is crucial to grasp the logic of the connection between the woman's perspective and the figure of the resigned, impotent Master. Lacan's answer to Freud's famous question "*Was will das Weib?* What does the (hysterical) woman want?" is: *a Master, but one whom she could dominate*. The perfect figuration of this hysterical fantasy is Charlotte Brontë's *Jane Eyre*, in which, at the end of the novel, the heroine is happily married to the blinded, helpless fatherlike figure (*Rebecca*, of course, belongs to the same tradition).

aged husband Sebastian and Devlin, in *Notorious.* (The notable exception here is *Under Capricorn,* in which the heroine resists the charm of a young seducer and returns to her aged, criminal husband after confessing that the crime her husband was convicted for was her own.) The third stage again shifts the accent to the male hero, to whom the maternal superego blocks access, thus prohibiting a "normal" sexual relation (from Bruno in *Strangers on a Train* to the "necktie murderer" in *Frenzy).*

Where should we look for the wider frame of reference enabling us to confer a kind of theoretical consistency on this succession of the three forms of (the impossibility of) sexual relationship? Here, we are tempted to venture a somewhat quick "sociological" answer by invoking the three successive forms of the libidinal structure of the subject exhibited in capitalist society during the past century: the "autonomous" individual of the Protestant ethic, the heteronomous "organization man," and the type gaining predominance today, the "pathological narcissist." The crucial thing to emphasize here is that the so-called "decline of the Protestant ethic" and the appearance of the "organization man," i.e., the replacement of the ethic of individual responsibility by the ethic of the heteronomous individual, oriented toward others, leaves intact the underlying frame of the ego-ideal. It is merely its contents that change: the ego-ideal becomes "externalized" as the expectations of the social group to which the individual belongs. The source of moral satisfaction is no longer the feeling that we resisted the pressure of our milieu and remained true to ourselves (i.e., to our paternal ego-ideal), but rather the feeling of loyalty to the group. The subject looks at himself through the eyes of the group; he strives to merit its love and esteem.

The third stage, the arrival of the "pathological narcissist," breaks precisely with this underlying frame of the ego-ideal common to the first two forms. Instead of the integration of a symbolic *law,* we have a multitude of *rules* to follow—rules of accommodation telling us "how to succeed." The narcissistic subject knows only the "rules of the (social) game" enabling him to manipulate others; social relations constitute for him a playing field in which he assumes "roles," not proper symbolic mandates; he stays clear of any kind of binding commitment that would imply a proper symbolic identification. He is a radical *conformist* who paradoxically experiences himself as an *outlaw.* All this is, of course, already a commonplace of social psychology; what usually goes unnoticed, however, is that this disintegration of the ego-ideal entails the installation of a "maternal" superego that does not prohibit enjoyment but, on the contrary, imposes it and punishes "social failure" in a far more cruel and severe way, through an unbearable and self-destructive anxiety. All the babble about the "decline of paternal authority" merely conceals the resurgence of this incomparably more oppressive agency. Today's "permissive" society is certainly not less "repressive" than the epoch of the "organization man," that obsessive servant of the bureaucratic institution; the sole difference lies in the fact that, in a "society that demands submission to the rules of social intercourse but refuses to ground those rules in a code of moral conduct,"[5] i.e., in the ego-ideal, the social demand assumes the form of a harsh, punitive superego.

We could also approach "pathological narcissism" on the basis of Saul Kripke's criticism of the theory of descriptions, i.e., from his premise that the meaning of a name (proper or of a natural kind) can never be reduced to a set of descriptive features that characterize the object denoted by it. The name always functions as a "rigid designator," referring to the same object even if all properties contained in its meaning prove false.[6] Needless to say, the Kripkian notion of the "rigid designator" overlaps perfectly with the Lacanian notion of the "master signifier," i.e., of a signifier that does not denote some positive property of the object but establishes, by means of its own act of enunciation, a new intersubjective relation between speaker and hearer. If, for example, I tell somebody "You are my master!", I confer upon him a certain symbolic "mandate" that is not contained in the set of his positive properties but results from the very performative force of my utterance, and I create thereby a new symbolic reality, that of a master-disciple relationship between the two of us, within which each of us assumes a certain commitment. The paradox of the "pathological narcissist" is, however, that *for him, language does indeed function according to the theory of descriptions:* the meaning of words is reduced to the positive features of the denoted object, above all those that concern his narcissistic interests. Let us exemplify this apropos of the eternally tedious feminine question: "Why do you love me?" In love proper, this question is, of course, unanswerable (which is why women ask it in the first place), i.e., the only appropriate answer is "Because there is something in you more than yourself, some indefinite X that attracts me, but that cannot be pinned down to any positive quality." In other words, if we answer it with a catalogue of positive properties ("I love you because of the shape of your breasts, because of the way you smile"), this is at best a mocking imitation of love proper. The "pathological narcissist" is, on the other hand, somebody who *is* able to answer such a question by enumerating a definite list of properties: for him, the idea that love is a commitment transcending an attachment to a series of qualities that could gratify his wishes is simply beyond comprehension.[7] And the way to hystericize the "pathological narcissist" is precisely to force upon him some symbolic mandate that cannot be grounded in its properties. Such a confrontation brings about

---

5. Lasch, *The Culture of Narcissism,* p. 12.
6. Cf. Saul Kripke, *Naming and Necessity* (Cambridge, Mass.: Harvard University Press, 1972).
7. It is against the background of this problem that we could perhaps locate the lesson to be drawn from Stanley Cavell's *Pursuits of Happiness: The Hollywood Comedies of Remarriage* (Cambridge, Mass.: Harvard University Press, 1981), namely a version of the Hegelian theory of repetition in history: the only proper marriage is the second one. First we marry the other *qua* our narcissistic complement; it is only when his/her delusive charm fades that we can engage in marriage as an attachment to the other beyond his/her imaginary properties.

the hysterical question, "Why am I what you are saying that I am?" Think of Roger O. Thornhill in Hitchcock's *North by Northwest,* a pure "pathological narcissist" if ever there was one, who all of a sudden, without any apparent reason, finds himself pinned to the signifier "Kaplan"; the shock of this encounter derails his narcissistic economy and opens up to him the road of gradual access to "normal" sexual relations under the sign of the Name-of-the-Father (which is why *North by Northwest* is a variation of the formula of *The 39 Steps*).[8]

We can now see how the three versions of the impossibility of sexual relationship in Hitchcock's films refer to these three types of libidinal economy. The couple's initiating voyage, with its obstacles stirring the desire of reunification, is firmly grounded in the classical ideology of the "autonomous" subject strengthened through ordeal; the resigned paternal figure of Hitchcock's next stage evokes the decline of this "autonomous" subject to whom is opposed the victorious, insipid "heteronomous" hero; and, finally, it is not difficult to recognize in the typical Hitchcockian hero of the 1950s and 1960s the features of the "pathological narcissist" dominated by the obscene figure of the maternal superego. Hitchcock is thus staging again and again the vicissitudes of the family in late capitalist society; the real "secret" of his films is ultimately always the family secret, its tenebrous reverse.

8. It is because *North by Northwest* repeats the logic of the Oedipal journey that it offers us a kind of spectral analysis of the function of the father, dividing it into three figures: Roger Thornhill's *imaginary* father (the United Nations diplomat stabbed in the hall of the General Assembly), his *symbolic* father (the CIA "Professor" who invented the *name* "Kaplan" to which Thornhill is tied), and his *real* father, i.e., the resigned, perverse villain Vandamm.

Filmography and Bibliography

Hitchcock Filmography, 1925–1976

Incomplete Films

1922 *Always Tell Your Wife*
Co-directed by Hitchcock and
Seymour Hicks. Screenplay by Hicks.

1922 *Mrs. Peabody (Number Thirteen)*
Screenplay by Hitchcock. (In his
interview with Truffaut, Hitchcock
describes this film as a "two-reeler" or
twenty-minute short.)

Silent Features

1925/rel. 1927 *The Pleasure Garden*
Screenplay by Eliot Stannard, based
on the novel by Oliver Sandys.

1925/rel. 1927 *The Mountain Eagle*
Screenplay by Eliot Stannard.

1926/rel. 1927 *The Lodger*
Screenplay by Eliot Stannard, based
on the novel by Marie Belloc
Lowndes.

1927 *Downhill*
Screenplay by Eliot Stannard, based
on the play by David LeStrange
(pseudonym of Ivor Novello and
Constance Collier).

1927 *Easy Virtue*
Screenplay by Eliot Stannard, based
on the play by Noel Coward.

1927 *The Ring*
Screenplay by Hitchcock and Alma
Reville.

1927/rel. 1928 *The Farmer's Wife*
Screenplay by Hitchcock, based on
the play by Eden Philpotts.

1928 *Champagne*
Screenplay by Eliot Stannard,
adaptation by Hitchcock, based
on an original story by Walter C.
Mycroft.

1928/rel. 1929 *The Manxman*
Screenplay by Eliot Stannard, based
on the novel by Sir Hall Caine.

Sound Features

1929 *Blackmail*
Screenplay by Hitchcock and Benn W. Levy, based on the play by Charles Bennett.

1930 *Juno and the Paycock*
Screenplay by Hitchcock and Alma Reville, based on the play by Sean O'Casey.

Murder!
Screenplay by Hitchcock and Walter Mycroft, based on the novel and play *Enter Sir John* by Clemence Dane and Helen Simpson.
(Hitchcock also directed a German version of this film, entitled *Mary.*)

1930/rel. 1931 *The Skin Game*
Adaptation by Hitchcock, screenplay by Alma Reville, based on the play by John Galsworthy.

1931/rel. 1932 *Number Seventeen*
Screenplay by Alma Reville, Hitchcock, and Rodney Ackland, based on the play by Jefferson Farjeon.

1932 *Rich and Strange*
Adaptation by Hitchcock, screenplay by Alma Reville and Val Valentine, story by Dale Collins.

1933 *Waltzes from Vienna*
Screenplay by Alma Reville and Guy Bolton, based on the play by Bolton.

1934 *The Man Who Knew Too Much*
Screenplay by Edwin Greenwood and A. R. Rawlinson, based on a story by Charles Bennett and D. B. Wyndham Lewis.

1935 *The 39 Steps*
Screenplay by Charles Bennett, Hitchcock, and Ian Hay (John Hay Beth), based on the novel *The Thirty-nine Steps* by John Buchan.

1935/rel. 1936 *The Secret Agent*
Screenplay by Charles Bennett, additional dialogue by Ian Hay and Jessy Lasky, Jr., based on the play by Campbell Dixon from stories by Somerset Maugham.

1936 *Sabotage*
Screenplay by Charles Bennett, additional dialogue by Ian Hay, Helen Simpson, and E. V. H. Emmett, based on the novel *The Secret Agent* by Joseph Conrad.

1937/rel. 1938 *Young and Innocent*
Screenplay by Charles Bennett, Edwin Greenwood, and Anthony Armstrong, based on the novel *A Shilling for Candles* by Josephine Tey (Elizabeth MacKintosh).

1937/rel. 1938 *The Lady Vanishes*
Screenplay by Sidney Gilliat and Frank Launder, based on the novel *The Wheel Spins* by Ethel Lina White.

1938/rel. 1939 *Jamaica Inn*
Screenplay by Sidney Gilliat and Joan Harrison, based on the novel by Daphne du Maurier.

1939/rel. 1940 *Rebecca*
Screenplay by Robert E. Sherwood and Joan Harrison, adaptation by Philip MacDonald and Michael Hogan, based on the novel by Daphne du Maurier.

1940 *Foreign Correspondent*
Screenplay by Charles Bennett and Joan Harrison, dialogue by James Hilton and Robert Benchley.

1940/rel. 1941   *Mr. and Mrs. Smith*
Story and screenplay by Norman
Krasna.

1941   *Suspicion*
Screenplay by Samson Raphaelson,
Joan Harrison, and Alma Reville,
based on the novel *Before the Fact* by
Francis Iles (Anthony Berkeley).

1942   *Saboteur*
Screenplay by Peter Viertel, Joan
Harrison, and Dorothy Parker, based
on an idea by Hitchcock.

1942/rel. 1943   *Shadow of a Doubt*
Screenplay by Thornton Wilder, Sally
Benson, and Alma Reville, based on a
story by Gordon McDonell.

1943/rel. 1944   *Lifeboat*
Screenplay by Jo Swerling, based on a
story by John Steinbeck.

1944/rel. 1945   *Spellbound*
Screenplay by Ben Hecht, adaptation
by Angus MacPhail, based on the
novel *The House of Dr. Edwardes* by
Francis Beeding (Hilary St. George
Saunders and John Palmer).

1945/rel. 1946   *Notorious*
Screenplay by Ben Hecht, based on a
theme by Hitchcock.

1946/rel. 1947   *The Paradine Case*
Screenplay by David O. Selznick,
based on the novel by Robert
Hichens, adapted by Alma Reville.

1948   *Rope*
Screenplay by Arthur Laurents,
adaptation by Hume Cronyn, based on
the play by Patrick Hamilton.

1948/rel. 1949   *Under Capricorn*
Adaptation by Hume Cronyn,

screenplay by James Bridie, from the
play by John Colton and Margaret
Linden, based on the novel by Helen
Simpson.

1949/rel. 1950   *Stage Fright*
Adaptation by Alma Reville,
screenplay by Whitfield Cook,
additional dialogue by James Bridie,
based on the novel *Man Running* by
Selwyn Jepson.

1950/rel. 1951   *Strangers on a Train*
Adaptation by Whitfield Cook,
screenplay by Raymond Chandler and
Czenzi Ormonde, based on the novel
by Patricia Highsmith.

1952/rel. 1953   *I Confess*
Screenplay by George Tabori and
William Archibald, based on the play
Nos Deux Consciences by Paul
Anthelme (Paul Bourde).

1953/rel. 1954   *Dial M for Murder*
Screenplay by Frederick Knott, based
on his play.

1953/rel. 1954   *Rear Window*
Screenplay by John Michael Hayes,
based on the story by Cornell
Woolrich.

1954/rel. 1955   *To Catch a Thief*
Screenplay by John Michael Hayes,
based on the novel by David Dodge.

1954/rel. 1955   *The Trouble with
Harry*
Screenplay by John Michael Hayes,
based on the novel by John Trevor
Story.

1955/rel. 1956   *The Man Who Knew
Too Much* (remake)
Screenplay by John Michael Hayes
and Angus MacPhail, based on a story

by Charles Bennett and D. B. Wyndham Lewis.

1956   *The Wrong Man*
Screenplay by Maxwell Anderson and Angus MacPhail, based on a story by Anderson.

1957/rel. 1958   *Vertigo*
Screenplay by Alec Coppel and Samuel Taylor, based on the novel *D'Entre les morts* by Pierre Boileau and Thomas Narcejac.

1958/rel. 1959   *North by Northwest*
Screenplay by Ernest Lehman.

1959/rel. 1960   *Psycho*
Screenplay by Joseph Stefano, based on the novel by Robert Bloch.

1962/rel. 1963   *The Birds*
Screenplay by Evan Hunter, based on the story by Daphne du Maurier.

1963/rel. 1964   *Marnie*
Screenplay by Jay Presson Allen, based on the novel by Winston Graham.

1965/rel. 1966   *Torn Curtain*
Screenplay by Brian Moore.

1968/rel. 1969   *Topaz*
Screenplay by Samuel Taylor, based on the novel by Leon Uris.

1971/rel. 1972   *Frenzy*
Screenplay by Anthony Shaffer, based on the novel *Goodbye Piccadilly, Farewell Leicester Square* by Arthur Labern.

1975/rel. 1976   *Family Plot*
Screenplay by Ernest Lehman, based on the novel *The Rainbird Pattern* by Victor Canning.

Television Films

1955   *Breakdown*
Screenplay by Francis Cockrell and Louis Pollock, based on a story by Pollock.

1955   *Revenge*
Screenplay by Francis Cockrell and A. I. Bezzerides, based on a story by Samuel Blas.

1955   *The Case of Mr. Pelham*
Screenplay by Francis Cockrell, based on a story by Anthony Armstrong.

1956   *Back for Christmas*
Screenplay by Francis Cockrell, based on a story by John Collier.

1956   *Wet Saturday*
Screenplay by Marian Cockrell, based on a story by John Collier.

1956   *Mr. Blanchard's Secret*
Screenplay by Sarett Rudley, based on a story by Emily Neff.

1957   *One More Mile to Go*
Screenplay by James P. Cavanagh, based on a story by F. J. Smith.

1957   *The Perfect Crime*
Screenplay by Stirling Silliphant, based on a story by Ben Ray Redman.

1957   *Four O'Clock*
Screenplay by Francis Cockrell, based on the story by Cornell Woolrich.

1958   *Lamb to the Slaughter*
Screenplay by Roald Dahl, based on his story.

1958   *Dip in the Pool*
Screenplay by Robert C. Dennis and Francis Cockrell, based on the story by Roald Dahl.

1958 *Poison*
Screenplay by Casey Robinson, based on the story by Roald Dahl.

1959 *Banquo's Chair*
Screenplay by Francis Cockrell, based on a story by Robert Croft-Cooke.

1959 *Arthur*
Screenplay by James P. Cavanagh, based on the story by Arthur Williams.

1959 *The Crystal Trench*
Screenplay by Stirling Silliphant, based on the story by A. E. W. Mason.

1960 *Incident at a Corner*
Screenplay by Charlotte Armstrong, based on her story.

1960 *Mr. Bixby and the Colonel's Coat*
Screenplay by Halsted Welles, based on the story by Roald Dahl.

1961 *The Horseplayer*
Screenplay by Henry Slesar, based on his story.

1961 *Bang! You're Dead*
Screenplay by Harold Swanton, based on the story by Margery Vosper.

1962 *I Saw the Whole Thing*
Screenplay by Henry Slesar, based on the story by Henry Cecil.

Selected
Bibliography

Bellour, Raymond. "Le Blocage symbolique." In *Communications,* Volume 23, pp. 235–350. Paris: Seuil, 1975.

Bogdanovich, Peter. *The Cinema of Alfred Hitchcock.* New York: Museum of Modern Art (Doubleday), 1963.

Bordwell, David, and Kristin Thompson. "*North by Northwest.*" In *Film Art: An Introduction.* Fourth edition, pp. 370–375. New York: McGraw-Hill, 1993.

Brill, Lesley. *The Hitchcock Romance: Love and Irony in Hitchcock's Films.* Princeton, N.J.: Princeton University Press, 1988.

Britton, Andrew. *Cary Grant: Comedy and Male Desire.* Newcastle upon Tyne, England: Tyneside Cinema, 1983.

Cavell, Stanley. "*North by Northwest.*" In *A Hitchcock Reader,* ed. Marshall Deutelbaum and Leland Poague, pp. 249–261. Ames: Iowa State University Press, 1986.

Denning, Michael. *Cover Stories: Narrative and Ideology in the British Spy Thriller.* London: Routledge & Kegan Paul, 1987.

Durgnat, Raymond. *The Strange Case of Alfred Hitchcock.* Cambridge, Mass.: MIT Press, 1974.

Hartman, Geoffrey. "Plenty of Nothing: Hitchcock's *North by Northwest.*" In *Easy Pieces,* pp. 93–107. New York: Columbia University Press, 1982.

Kapsis, Robert E. *Hitchcock: The Making of a Reputation.* Chicago: University of Chicago Press, 1992.

Keane, Marian. "The Designs of Authorship: An Essay on *North by Northwest.*" *Wide Angle* 4, no. 1 (1980): 44–52.

LaValley, Albert J., ed. *Focus on Hitchcock.* Englewood Cliffs, N.J.: Prentice-Hall, 1972.

Leitch, Thomas M. *Find the Director and Other Hitchcock Games.* Athens: University of Georgia Press, 1991.

Leff, Leonard. *Hitchcock and Selznick.* New York: Weidenfeld & Nicolson, 1987.

Modleski, Tania. *The Women Who Knew Too Much: Hitchcock and*

Feminist Theory. New York: Methuen, 1988.

Naremore, James. "Cary Grant in *North by Northwest.*" In *Acting in the Cinema.* Berkeley and Los Angeles: University of California Press, 1988.

Rohmer, Eric, and Claude Chabrol. *Hitchcock: The First Forty-Four Films,* trans. Stanley Hochmann. New York: Frederick Ungar, 1979.

Rose, Jacqueline. "Paranoia and the Film System." In *Feminism and Film Theory,* ed. Constance Penley, pp. 141–158. New York: Routledge-BFI, 1988.

Rothman, William. *Hitchcock: The Murderous Gaze.* Cambridge, Mass.: Harvard University Press, 1982.

Ryall, Tom. *Alfred Hitchcock and the British Cinema.* Urbana: University of Illinois Press, 1986.

Spoto, Donald. *The Art of Alfred Hitchcock: Fifty Years of His Motion Pictures.* New York: Hopkinson and Blake, 1976.

———. *The Dark Side of Genius: The Life of Alfred Hitchcock.* New York: Random House, 1983.

Stam, Robert. "Hitchcock and Buñuel: Authority, Desire, and the Absurd." In *Hitchcock's Rereleased Films: From Rope to Vertigo,* ed. Walter Raubicheck and Walter Srebnick, pp. 116–146. Detroit: Wayne State University Press, 1991.

Truffaut, François. *Hitchcock.* New York: Simon & Schuster, 1967.

Wexman, Virginia. "The Critic as Consumer: Film Study in the University, *Vertigo,* and the Film Canon." *Film Quarterly* 39, no. 3 (Spring 1986): 32–41.

Wollen, Peter. "*North by Northwest:* A Morphological Analysis." In *Readings and Writings: Semiotic Counter-Strategies,* pp. 18–33. London: Verso, 1982.

Wood, Robin. *Hitchcock's Films Revisited.* New York: Columbia University Press, 1989.

iek, Slavoj. *Looking Awry: An Introduction to Jacques Lacan Through Popular Culture.* Cambridge, Mass.: MIT Press, 1991.

———, ed. *Everything You Always Wanted to Know about Lacan (But Were Afraid to Ask Hitchcock).* London: Verso, 1992.

DATE DUE